THE WOMAN IN THE RED DRESS

MINROSE C. GWIN

The Woman in the Red Dress

Gender, Space, and Reading

UNIVERSITY OF ILLINOIS PRESS
URBANA AND CHICAGO

Manufactured in the United States of America
C 5 4 3 2 1
∞ This book is printed on acid-free paper.

Library of Congress Cataloging-in-Publication Data
Gwin, Minrose.
The woman in the red dress : gender, space, and reading / Minrose C. Gwin.
p. cm.
Includes bibliographical references (p.) and index.
ISBN 0-252-02732-9 (cloth : acid-free paper)
1. American literature—Women authors—History and criticism—Theory, etc. 2. Feminism and literature—United States. 3. Women and literature—United States. 4. Fathers and daughters in literature. 5. Space and time in literature. 6. Women—Books and reading. 7. Sex role in literature. 8. Incest in literature. 9. Women in literature.
I. Title.
PS147.G88 2002
810.9'9287—dc21 2001004575

Contents

Acknowledgments

I thank Ruth Salvaggio for her appreciation of these dense thickets and for many hours generously given to the projects of keeping them still wild but navigable. Her thoughts on language, beauty, and love have shaped this volume in no small way.

Having left the University of New Mexico as this book was going to press, I feel especially mindful of my debts to former colleagues and still steadfast friends. For their encouragement with this body of work and their support, I thank Diana Robin, Susan Dever, Carolyn Woodward, Gail Houston, Michael Fischer, Gary Harrison, Jesse Alemán, Beverly Burris, Sylvia Rodriguez, Patricia Clark Smith, and Marta Weigle. I am grateful for the important intellectual companionship offered by the UNM Cultural Studies Series of Lectures, under whose auspices I twice presented pieces of this work, and for a series of doctoral students in English and American studies whose own travels in space theory have been both stimulating and sustaining: Jill Cowley, Shari Evans, Gloria Larrieu, Mónica Torres, and Elizabeth Wright. For her insight into Toni Morrison, I am indebted to Kimberly Stanley, coteacher and friend.

Over more than a decade in Albuquerque, I have found myself sustained by good friends. I am especially thankful for the celebratory spirits of Helen Damico, Angela Boone, Mary Bess Whidden, and Mary Power.

I also appreciate sabbatical leave, course release, and travel grants from the University of New Mexico.

The Woman in the Red Dress developed as a series of scholarly papers and articles. Specific acknowledgments are included with the notes for each chapter. Generally, I am very much indebted to the exacting, thoughtful critique of the readers of this manuscript for the University of Illinois Press: Linda Wagner-Martin and Rita Felski. I appreciate the precision of their insight and recommendations; the manuscript is much better for them. I also feel fortunate indeed to have the opportunity to work with such a talented and visionary editor as Joan Catapano at the University of Illinois Press.

I also want to thank and acknowledge the following authors and presses for permission to publish certain writings and materials:

Ron Kolm, for permission to reprint his poem "Suburban Ambush," which has appeared in numerous publications (usually in collaboration with a visual artist as part of an ongoing performance piece), including Art Spiegelman's *Raw,* Jim Fleming and Peter Lamborn Wilson's *Semiotext(e) USA,* the periodical *New Observations,* and Robert Siegle's critical book, which takes its title from the poem.

Elaine Kraf, for permission to reprint three illustrations from her novel *Find Him!* (New York: Fiction Collective, 1977), 78 (giraffe), 80 (musical score), and 183 (questionnaire).

West End Press, for permission to reprint Cherríe Moraga's poem "Dedicación" from her book *Giving Up the Ghost: Teatro in Two Acts* (Albuquerque, N.Mex.: West End Press, 1986). © 1986 by West End Press.

Wesleyan University Press, for permission to reprint lines from Joy Harjo's poem "Deer Dancer" in her book *Mad Love and War* (Middletown, Conn.: Wesleyan University Press, 1990). © 1990 by Wesleyan University Press.

THE WOMAN IN THE RED DRESS

Prologue: Uncle Wiggily's Airship

Between the time I was born and my sixth birthday I never went anywhere I can recall. I was born in Tupelo, Mississippi, to a mother without a husband, or rather to a mother with a husband who was rapidly doing a disappearing act, a dashing young ("too young") aviation cadet named Al, who dashed right off and was never seen again in those parts.

From as early as I can remember, my mother and I lived with my grandparents in a large, square brick house surrounded by huge oaks, pecans, and mimosas on the corner of two pleasant streets several blocks from downtown. On steamy summer nights we would all sit out on the long front porch, swatting mosquitoes and swinging in the big swing. I would put my head in my grandmother's lap and listen to the screech of the swing and the creak of rocking chairs. The grownups, neighbors and family, would be debating the state of the Presbyterian church or telling stories of the Bataan Death March and other horrors of the most recent war. Sometimes my grandfather would tell stories about his grandfather, the one who came to North Mississippi as a boy in 1840 and turned into a lawyer on horseback who galloped up and down the dusty Natchez Trace carrying his legal papers in his saddlebags. Alice Anderson, the blind widow in the big white house next door, would throw open her French doors and play Rachmaninoff on her grand piano, and my mother, whose mezzosoprano voice was in much demand for church weddings, would sing a song in another language made up of long-held vowels.

It was a good house, one of the few left standing after the 1936 tornado swept through town, leaving a dead baby girl blown into a bush, not to be found until days later, and a mass of wounded and homeless. The house became the town hospital by default. Victims were stretched out on my grandmother's kitchen table. Limbs were severed there, broken bones set, tree branches extricated from the wounded. I hadn't been born then, but I knew the stories by heart. The tornado sounded like a freight train coming at full speed. All the windows in the house exploded. Fortunately everyone had gotten down to the basement after seeing the yellow sky, feeling the throbbing stillness, and hearing the sound of the roaring engine of destruction. For months after, the lost and wounded slept on the floor all over the house. My mother said she would have to step over them, casts and all, to get to the bathroom in the night.

During my first years my grandfather would read to me every night. I would sit next to him on the sofa in the cool, dark living room, the chosen book in his lap. I would turn the pages. We read all the Uncle Wiggily books. The old gentleman rabbit had a bad case of rheumatism, but, armed with his trusty crutch and valise, he knew how to get around, traveling in the most splendid and hazardous ways. He flew in airships that took him from one adventure to the next; he got stuck in mudholes; he fought off alligators from a paper boat; he cured Grandfather Goosey Gander's epizootic with a cup of catnip tea; he was saved by a colony of courageous ants from a bad giant who wanted to eat him for dinner but ended up having baked beans instead.

Uncle Wiggily gave me a lust for travel. In dark closets I secretly packed my mother's handbags and pretended they were my traveling valises. I would get my grandfather's cane and tote it and my bulging valises to the top of a mimosa tree outside the kitchen window. I would twirl the mimosa blossoms against my nose and smell the sweetness of cherry blossoms in Asia. I believed I was mounting the skies in my own airship, ready, like the old gentleman rabbit, to find my fortune and look for adventures with fellow creatures, good and bad.

My travels came soon enough, but they were not what I anticipated. When I was six, another flying man came to pilot me and my mother away. He had been in the navy. What he did particularly well was landing fighter bombers in a split second on aircraft carriers. "In a split second," my mother would repeat, and her eyes would glow. He was blond with clear blue eyes you could see through. He always brought me a pack of Juicy Fruit. I later noticed that he looked like a lankier version of Alan Ladd. He didn't say much, but when he did, his voice was hoarse and rough. One night, before they married in my grandparents' living room (with my mother in pink since it was her second time), I went to sleep in my grandfather's velvet chair and dreamed this man's face above the mantle. Slowly it turned into a skull, and I woke up to see the last of it flickering away in the fire's glow. After the honeymoon trip to New York City, where she got lost in Bloomingdale's and hours later her new husband found her sobbing next to an escalator, Mama packed her bags and mine. My life in the cool, dark, spacious house of my grandparents, who wept when my mother spanked me, was over.

My stepfather was a traveling man. Like the absent father of Tennessee Williams's imagination, he had fallen "in love with long distance." The next six years we moved so many times I lost count. One year I had grade school pictures from three schools. Some places we lived I never even got to school because I would get sudden onsets of sore throats, coughs, swollen glands that lasted for weeks, even months. From my grandparents' rambling two-story house with nooks and crannies up and down, we were plunged into tighter spaces. Tiny apartments surrounded by concrete. Houses behind houses. Loaned houses with odd smelling furniture from relatives whose eyes always looked past mine to something over my shoulder.

Whenever my stepfather forfeited another job or ran out of rent money, we would head out for another place, usually around dusk, when the mothers in the apartments would be calling their children through lighted windows for supper and baths. The time of day a dear familiarity drifts through the coming dark. We ran into a wild boar on a dark road in Louisiana; I fell out of the backseat, where I was sleeping, and hit the floor with a thud that kicked the breath out of me. We were stranded until morning. We saw the bluebonnets in bloom in the oil fields of Texas, slapped our wheels in mud over long, straight roads across the Mississippi Delta. My little brother was almost born in the backseat of the car as we tore across the city of Houston, Mama screaming bloody murder, to get to a hospital.

After several years of such travels, my mother's full lips began to purse and she began to scream. She bristled with implements: barbed metal curlers sprang from her head; vacuum-cleaner wands, hairbrushes, switches, from her hands. Her rage, whether directed at me or my brother and sister—by then my stepfather had taken to the roads fulltime to sell things, so he was hardly ever there—made our diminished spaces feel full. More years passed, and she began what would be a thirty-year journey into her own dark place, from which she was never to emerge. She died in transit, in the back of an ambulance sent from nursing home to hospital.

As a girl I began my own travels. I read, and I read fast and hard, traversing as expeditiously as possible the long line of words that led somewhere else. I read everything I could get my hands on. I staggered along sidewalks under immense loads of novels from local libraries. A week later I would stagger back to exchange loads. If a book didn't take me somewhere else within a few pages, I tossed it and began another. I never read a book twice, nor did I linger over a good one. I needed to be off on another airship.

I am telling this story because I want you to know this is writing that comes from a long distance. I might say I travel these spaces to make my way home, but that's not really it. I travel to hear stories of other homes and stories of other journeys. For me, reading is like looking into that last lighted window as one leaves the neighborhood.

Introduction: The Woman in the Red Dress

> What is it about space that invites self-forgetting, that solicits these delicious misprisions about boundaries, origins, solidarity, and the politics of community?
>
> —Patricia Yaeger, "Introduction: Narrating Space"

> Being in space is not easy.
>
> —Gillian Rose, *Feminism and Geography: The Limits of Geographical Knowledge*

Why are spatial metaphors so captivating? Perhaps because space is never empty but always palimpsestic and mobile; "it" is never a single effect but rather a social, transhistorical production, a crosshatching of meanings and actions, longings and oppositions, distances and proximities. Perhaps because space leads to thoughts about the makings of identity and social relations, one's placement on this dying planet, one's interiority marked and shaped by history and circumstance and encounter. Contemplating space, I may not end up going where I had intended to go. I may indeed find myself the terrain rather than she who set forth, the traveled rather than the traveler. Like the recent conceptualizing of space as an ever-shifting field of geographical, social, and psychological busyness, spatial metaphors are perpetually paradoxical, seeming to situate us in "the real world" even as that world is permeated with signs of history and long-absent passengers, alluring and prohibited borders, imagined abysses of incommensurability—so that reality itself is always moving toward somewhere else.

I begin this book with questions of metaphor because, in theorizing space, one finds metaphor unavoidable. In contemporary critical theory the term *space* has come to describe not an entity that contains something else but the swirl of social relations and productions in particular locations, whether these locations be material, cultural, or even psychological. Defined this way, space is already metaphoric, laden with the instability and paradox that accompany such relations and productions. Indeed, although I situate *space* as a noun in this book, it is always on the verge of becoming a verb, and an oily one at that. Just when I think I have it neatly packed away, it slides out of my trusty valise and is, before I know it, on its way to becoming something else. "But what do you *mean* by space?" I am asked. Whatever answer I give is never quite right, never quite *it*.

"How to say it? In this language there are no words for how the real world / collapses," writes Native American poet Joy Harjo.[1] Her poem "Deer Dancer" is about the way space can be heavy, laden as it inevitably is with history and myth, even as it is light, having been altered through filters of motion and beauty and possibility. "Deer Dancer" is the story of a woman, perhaps wearing a stained red dress, perhaps not, who walks into "the bar of broken survivors" and dances naked on a table, awakening an epiphanic delight in those who watch: "We were Indian ruins. She / was the end of beauty" (5). This double-edged jolt of pleasure is both historical and mythical; the stranger is recognized as a tribal member, "her family related to deer, if that's who she was, a people / accustomed to hearing songs in pine trees, and making them hearts" (5). The pleasure and recognition of the participants in this poem are tied to a multitude of ritualistic Deer Dances performed in concrete and distinctive ways to celebrate the importance of the deer to the survival of Native American peoples:[2] this woman is *known* in this specific way; she is "the deer who crossed through knots of a curse to find / us" (5–6). In the woman's dance and the watchers' response ("She shook loose memory, waltzed with the empty lover we'd all become") is a multiple sense of fluctuation, of imaginative motion, but with roots in the real world. Those "Indian ruins" who watch are "broken survivors . . . of poison by culture." They are firmly located in time and space in "that bar in the middle of winter . . . on the coldest night of the year," but they also find themselves *re*placed somewhere else. They return to who they are and yet become more than who they are. In their watching, they are found by the one they seek, "the woman inside the woman," the deer who crosses over, pursuing what is best and beautiful in them.

The fluctuation of identity enacted in Harjo's poem—the spreading of the one over the many and the many over the one, the motion of transformation—can be, and often is, a moment of specific political intervention. It is a highly charged hiatus in which anything can happen, and it is impelled, dually, by the experiencing of space as a series of social productions in time and by the flight of imagination that makes such an act not only possible but also inescapable. Drawn from Harjo's historically diasporic experience as a member of the Creek Muscogee tribe, as well as many other complex personal events and commitments in her life—her extraordinary ability as a musician and her personal sense of displacement, which pervade her poetry—"Deer Dancer" brings a wholly particular cultural and legendary history to the moment of transformation when the woman in the red dress (maybe) travels into myth, and misfits become part of a ritual that refigures not only the material space they inhabit and produce but its crosshatchings in time—past, present, and future.

What is critical here is that, while Harjo acknowledges that she wasn't there in the bar, she places herself in the story. Did she hear this story of the dancing woman, and if so, where? At a party? A family celebration? A bus stop? On an airplane? Did she read it in a letter? Did one of her children hear it from a friend? Did she make up the story? Is it not "true"? It seems true; it seems real. Harjo travels into that material, cultural space and becomes the "we" of the tribe and the "we" of the bar ("But I imagined her like this" [6]). She situates that imagined spatial experience in time—past, present, future—when the woman steps onto "a table of names," begins to dance, and then takes off her clothes. Harjo's genius as a visionary poet (and musician) rests in the way she simultaneously preserves and relinquishes geographic and cultural borders.[3] In this poem she radically reproduces specific spatial configurations (the bar, the tribe, the story) and sets them into flight, impelling the plural first person, the tribal we, to shake loose and travel. While remaining distinctive historically and culturally, this we also elongates in both space and time, the one incredible moment of plenitude and extension when "the myth slipped down through dreamtime," and, in its motion through space, we too imagine "not a stained red dress with tape on her heels but the deer who entered our dream in white dawn, breathed mist into pine trees, her fawn a blessing of meat, the ancestors who never left" (6).

I hover over this beautiful poem because I want this book to be poised in such moments of the imagination, in all their consequence, moments in which the real world collapses and yet is somehow still heavily present.

Such moments bring into being the field of social relations that is space, and space provides a way of thinking about such simultaneous, and perhaps seemingly paradoxical, locations and dislocations of identity in the historical moment and beyond that moment. This book is engaged in such moments, when imaginings of space pervade the processes of reading and the theorizing of gender. There is still a common feminist assumption that one reads imaginative texts to confirm one's own identity. In this context, I instead will make a case for reading literature as a way of experiencing otherness—those other houses one sees when passing through the neighborhood and knows one might have lived in. I want to suggest also that the foregrounding of space as represented dually, in narrative itself and in the act of reading it, can bring us into this experience of otherness in a form of "space travel" that sustains both aesthetics and politics in the act of reading.

Much recent thinking about space emphasizes that space is not an empty container that holds human activity but rather multiple fields of interaction created by social arrangements among individuals, groups, and nations—arrangements that are always shifting and have everything to do with power relations, geographical locations, access to mobility, and a countless host of other factors. Considered this way, space, like the woman in the red dress, is always unstable and problematic; it is itself a configuration of fluctuating social relations that are constantly being unraveled and rewoven.

So space, as we encounter it through imaginative engagement, is indeed strange, but its strangeness can turn us not away from but toward a contemplation of the social relations that shape it, and us. Literature and art lead us into this arena of contemplation in a way that history does not. Henri Lefebvre offers Marxist warnings against the networks of desire that space sets into motion, and not unrelatedly, he cautions against literature and literary analysis as methods for thinking about "real" space. My project here, however, is to foreground the deep engagement that reading can become as a way into space that is not so much real as it is true to the complexity of real life. The pleasures and politics of space's strange productions in literature open to new ways of thinking and theorizing about gender. The imaginative encounter with and contemplation of space as a site of social relations can move us, and move us strangely, not so much to points either false or true but to a place *of intense contemplation,* a place of thick complexity where, as in Harjo's bar, anything is possible, where history and imagination converge.

This book locates its inquiries and readings in the compound splicings between real and imagined spaces and the ways in which those fluctuations and interchanges we call "space" intersect with language and stories, as in Harjo's poem—stories that enact spatial representation and production through their stirrings of the imagination. Distinctly specific (culturally, geographically, historically, or psychologically) as they are (*this* bar, *this* woman, *these* ancestors, *these* multiple rituals of deer dancers and Native American stories of transformation), such cognitive moments are also largely transgressive, for they call into being those gaps, ruptures, fissures in the fabric of lived experience and social relations, disjuncture and contingency, all that lies not only within and without but also *between.*

My argument is driven by a belief that there is distinctive pleasure in cognitive motion, the teeter of the imagination's aeronautics in the moment of liftoff, and that this kind of pleasurable engagement is a powerful force that can fuel cultural transformation. Metaphor, in the original sense of the word, enables travel, conveying a sense of one's mobility, of being borne from one point to another.[4] Metaphor can become the motion between meanings that often destabilizes both sets of meanings instead of making one more fixed or knowable.[5]

A glittering galaxy of metaphoric configurations has materialized from the "space talk" that emerged in the final decade of the twentieth century. Theorizing about space, as well as the use of spatial language, has proliferated in social and cultural theory. Space talk abounds with gaps, geographies, "women's spaces," queer space, borders, openings, abysses, *aporias,* interstices, *chora,* curves, edges, terrains, landscapes, topographies: all evocative of something alluringly both of and beyond the cartographies of language. Feminist theory and literary studies of recent years also record a profusion of spatial rhetoric and an ongoing fascination with the spatial configurations of women's writings.[6] Such inquiries and the language in which they are couched have been a natural outcome of the postmodern complications of subject-object relations, especially the understanding that subject and object positions can be both transitory and internal. Language that partakes of and marks such dimensions can propel us into new terrain, perhaps because space is strange, unpredictable. Contemplating space as it is evoked imaginatively in literature makes one aware of the vulnerability of borders and thus summons feelings of placement and displacement and the desires and longings that cling to such feelings.[7]

One serious question that emerges from such discussions is whether theoretical deployments of spatial metaphors, and such metaphors' sly capaciousness, have promoted detachment from location (itself a slippery term) as a site of analysis. Space is complicated; sometimes spatial metaphors do not translate that complexity. The unproblematic construction of space philosophically engendered by Newton, Descartes, and Kant creates a fixed absolute—an empty container of individuals and histories. It requires no great leap to see how an absolutist view of space (and time) relates to large systems of unequal power relations (Smith and Katz 75–79).

With the recent problematizing of the concept of "place" (and contingent terms such as "location" and "position") as a site of authenticity, stability, and nostalgia, this has become a more complicated question than it might seem, however vehemently the postmodern turn to space talk has been faulted for being often unexamined and dehistoricizing. An example of such critique is Angelika Bammer's extremely provocative introduction to *Displacements: Cultural Identities in Question,* in which she argues that postmodern discourses of otherness have so vigorously seized on displacement as a trope that "it would appear, almost by definition, that to 'be' in the postmodern sense is somehow to be an Other: displaced." Differences created by historically located experiences for certain groups of people are erased by being universalized; specific discriminatory experience for specific groups of people in specific places "is appropriated for the purposes of elaborating a new, postmodernistically hip version of the universal subject" (xii–xiii).

Caren Kaplan sees similar problems in postmodern theoretical discourse, warning that "terms such as 'borders,' 'maps,' 'location,' 'space,' and 'place' do not necessarily liberate critical practices from the very conundrum of aestheticization and universalization that spurred a search for alternative metaphors and methods in the first place" (*Questions* 144). Kaplan echoes some geographers' concerns that, as meaning has become increasingly destabilized in literary and cultural studies, a dehistoricized and unexamined concept of space has appeared in the form of various spatial metaphors used in critical discourse;[8] in short, spatial language needs regrounding in the material and historical.[9]

Kaplan recounts the evolution of her own work away from inquiries into literature when, after writing her dissertation on post–World War II travel memoirs, she "became dissatisfied with close readings of literary texts" and moved back to political, economic, and social theory (6), specifically interdisciplinary cultural studies. My own experience has led in an opposite direction. Working in the field of feminist literary analysis, I have been strongly drawn to the progressive political imperative of cultural studies, but I have worried about politicization at the expense of complexity, just as these scholars have been concerned (rightly so, I think) with a lack of complexity and social and historical grounding in certain uses of spatial language. My concern is not just the complexity of texts and disciplines, which is certainly worth worrying about all by itself, but the complexity of imaginative experience and its bearing on identity. Like space, language is tricky and strange. Like space, it can disavow its constitutive power and assume deceptively innocent transparency.

If one thinks of space as a field of social relations always on the move, then metaphor is not only available but inevitable because it enacts that mobility. Metaphor can serve the valuable analytic function of making visible the invisibility of power and its relation to language. To limit what we call "space" *only* to its material and historical manifestations, then, is to overlook how language and power are implicated in social relations and how social relations are implicated in the construction of our interior lives (which, of course, turn back to become reflected and refracted in language). So space is interior and unknowable as well as present and observable in manifest action, in history.

Space flies like a migratory bird between the interior and the exterior. Space travels.[10]

As an analytical model dependent on mobility and depth, space can take us somewhere else. As such a traveler, space has profound consequences for the reconceptualization of gender. The imaginative contemplation of space can take us somewhere specific—historically, culturally, and geographically. It can also take us not just into the complex interiority of gender in the contexts of social relationships, locations, and identities but also into gender's own indefatigable mobility.

Addressing this latter point, Susan Stanford Friedman's important book *Mappings: Feminism and the Cultural Geographies of Encounter* offers extended discussions about the directions in which studies of gender and feminist critical practice need to move. Basically she argues that feminist theorizing needs to become more located, complicated, and multilayered. In the twenty-first century, feminist thinking needs to bring into play material realities *and* intellectual discourses; it needs to be situated in complex notions of identity and culture, borders and borderlands, space and time. Friedman, a literary critic, believes that feminists must learn to think "geopolitically"; that is, we need to learn the skill of "identifying the political meanings of space as a distinct constituent of identity and societal systems" (110). She believes that literature can illustrate such layerings if read with attention to history and location.

This insistence on complexity and nuance lies at the heart of geographer Doreen Massey's *Space, Place, and Gender,* to which I will circle back in a moment. Massey considers how "those envelopes of space-time in which and between which we live and move (and have our 'Being')" are permeable, mobile, and interconnected (122) and how recourses to place as a source of authenticity, nostalgia, and stability can lend themselves to reactionary politics, as well as essentialist models of gender. If space itself can travel between surface and depth, past and present, materiality and metaphor, how far can its capaciousness take us in the analysis of gender? Recent thinking about space as specifically located in geography and history has important implications for feminist thinking about the world because it offers a complex conceptual model about that world. I believe, though, that the travels of space in and through language and narrative, specifically through the reading of literary texts, can also draw us toward more complex imaginings of gender. Space shapes the unfolding of narrative time, just as history and materiality shape the unfolding of space. When a Eudora Welty character chats with the ladies in a local beauty shop in Hazelhurst, Mississippi, the story that emerges (which isn't always the story the narrator thinks she is telling) is made by the material space of the beauty shop itself, the rural southern environment in which everyone knows everyone else's business, the gendered and racialized textures of culture and geography, history and place.

More specifically, Gcina Mhlope's "The Toilet," a story of circumscribed material and historical space narrated by a black South African woman, depends for its meaning on the very physical colonial restrictions of apartheid, a geography of black and white.[11] The young narrator, who is secretly living with her sister, a live-in domestic worker in Johannesburg, must hide herself from her sister's employer, a white woman with orange hair, a swimming pool, and two large fierce dogs. During certain hours the young woman hides in a public toilet that she makes her private space, passing the time by reading books and writing poems and stories. What is small and unpleasant—the material space of the toilet—becomes large and largely pleasurable through an act of the imagination; what is large—the brutal and confining landscape of racist colonialism—becomes, at least temporarily, stunted and insubstantial as a result. Mhlope's story pivots on this reversal of largeness and smallness; its spatial narrative connects identity and history as they are charged by material, cultural, and cognitive fluctuations and inversions.

Like Harjo's "Deer Dancer," Mhlope's is a story about the motion and expansiveness of the imagination. Such spaces are historical and material, but they also enact specific imaginative interventions with the historical and material. In literary texts such as these, history, materiality, and imagination are not cast in opposition. Instead there is a pentimento effect, the layering of an image that has been painted over again and again and whose various mutations can be seen through the surface effect.[12]

Traveling such stories and their intricate crosshatchings in space and time (indeed, the whole concept of readerly mobility, not to speak of access to literacy) gives pause, especially the terms under which travel can, or cannot, proceed—its economic and philosophic implications, its cultural and personal contexts.[13] In employing the metaphor of travel to discuss how reading moves us, I particularly want to rethink the relationship between space and the work of the imagination rather than simply to offer "a multiplication of absolute spaces,"[14] which can be had through ahistorical readings of texts. However, as I will later discuss at length, the issues of mobility and position attendant on the trope of travel may be complicated and perhaps even reversed by its usage vis-à-vis reading and the pleasures of reading, as well as by *their* complicated relations to gender and identity. The reading of imaginative writing can lead into rather than away from the vastly multiple material, social, and cultural spaces that create and are created by the complexity and intricacy of social relations, which are themselves always changing.

There can be deeply serious fluctuations of identity that occur in reading. I want to know where that kind of fluctuation can lead in a collapsing real world where both theory and politics sometimes fail us. Narrative opens these sites of practice, of becoming. These may be fictive spaces, in the sense that they represent visible and invisible social practice and psychological machination, but they also can be more true than true, for they map interior geographies that are not real but lead us to an interior reality that is both about and embedded in the real. (It is instructive that Neil Smith and Cindi Katz, both social scientists, note that, until very recently and for most of the twentieth century, it was physics and art, not geography and other social theory, that explored the relativity and relationality of space [74]).

Even in their most rarefied forms, literary texts are of the world and engage the world in complicated and various ways (Said 35). Read, for example, either John Blassingame's or Eugene Genovese's well-documented histories of slavery and then Toni Morrison's *Beloved.* Which of these books leaves you with a sense of what slavery *was*? the touch, the smell of slavery? the mother's predicament under slavery? the thickness of the bit? We travel such texts, but they also travel us, in ways so utterly complex and terrifying, and yes, beautiful, that we can never adequately assess them. Who is the someone else who returns from the journey of reading *Beloved,* I may ask myself, for she is not the one who embarked. Reading such texts makes space and time mobile; it enacts and extends that mobility infinitely. The narrow space that is Sethe's kitchen becomes elongated into the historical and cultural past, and into her and the readers' very different futures. In analyses of social orderings, such narrative enactments of space are crucial to an understanding of how real lives are made and remade within multiple locations and histories, and of how gender and sexuality, race, and class are at once circumscribed and destabilized discursively within and between those locations and histories.

But space, as Lefebvre points out, is never innocent, although it can offer many illusions, not the least of which is transparency. Lefebvre's conceptual model insists that social space is not an abstraction or a container but a social production; it is not empty, it possesses hidden features, it is inextricably embedded in time, it has a history. He likens space to money; it is real in that its representational value is so strong that it makes all the difference. One of the most important questions posed by Lefebvre concerns the relations between social space as productions of the outside—those physical and social spheres in which we find ourselves implicated—and mental space as productions of the inside, our interior realities (28). This duality of out/in can be translated into the familiar question of the relations between materiality and metaphor.

My argument, as I have said, is that these two are neither oppositional nor mutually exclusive. It is certainly not a new idea that these spatial practices and their intricate relations to power are always embedded and negotiated imaginatively and in language,[15] even though what Yaeger would call their "irreducible strangeness" (5) and what Lefebvre calls their "encrypted reality" (28) always exceed our ability to explain. What does this incommensurability imply? First, that the postmodern turn in cultural geography toward new conceptual models and the spillover into other disciplines of what Edward Soja has variously called an "ontological spatiality" and a "spatialized ontology" (8) have complicated spatial metaphorization as a juncture between social space and mental space, out and in.[16] Second, that these seepages in the relations between out and in tend to warp their purity, their separateness into . . . something else, an opening into new conceptualizations of identity and social relations. Contemporary thinkers in multiple disciplines—social geographers, historians, architects, philosophers, literary and film critics, psychologists, urban planners, anthropologists, and others—have not been hesitant to cluster around such an opening. Consider these titles of the past decade: *Geographical Imaginations; Sexuality and Space; Space, Time, and Perversion; The Production of Space; Postmodern Cities and Spaces; Geographies of Exclusion; Postmodern Geographies: The Reassertion of Space in Critical Social Theory; The Geography of Identity; Feminism and Geography: The Limits of Geographical Knowledge; Space, Place, and Gender; Writing Women and Space; Reconfigured Spheres: Feminist Explorations of Literary Space; Gendered Spaces; Queer Space; Queers in Space; Remapping Memory: The Politics of TimeSpace; Place and the Politics of Identity; Mappings: Feminism and the Cultural Geographies of Encounter; Thinking Space; New Frontiers of Space, Bodies and Gender.*

Drawing on Lefebvre and Foucault, Soja seems to see this opening as positioned philosophically somewhere between two persistent illusions that have dominated Western perceptions of space: the "illusion of opaqueness," wherein one sees "only a superficial materiality, concretized forms susceptible to little else but measurement and phenomenal description: fixed, dead, and undialectical," and alternatively, "the illusion of transparency," which dematerializes space into pure representation. Making space mean only what we want it to mean blinds us to "the social construction of affective geographies" and to the ways in which social relations are concretized and embedded in space. For example, as Pamela Ryan points out in regard to Mhlope's story "The Toilet," one must read this and other stories by South African black women with some understanding of their "literal lack of space": their compression between "the external forces of apartheid and colonialism, on the one hand, and . . . a deeply entrenched system of male dominance, on the other" (97). If one reads this story thinking only of gender, one misses the story itself.

Soja wants to break through perceptions of space as opaque or transparent to a contemplation of "the meaningful existential spatiality of being and human consciousness" (7). Perhaps part of what he means by this is a sense of one's own and others' identities as being paradoxically both located and mobile, here and there. One's own sense of being and location in the world is always under imaginative, linguistic construction. In her feminist critique of the field of geography, *Feminism and Geography,* Gillian Rose, for example, expresses a yearning for an "elsewhere." She is uncertain about the precise nature of such a space but knows that "it would not be like here and now"; imagining this elsewhere would allow women to feel safe and powerful, "somewhere beyond capture" (143). Feminist critique, Rose believes, "depends on a desire for something else" (138).

Yet the conceptual conundrum that contemporary, third-wave feminism seems to have inherited from its predecessors is the propensity to contour and solidify that something else so that it cannot travel or mutate. Thus arrested, something else may become what Yaeger calls "themed space," space that is "precolonized and prefabricated around an idea or point of view" (18). This tendency to freeze and contain the promise of alternative ways of conceptualizing gender and gendered arrangements is perhaps understandable: as Yaeger points out, "clever theming guarantees coherence and readability and, as an ecstatic bonus, has the capacity to be embodied or expanded; themes promise communal plenitude and coherent extension in space" (18). Yaeger's examples of themed space come from popular culture: the Magic Kingdom of Disney World, program notes of a fashion designer creating rhythms and colors of urban Africa, television journalists visiting the ghetto in safari jackets. These are spaces that connect performative simulacra with capitalist seductions. We are made to want to travel such spaces and to pay for our desire to do so. Theming "gratifies much more than a whimsical desire for homogenized, coherent space; it suggests a longing for incorporation, a longing to inhabit credible space" (18).

Massey also wonders about this nostalgic longing for a stable "place called home" (10) and worries that such homes (examples within feminism might include lesbian space, queer space, colonized space, the space of victims, the space of survivors, border space, the space of women of color and its multiple variations, outsider space, insider space, feminist community, women's studies) work against a conceptualization of place and identity that allows women mobility, literal or imaginative. One might indeed ask about the extent to which these places called home have been and are themed Magic Kingdoms that have materialized out of longings for coherence and incorporation and about the degree to which they are creations of the kind of mobility and interconnections that Massey advocates. To what extent do they mark a release from women's confinement and exclusion or, alternatively, embody fixed notions of identity and place that freeze and isolate gender as a category?

What is unmistakable is the imaginative dexterity of feminist efforts to ground but also restructure social relations within certain spaces, creating those spaces as pure representation, but representation that matters (as representation always does). Another kind of blindness about space occurs, however, when those spaces are assumed to be transparent or opaque—when they cannot be understood as specifically located and produced, as having certain blandishments and certain dangers. Or the spaces constituted by social relations may be seen as natural, lacking our own active constructed realities, in the way we put our own desires and resistances into play in their construction. "Theming," in Yaeger's sense of the term, depends on a notion of space as transparent. Drawing on Lefebvre, Alison Blunt and Gillian Rose show how "different epistemological claims about women's identity produce different interpretations of space itself" (5); one might add that the causal relationship here is reversible. As Blunt and Rose point out, essentialist notions of women, as well as universalist ideals of global sisterhood, both rely on and create transparent space that in turn tends toward homogeneity and a totality of knowledge. Complexity, difference, complication, and diversity are all absorbed confidently within these boundaries. To extrapolate to literary studies, Carla Kaplan's *The Erotics of Talk: Women's Writing and Feminist Paradigms* remarks on how the construction of themed spaces in critical analyses of women's writing has sometimes resulted in predictable rather than nuanced textual readings. Feminist readings with liberatory and recuperative themes, Kaplan argues, while serving certain important purposes, may celebrate unilateral notions of "the 'voice' of 'subversion' [and liberation?] which often take for granted identifications and linguistic effects that in fact cannot be presupposed" (147). Such readings do not take into account the complexity of a piece of narrative writing, because they erase the complications always attendant in motive and voice, not to speak of the extremely complex and multilayered social interactions that the author has encountered and in which she has engaged.[17]

What, then, are the relations between space (spatial representations *and* representations of space) and cultural critique, or between space and the multiple dimensions of gender, or between space and my subject—namely, women's narrative writings? Yaeger, also a literary critic, argues that the postmodern rethinking of space has profound implications for the field of cultural studies (25) and that the new cultural geography's insistence on the complex, hybrid nature of location and place "offers an important antidote to some of the dead-end binarisms within cultural studies" (15).[18] Massey's work is an important example of such interrogations, one with provocative implications for thinking about the spatial dynamics of women's narrative and feminist reading. (Interestingly, Massey, herself a geographer, turns to contemporary women's literature—for example, Morrison's *Beloved*—to elaborate her case.) Massey's larger argument is that space, typically coded feminine, must be rescued from a position of "stasis, passivity, and depoliticization" and reconceptualized in relation to time, typically coded masculine (6). Such a reconceptualization avoids opposing the spatial to the temporal as absence to presence but rather links spatiality to power in the social realm, thereby opening to an examination of "the spatiality of power itself" (4). The result of thinking simultaneously in terms of space and time is that one is able to see the dynamism of social relations and thus observe what Massey calls "the existence in the lived world of a simultaneous multiplicity of spaces: cross-cutting, intersecting, aligning with one another, or existing in relations of paradox or antagonism" (3). One is able to conceptualize not only dimension but also layers of dimension (such as those one finds in reading).[19]

Where can such a mobile and multidimensioned spatiality take us? To place and gender, simultaneously. According to Massey, the same gendering that creates the binary model wherein time is masculine (e.g., "history, progress, civilization, politics and transcendence") and space is feminine ("the opposites of these things") also operates through a series of dualisms that are connected to time and space. Hence Massey writes, "the exercise of rescuing space from its position, in this formulation, of stasis, passivity and depoliticization, therefore, connects directly with a wider philosophical debate in which gendering and the construction of gender relations are central" (7). Massey wants to examine not so much how space is coded as feminine but how the dualistic distinction between space and time relates to and propels other binaristic thinking, especially polarizing distinctions between genders. She observes that the ways in which gender inhabits space and place and is inhabited by them are complicated and reflexive. Spaces and places "are gendered through and through" in myriad and multiplying ways that vary depending on history and culture, our senses of these spaces and places, and other related matters such as degree of mobility. Moreover, "this gendering of space and place both reflects *and has effects back on* the ways in which gender is constructed and understood in the societies in which we live" (186). One might add that the polarization of male time versus female space also results in the failure of a complex social analysis that would bring together the local and the global.

I thus suggest, as have Massey and Friedman in somewhat different contexts, that foregrounding space in feminist thinking can be enormously helpful in understanding the complex textures of life and living. It does so because space can be strange, as strange as life. Let me give an example from a "true" story related by Judith Butler. The pool at Butler's community center in a Jewish neighborhood in Baltimore is filled with older women, blue concentration camp tattoos on their arms, flashing huge "compensatory thighs." The scene is a "hydro-aerobics" class, and the women dance in the water "with obvious pleasure" to a remake of Tommy James and the Shondells' "Mony Mony," from, as Butler notes, an adolescence they never had. In the locker room these same women inspect Butler's body "and offer advice." The attendant thinks she's a man and in the wrong locker room. The women want to know why she doesn't shave her legs and whether she is married yet. Here the spaces of exile and "home," past and present, pain and pleasure, are inextricably and complexly blended for everyone involved. In describing the scene in the pool, Butler herself feels a "collapse of temporal frames" and finds in that collapse an "occasion for affirmation." She dives in, joyfully, it seems ("Skeptical Feminist Postscript" 236). In the community center pool, as in Harjo's bar on the coldest night of the year, the real world does indeed collapse, and something else comes into being, another space in which time and history—both lived and imagined—are at once deeply present and presently transfigured. This is a cognitive process that is specifically located yet mysteriously destabilized and destabilizing. Here, as in Harjo's poem, there is the multiple story, laden with complexity and nuance—historically, geographically, socially—and there is *only* language to "say it"; that is all that is available to articulate this collapse into something that is both beautiful and terrible, something that language can't say but must.

How to limn this complexity? Dive into it? If, as Butler's story illustrates, the spatial can be rethought as composed of layers and cross-layerings of the web of social relations in space and time, then place may be seen in the way Massey suggests: as "a particular articulation of those relations, a particular moment in those networks of social relations and understandings . . . open and porous" rather than frozen, bounded, and static. As Massey points out, such a view of space-time and place as open-ended and overlapping has obvious implications for exclusivist or essentialist claims to places, positions, or identities (nationalistic or local) and "challenges any possibility of claims to internal histories or to timeless identities" (5). The identity of place is continually formed and re-formed out of the unsettled qualities of space-time and depends on its own articulation of those complexities.

Such a concept of place inevitably leads to an antiessentialist, problematic construction of identity and identity politics that is not bound by anchored and conclusive notions of place, whether national or local. The "character" of a place is found in the different layers of past and present, here and there, within and without, over time and space. Massey believes that we can understand the character of a place only by "linking that place to places beyond" and by conceiving "a global sense of the local, a global sense of place" (156). Such a definition can also be brought to bear on identity and gender and the linking of both "to places beyond." The woman in the red dress—where did she go in her climb up "the stairway to heaven" (6)? How far did she reach? Harjo writes that the woman's dance made people not just *see* but also change. For some, like Henry Jack, who "could not survive a sober day," this is "a miracle" (5).

Such happenings in and through space—while mobile, paradoxical, and intersecting—are nonetheless quite specific and local. As Henrietta Moore has shown in the field of anthropology (and as Massey herself shows in her discussions of urban environments in England), that which we call space can indeed be read as a text of specifically located social productions and relations. The contemplation of *representations* of such spatial texts—Butler's pool or Mhlope's toilet, for example—provides an opening in critical theory and literary analysis of the kind Massey sees in geography and cultural studies—a way in, not only to the trickiness of any piece of writing worth its salt but to the crucial levers between social relations and language, location and imagination.

Space is always tied to power relations, which are clearly a subject of crucial interest for feminism and feminist theory. The serious contemplation of space provides a way into the dynamics of power, for as David Sibley reiterates, following Foucault and Lefebvre, the rituals of spatial organization are always implicated in power dynamics and social control, as well as in the construction of deviancy: "Self and other, and the spaces they create and are alienated from, are defined through projection and introjection. Thus, the built environment assumes symbolic importance, reinforcing a desire for order and conformity if the environment itself is ordered and purified; in this way, space is implicated in the construction of deviancy. Pure spaces expose difference and facilitate the policing of boundaries" (86). Sibley, in fact, calls for "an anthropology of space" to analyze the problem of exclusion and exclusiveness (72).

It goes without saying that feminism's most trenchant interrogations have concerned the spatial problems of exclusion and confinement—being locked out or locked in.[20] In the twentieth century these interrogations were marked by memorable moments:

- Virginia Woolf's famous complaint in *A Room of One's Own* about not being allowed to enter the "Oxbridge" College library and her question about whether it's better to be locked out of such a place than locked in;
- Luce Irigaray's haunting lament, "Everywhere you shut me in. Always you assign a place to me. . . . You mark out boundaries, draw

lines, surround, enclose. Excising, cutting out" (*Elemental Passions* 24);
- — Legal theorist and historian Patricia Williams's description of her "round brown face" pressed to the window of Benetton's in Soho, inside of which a gum-chewing white teenaged clerk deemed her too dangerous to buzz in (44);
- — Gloria Anzaldúa's complexly articulated strategies for living in border space as a queer Chicana "by developing a tolerance for contradictions, a tolerance for ambiguity" (*Borderlands* 79);
- — Arundhati Roy's brilliant narrative of postcolonial but caste-bound India, where "History and Literature [are] enlisted by commerce" and "ancient stories [are] collapsed and amputated" both in space and time so that tourists can see a highly condensed and uncomplicated "ethnic" dance while sipping drinks around the pool (*God of Small Things* 120–21)

Especially in the field of geography, where space is precisely the point, feminist scholars have focused on what Rose calls "the gender of geography" (5). Rose's claim that disciplinary productions of knowledge have excluded both women as its producers and women's issues as its objects has been a mantra for women's studies over the past three decades. Rose contends that this erasure of women creates a disciplinary situation in which "to think geography—to think within the parameters of the discipline in order to create geographical knowledge acceptable to the discipline—is to occupy a masculine subject position" (4). (It may be noted that feminist disciplinary critique comes a bit late to geography, following feminists' similar observations about other disciplines in the 1970s and 1980s—well-known examples, among many, include Irigaray's challenges to psychoanalytic theory in *Speculum of the Other Woman* [1974] and *This Sex Which Is Not One* [1977]; Judith Fetterley's critique of American literature and literary history as masculinist constructions in *The Resisting Reader* [1978]; Williams's searing interrogation of law and law enforcement in *The Alchemy of Race and Rights* [1991]; and Scott's focus on the meaning-making properties of language in constructing history in *Gender and the Politics of History* [1988]). Rose calls for "a politics of paradoxical space" that "does not replicate the exclusions of the Same and the Other" but acknowledges a proliferation of differences within and beyond gender, a "radical heterogeneity among women, which is a space for struggle and resistance" (137, 136).

Paradoxical space. Yes, the woman in the red dress performs struggle and resistance, but the poem also destabilizes the ground on which struggle and resistance stand by complicating gendered alignments and constructions, both culturally and erotically. In this poem, survival, erotics, and gender are specifically linked, but in complicated ways. Among Native Americans of the Southwest, Deer Dances are an important cultural event signifying a connection to the natural world and the importance of deer in ensuring survival (Frisbie 82). Several of the southwestern Deer Dances (including those at Santa Clara and San Juan Pueblos in New Mexico, a state in which Harjo lived for several years), are performed by male dancers. Often women watch and even chase the men into the woods.[21] Paula Gunn Allen's story "Deer Woman," which builds on a Cherokee story, has two men leaving a bar with two strange women before noticing that the women have hooves instead of feet. Other deer dancer stories have focused on the potentially violent nature of Deer Woman: in a number of Omaha Deer Woman stories, those who follow Deer Woman into the woods are found dead, often by castration, the next morning (Evers 45), and among the Oglala Lakota, Deer Woman is often said to kill the men she seduces (Lang 230). Perhaps even more interesting are some Dakota, Ponca, Omaha, Oto, Pawnee, and Creek stories where Deer Woman is a prime cause of male homosexuality (Evers 38).

Against this background of Native stories, Harjo's gaze and the gaze of other women in the poem ("She was no slouch, and neither were we watching" [6]) complicate and ignite the poem's erotic field. Not only is the woman specifically located in material and cultural spaces, but gender—the energy she generates as a woman, probably a Native woman, who performs struggle and resistance, beauty and desire, in a cold, dismal bar out in the middle of nowhere—becomes a space of imagined social and erotic relations that produces complexly subversive encounters with the unexpected, the miraculous, perhaps even the dangerous and forbidden.

So the woman in the red dress travels.

As subject matter, space has no limit; hence its challenge. My inquiries herein are shaped around the triad of space, narrative, and gender. In negotiating the distances and contiguities between Yaeger's postmodern engagements with spatiality and Rose's real-space admonishments that are poised, frozen, alongside each other in the dueling epigraphs of my introduction, this book is composed of three discrete but overlapping parts—all meditations on certain spatial dynamics, interior and exterior, of contemporary women's narrative writing. I believe that these representations of space in narrative, which itself depends for its very life on multiple locations—cultural, geographic, historical—and on our desire as readers to move through time and space, may return us to Massey's desire, which I share, for a connection with what is contingent and permeable about both space and gender, for that opening, that something, that someone, that somewhere, else that rides the motion of the imagination.

Yet this book is as much about the permeability of reading as it is about the spatial dynamics of textuality, how reading itself may create a dimension that brings readers and writers into crucial confluences that help us travel and negotiate the differences of lived social relations, of collapsed realities. What I hope to illustrate in a variety of contexts and examples is that writing and reading contour these envelopes of space-time. Sometimes when we read, we become those we are not. It is my belief that this perpetual displacement and replacement of identity—this often disconcerting disalignment of the self's borders through reading literature—can lead to a more precise and profound understanding of our own social locations and relations as well as those of others and, further, can make us aware of the always thick overlays of location and relation.

In *Ruined by Reading* Lynne Sharon Schwartz argues for the passion and possibility of reading as "escape from the boundaries of our own voices and idioms" (112). Such reading, she believes, brings space and time together, teaching us to "sit still" and "confront time head-on" (115), thereby opening a space for "the story itself, with its own inner life that occupies the vast spaces of our own" (111). My argument is that such reading, because it *is* pleasurable, cannot help but be politically consequential by dislocating us from within the boundaries of our own experiences. It is this movement of leaning into the inwardness of the one who is not I that can inspire respect and trust, that can teach me something—though certainly not everything—about not always being *here.* It can also change what I think of as here. Schwartz writes that when she was a child, reading provided a way to make her life her own (119); I suggest that reading is a way to make one's life and one's self both more and less than one's own through a meaningful act of dislocation from known geographies.

It is to be hoped that such an act of dislocation will allow the reader some access into different historical and cultural spaces, but it is not so much destination (whether the woman in Harjo's poem really wore a red dress or was really from a recognized tribe, or Morrison's "historical accuracy" in *Beloved*) but the act of dislocation itself that is self-altering.[22] On this point my approach differs from Friedman's discussions of literature for illustrative purposes in the context of what a transnational feminist critical practice might become. My focus is how some literature works in such mysterious ways, not only to *move* us, in the most multiple and complicated sense of the word, from one place to another but also, in that process of travel, to *change* us so that we are never quite the same again. "Literariness," Barbara Johnson observes in *The Feminist Difference,* resists the simplistic, the binary. It is this resistance that makes literature important for feminism, "because literature can best be understood as the place where impasses can be kept and opened for examination, where questions can be guarded and not forced into a premature validation of the available paradigms. Literature, that is, is not to be understood as a predetermined set of works but as a mode of cultural work, the work of giving-to-read those impossible contradictions that cannot yet be spoken" (13).

Such contradictions are readily apparent in my choice of texts, which all in one way or another enact women's many and varied experiences of enclosure, confinement, and restraint. What I have found, however, is that when a space seems really closed, it may open in some other way, internally perhaps, always mysteriously, sometimes only on the wings of the imagination. Despite their mystery, such spatial moves need to be charted because they reflect the subtle shifts in identity and perception that bring about mutation and transformation; they produce mirror images that return us to the world and suggest that the world can be changed. I have chosen these texts because they do just that. They show us how tight spaces can open precipitously, on the wings of the imagination, to reimagined social relations.

Although throughout this book I distinguish among spaces—material, narrative, textual, metaphoric, cultural—I have a general perception of space as a field of productivity that is mobile, ambiguous, and always in the process of being temporalized. This I take from those whose thoughts on space I have discussed, as well as from Michel de Certeau, who imagines space as "composed of intersections of mobile elements . . . actuated by the ensemble of movements deployed within it . . . like the word when it is spoken, that is, when it is caught in the ambiguity of an actualization. . . . In short, *space is a practiced place*" (117). So when I say space, I am actually thinking more in terms of what Massey calls space-time. The social and aesthetic productions that make space never occur outside time because these productions are themselves temporal.

With this sense of mobility in mind, I turn in these pages to a certain kind of reading I call space travel. Its characteristics are an acute absorption in the stories I read; an attention to representations of the female body's grounding in the local and specific as well as women's experiences *of* the spaces we inhabit and create; and finally, a flavor of the imaginative excitement Yaeger describes—a space flight of sorts—precipitated by writing and reading that pose gender as a mode of travel, not a destination. Yaeger calls for a poetics of geography; herein I try to map a geography of poetics, charting those spatial representations and practices in writing and reading that dislocate us from our own lived lives and geographies, that travel us as we travel them, and that, in doing all this, make us find pleasure in the traveler who has come to inhabit and alter us—sometimes to haunt us.

This motion of the imagination, through its encounters with space, is both a collapse of and an encounter with reality, a complex, narrative geography of where we seem to be, where we might have been, and where we might go. It is like the moment when the woman in the red dress travels from the bar table into myth and takes everyone with her—rooted in the real world, yet in flight.

1 *Space Travel: Reading Helplessly*

Yesterday I finished reading Rosellen Brown's *Tender Mercies,* a novel about a woman named Laura who becomes almost completely paralyzed when her husband accidentally runs over her in a boat while she is swimming. Laura can barely move one hand. She reads books by shoving the pages over with her whole hand, "like a bear tipping a honey pot" (159).

During the day Laura reads books about "untouchable matters." At night she dreams of flying, of floating, her limbs waving, her hair blowing in the wind. She dreams she is a woman in motion.

Last night, with *Tender Mercies* on my bedside table, I dreamed, after a full day in an able body, of immobility, the space of the wheelchair, of being unable to get through doors. I dreamed I was rolled in to my high school class reunion, my head bent over like a lily.

In introductory remarks at a reading of *Beloved* in 1988, Toni Morrison spoke about how she tried to take her readers in her hand and gently pull them into the historical space of more than two hundred years of North American slavery. This was, as she said, a space "which under its best conditions was unthinkable." Both she and the reader, she said, needed to do what the slaves had done: "enter that space *helplessly.*"

> Just to imagine it on a very day-to-day basis and then to translate that imagination into language that could hold it just hold it, not compete

> with it, but just hold it because that's all you want the language to do under those circumstances and finding finally a simple sentence that could say it just right, waiting for the language to arrive and the picture to arrive and then hoping that there had been some seduction on the part of myself as writer so that the reader can enter into this place without fear and trepidation and do what they had done—that is the slaves (I had to do what they had done; I wanted the reader to do what they had done) which was simply to enter that space *helplessly,* with nothing to help you, except one day at a time, one page at a time: feeding the information, retreating from it, dealing with it, going back to it so that there is nothing but the aid and succor that the voice of the narrator provides so that we are all—myself as a reluctant writer, readers as perhaps diffident readers, the characters as people who never ever speak to anybody unless forced to, who spend all of their time trying not to say it, not to remember it, not to have it seep in. So all of us—characters author reader—are invited on a journey nobody really wants to take and the only thing that can save us all is the language that must arrive honest, clean, straight-up, and trustworthy. (Remarks)

These are thoughts in this first chapter about what it means to read as a commitment to the unknown, how one might "enter that space *helplessly.*" In a study of the gendering of space among the Marakwet of Kenya, anthropologist Henrietta Moore has argued that material space can be read as a text. To understand space as a text, Moore says, is "to conceive of the spatial order as something more than merely the physical manifestation, or product of, activities conducted in space. Spatial texts may, therefore, be said to have both a history and a future" (*Space, Text, and Gender* 81). As it looks both forward and backward, space is therefore always imbricated with narrative. Moore is interested in reading space as a narrative of social relations. Conversely, I will be reading narrative texts as productions of material and cultural spaces that partake of time in a number of complex ways, not the least of which is that the social relations which create them have a history in the real world.

It is my hope that this book travels wider and wider circles from beginning to end. In this chapter my discussion foregrounds theories of space, gender, and reading on the one hand and specific readings of literary texts—texts in which space itself is foregrounded—on the other. As I've said, I see the intersection of reading and space as an important site for understanding gender in complex and laden ways: locating gender in specific social relations, geographies, and histories but also *dis*locating gender in terms of how it can be imagined. This process of dislocation that reading by its very nature offers is of consequence, not only because it enables the reader to "travel" and become the site of travel, not only because it embodies the thick reality of women's lives, but because it sets the imagination to the exacting task of thinking gender differently.

Thinking gender differently has in recent years taken on multiple meanings. It has become a widely held assumption that positionings as women must be conceived relationally, palimpsestically, and globally. As Moore has stressed, "identity and difference are not so much about categorical groupings as about processes of identification and differentiation" (*Passion for Difference* 2).[1] A second and not unrelated way of thinking gender differently pivots on Judith Butler's groundbreaking work in queer theory. Butler considers how both gender and body need to be reconceptualized as both constructed and performative; hence: "If gender is the cultural meanings that the sexed body assumes, then a gender cannot be said to follow from a sex in any one way" (*Gender Trouble* 6). Indeed, "there may be forms of 'gender' within homosexuality which call for a theorization that moves beyond the categories of 'masculine' and 'feminine'" (*Bodies* 238). Interestingly, in *Bodies That Matter* Butler, like Massey and Moore, uses literary readings to ground and situate her argument that both gender and bodies are governed by the regulatory practices that produce them.

Reading literature has functioned in such feminist arguments as illustrative of the complicated transmutations of gender and the idea of gender. My incursions into specific texts, however, are less about grounding an argument than about tracing the process of the imagination as it travels the spatial/narrative dimensions of gender. Rethinking gender requires imagination, just as bringing gender theoretically to its full complexity requires imagination as well as knowledge. Reading (and hearing) stories is a way of knowing through imagining, and when reading attends to space in narrative and the spatial configurations of our own responses to narrative, it is possible to bring the cognitive and embodied experience of what Rose calls "being in space" to the foreground in one's own experience of the world, one's own critical practice. The move from empiricism to imaginative thought—materiality to metaphor—and vice versa occurs mysteriously, powerfully. It is hard to trace or describe because such moves are, indeed, always on the move. How the spaces of a single book may travel to and through one of us to many of us, and to many more of us, is beyond comprehension or measure.

Yet such spaces also can be precise and material. As Moore and others have shown, material space is not arbitrary but rather a complex text of the social relations that both form materiality and move within it. This complexity becomes even thicker in a literary text that is itself focused on material space. When I teach Harriet Jacobs's *Incidents in the Life of a Slave Girl,* I try to reconstruct in rough form the confining space in which Jacobs lived for seven years, a nine-by-seven-foot area with only three feet of headroom at its highest point. I encourage students to enter it and imagine themselves in it through heat and cold, wind and rain—for seven years. This seems a necessary thing to do, both because of Jacobs's careful attention to the measurements and description of the garret and because of the relationship of the garret to the outside, where her master and mistress terrorize her.

Jacobs wants her nineteenth-century readers to understand just how small her garret was and how insubstantial:

> A small shed had been added to my grandmother's years ago. Some boards were laid across the joists at the top, and between these boards and the roof was a very small garret, never occupied by any thing but rats and mice. It was a pent roof, covered with nothing but shingles, according to the southern custom for such buildings. The garret was only nine feet long and seven feet wide. The highest part was three feet high, and sloped down abruptly to the loose board floor. There was no admission for either light or air. (114)

How does it feel to be in the garret? To be unable to stand upright?

> To this hole I was conveyed as soon as I entered the house. The air was stifling; the darkness total. A bed had been spred on the floor. I could sleep quite comfortably on one side; but the slope was so sudden that I could not turn on the other without hitting the roof. The rats and mice ran over my bed. . . . This continued darkness was oppressive. It seemed horrible to sit or lie in a cramped position day after day, without one gleam of light. Yet I would have chosen this, rather than my lot as a slave. (114)

As time goes by, Jacobs writes, her misery increases: "I was tormented by hundreds of little red insects, fine as a needle's point, that pierced through my skin, and produced an intolerable burning. . . . The heat of my den was intense, for nothing but thin shingles protected me from the scorching summer's sun. . . . when winter came, the cold penetrated through the thin shingle roof, and I was dreadfully chilled. . . . my shoulders and feet were frostbitten" (114–15). Eventually Jacobs bores an inch-sized hole in the wall of the garret, allowing her to watch her children playing below and to watch Dr. Flint's comings and goings. In doing this she creates a spatial reversal. She has inverted the panoptic situation she had found herself in; she becomes the watcher rather than the watched. A sculpture exhibited several years ago at the Whitney Museum in New York reconstructed Jacobs's space, interestingly enough, in the shape of a giant eye which could be entered and looked out of—a material space that enacted in its own dimensions, in the largeness of the eye, the power reversal of Jacobs's spatial move.[2] Her small space becomes large because, although she suffers physical and mental anguish, she has evaded the more constricted and dangerous social relations of a woman who is a slave in the house of a man intent on raping her. At the same time she has enacted for her readers the cultural space of African American women's experience, both the compression of that experience—women's terror of open space, whether on a slave ship or in the master's house—and women's powerful turn to spatial protection, whether in the form of a garret or some other form of resistance. Claustrophobic enclosure, certainly painful in itself, nonetheless makes possible this reversal.

One can carefully examine the sketch of Jacobs's hiding place in Jean Fagan Yellin's edition of Jacobs's book. One can note that it is three feet high *only at its highest point, which itself is not directly above the flooring where Jacobs might have stood bent over.* One can just as carefully contemplate Jacobs's stubborn resistance within the material spaces of her life, how even at the end of her story, when she has escaped to the North and her freedom has been purchased by a white woman, she resists the notion that what was truly always hers, her freedom, has to be secured with money.

Jacobs's narrative urges the embodied imagination, the imagined body.[3] It invites imaginative entry into material and cultural space, just as it invited readers of the nineteenth century, especially white women of the North, whom Jacobs often addresses in her text, to enter, as confined bodies, its representations of space as a paradoxical site of enclosure and freedom. Although her purposes were socially and psychologically complex, Jacobs addressed these women chiefly because they could exert influence, not because they were her ideal readers. So this is a spatial text with a specific history of readership and power built into its historical relations between writer and readers. Thinking about such relations—reading them as a spatial text, much as Moore reads material space as an anthropologist—is helpful in evaluating the material and cultural spaces Jacobs inhabited and their ideological constructions. Jacobs's story, by encouraging contemporary readers like myself to enter it as a site of cultural production, ends up reading and critiquing our reading practices.

This is then a complicated relationship among readers past and present, text, space, gender, location, history. What does it really mean? What does it matter? My travel into Jacobs's material spaces and their travel into my contemporary cultural spaces serve both to lengthen and shorten the distance between her world and my own. Reading her words, her life, brings me to a point at which I can imagine, in very embodied ways, both her cultural enclosure and her resistance to enclosure. But my work lies not only in reading, but in traversing that distance which lies between Jacobs and myself, to measure and assess it, even as it enters and transforms my understanding of who she was. The distance between. History, race, location. Being simultaneously inside and outside such a text as Jacobs's requires reading one's own social relations and histories, even as identity and position themselves fluctuate in the process of that reading.

Such a reading practice thickens the enigma that gender poses as a dense relational construction. Let me hasten to say that I do not propose reading as a substitute for political action or interaction or claim this kind of reading as specifically or exclusively feminist. An observation about the value of reading comes, for example, from C. S. Lewis, who believes that we read to "seek an enlargement of our being. We want to be more than ourselves . . . [,] to go out of the self, to correct its provincialism and heal its loneliness" (137–38). Lewis rejects the view that literature is to be valued for its truth value or its cultural work, or that literature liberates its reader from the borders of self. The kind of reading I am suggesting, however, does all this and therefore can be politically efficacious because it propels the reader into a state of dislocation, perhaps even into a state of loneliness. The reader is acted on, drawn into another's space, altered. This, as Johnson notes in her strong endorsement of literature's importance to feminism, is indeed "cultural work" (*Feminist Difference* 13).[4]

In terms of the cultural work of this project, reading not only urges motion; it urges a rethinking of gender as motion. Like reading, gender becomes not a fixed site or position, not even a complexly relational construction, but a mode of travel. Literature is its unpredictable flight path, and as the texts I will be reading show, "being a woman"—whatever that may come to mean over time and place and circumstance—necessitates imaginative travel. That the imaginative process of reading is, and indeed must be, richly pleasurable—that it is an aesthetic process at its very core—does not deprive it of social consequence. That it can be consequential in the social realm does not rob it of its beauty and power to give us immense pleasure. Toni Morrison's *Beloved,* for example, is nothing if not beautiful.

Real and imagined spaces and borders of identity are themselves not only permeable but also mobile; their mobility has implications for the ways in which we continually construct ourselves (and others). Space has everything to do with this process. Both material and metaphoric spatialities can reveal seemingly innocent inscriptions of power in human relations.[5]

Because such reading can be both solitary practice and communal experience, aesthetic production and cultural work that imbricates material and metaphoric spaces, it relies on a corporeal imagination. By this I mean a sense of how physical bodies, as well as social relations, inhabit and make the tangibility of space and how lived and imagined genders and bodies converge with representational practices of theorizing and imagining gender. Rosi Braidotti argues that the body is "one's primary location in the world, one's primary situation in reality" (*Nomadic Subjects* 219). That location and its situation are never stable, however, but rather always being negotiated among the corporeal, the constructed, and the imagined. The body travels, and not just literally.

What is reading for if not to bring the embodied imagination to these unsettling connections, these dreams? These other spaces we inhabit and these other identities who inhabit us? As Joseph Urgo says, "Literary recognition is not a matter of mirrored reflection but an abrupt encounter with something we thought we had lost, some way of thinking possessed by someone else, in another place, at some other time" (258). This is the pleasure—and the seriousness—of reading imaginative writing. It is like unexpectedly encountering the woman in the red dress and knowing, somehow, that one has seen something more than a woman in a red dress. One has perhaps seen a path into the forest from which one might never emerge.

In the preface to this book I described the way I learned to travel through reading.[6] A woman from an immigrant Italian family of eight children tells me how she and her mother made a poster for a book fair. They painted a picture of a female genie on a magic carpet, along with the poem they composed together:

> I couldn't travel around the world.
> I didn't have the fare.
> But I read lots of books
> and they took me everywhere.[7]

It goes without saying that many women throughout history and across cultures haven't been able to travel freely. But the genie on my friend's poster is telling. Is it possible that some or perhaps many women, because of lost and limited opportunities to travel, have become particularly adept at "traveling" through reading and hence at *re*materializing the metaphor of travel? For example, Anzaldúa writes: "When I was seven, eight, nine, fifteen, sixteen years old, I would read in bed with a flashlight under the covers, hiding my self-imposed insomnia from my mother. I preferred the world of the imagination to the death of sleep. My sister, Hilda, who slept in the same bed with me, would threaten to tell my mother unless I told her a story" (*Borderlands* 65). Similarly, Frances Murphy Zauhar confesses to having grown up with her nose in a book and cites "other pernicious examples of *excessive female reading*" (105–6). Her essay is part of a 1993 anthology entitled *The Intimate Critique: Autobiographical Literary Criticism,* whose contributors share the conviction that, contrary to what we've been taught about the reader's authority as dependent on disengagement from a text, feminist readers need to get back to the original emotional engagement we had with books—that reading, as well as writing, is a way of rescuing ourselves from our own wounds (Graulich 188), our loneliness. For some it may be a way of rescuing the erotic power that, as Audre Lorde has said, so many women have repressed to live in a world that denies the erotic.[8]

Certainly narrative and storytelling create desire. Stories are told *to* someone; listeners or readers are invited into a shared space. In Zora Neale Hurston's *Their Eyes Were Watching God,* Janie Crawford sits on the back step and tells her story to her "kissin' friend" Phoeby, and while she does so, Phoeby, a "hungry listener" who hasn't been anywhere, "dilate[s] all over with eagerness" to travel the spaces of Janie's life: "They sat there in the fresh young darkness close together. Phoeby eager to feel and do through Janie, but hating to show her zest for fear it might be thought mere curiosity. Janie full of that oldest human longing—self-revelation. Phoeby held her tongue for a long time, but she couldn't help moving her feet. So Janie spoke" (7).

Phoeby's form of travel is both imaginative and visceral. There is intimacy within this space between teller and listener, the production of mutual pleasure and travel, unlike the patriarchally controlled spaces (the field, the store, the house) Janie inhabited during her first two marriages.[9] At the same time, the sociality of the space between Janie and Phoeby as black women in a black community talking about relationships with black men has its own ideological exigencies and its own cultural history. Carla Kaplan believes that "reading *Their Eyes Were Watching God* as a story of communal reintegration and reconciliation mediated through the positivity of love and voice occludes the ways in which Hurston's revision of the romance narrative (denying Janie her conventional lover-hero and granting her a heroine-listener instead) works to *deepen* rather than reduce the contradictions cutting across it" (121). Janie's story creates not one but many hungry listeners of contradiction. We, as readers, may find ourselves, and our hunger, both outside and inside the space of telling and listening, both included and excluded. Yet the space of Janie's story of heterosexual desire, couched as it is within the complex workings of several black communities and the closeness between two black women, nonetheless travels to encircle us. We may travel from other places, other histories, all with their own contradictory inclinations, to find ourselves inside the store with Janie, down in the muck with Janie, in the courtroom with Janie, hunkering down on the porch steps with Janie—like Phoeby, "eager to feel and do through Janie" (6). We simply can't help it.

This is sometimes what happens when we read. There is a shift in identity that opens the path for imaginative encounter. In a discussion of American Indian orality, Marilou Awiakta finds "there is *no psychic distance* between the singer and the song; listeners share the web of context and experience" (194).[10] Yet in a story like Janie's, like Hurston's, hungry listeners may find that distance also has a story to tell. Mae Gwendolyn Henderson suggests that Janie's earlier challenge in addressing an all-white male jury in her murder trial is the challenge of the black woman writer—"namely, to speak at once to a diverse audience about her experience in a racist and sexist society where to be black and female is to be, so to speak, 'on trial'" (21). This is, of course, Jacobs's task as well, as she is acutely aware when she repeatedly asks white women of the North to consider the very real distance between her experience as a slave and theirs as free women. Hurston therefore creates both inclusive and exclusive space in her novel. That space has a history; it folds in time, location, circumstance. Hurston's novel requires an enclosure of the reader within textual space at the same time that the reader remains aware of cultural and material spaces—reader's, writer's, and characters'—and their ideological underpinnings and histories that enmesh the story and its readings and readers.

With women's published fiction and autobiography growing by leaps and bounds in small press, university, and world trade markets in the first decade of the twenty-first century, reading literature seems a somewhat conspicuous way to explore large and vexing questions about gender in a seemingly unlimited heterogeneity of cultural spaces.[11] Books such as Suzanne Juhasz's *Reading from the Heart: Women, Literature, and the Search for Love,* Lynne Sharon Schwartz's *Ruined by Reading,* and Lynne

Pearce's *Feminism and the Politics of Reading* have combined personal and theoretical approaches with the project of feminist reading. Pearce believes that the reading process has a mind of its own and, much as we would like to try, can never be completely marshaled for politically efficacious ends (38). The emotional complexity of reading summons us to become what Pearce calls "implicated" readers because we are drawn into the text in complicated, apolitical (sometimes antipolitical) ways. There is, as I hope to show in this chapter, readerly investment—and investiture—not only because we become, as Pearce notes, emotionally involved in a text but also because we find pleasure in that linkage. There is something about such fluctuation and flight, as I have said, that is almost impossible to describe. This sense of motion, this space travel, has to do with imagination and identity: how fluctuation within the self, and the world, is always possible if one can just think it.

It may seem anachronistic to say that reading and teaching literature by women is more crucially important than ever before. Women's writing is still underrepresented, however, and feminist critical thought, after its incredibly generative seepage into all forms of contemporary critical discourse, is now considered "post." On the international scene the Modern Library's ranking of "the 100 best novels in English of the twentieth century" is an ethnocentric list featuring works by such choices as Jack London, Richard Hughes, and Erskine Caldwell while omitting those by Toni Morrison, Eudora Welty, Zora Neale Hurston, Annie Proulx, Alice Walker, Margaret Atwood, Leslie Marmon Silko, Djuna Barnes, and other modern and contemporary women writers. Of the one hundred novels chosen, only eight were written by women authors, one of whom—Edith Wharton—is cited for two books.

The Barnes and Noble bookstore in Albuquerque, New Mexico, where I lived until recently, sports a huge mural running across the top of one enormous wall and depicting early twentieth-century writers in a cafe, Parisian-style. The Great Authors sit at tables, sipping, chatting (about Great Literature surely), and smoking. The seated figures have their names emblazoned under them: Hemingway, Orwell, Nabokov, Joyce, Fitzgerald (Scott, not Zelda), Parker (Dorothy), Faulkner, Steinbeck, Eliot (T. S.), Singer, Kafka, Neruda, Hughes (Langston), Tagore (Rabindranath), and Hurston (the last three, all people of color, sit together at the table on the far right). Sprinkled in with these thirteen male and two female authors are three women with big hats over their faces. Under these hats the No-Name Women have blurred faces, which make it perfectly clear that they are Nobody. Or perhaps they are Shakespeare's sisters, or the male authors' main squeezes. Here's who they are not: Radclyffe Hall, Virginia Woolf,

Gertrude Stein, Nella Larsen, Willa Cather, Djuna Barnes, H.D., Mina Loy, Elizabeth Bishop. And so on.

What is especially interesting is that the mural does not just omit women writers such as Woolf but replaces them with the No-Name Women with blurred faces. So this was not a matter of space—the usual argument for the lack of certain authors in anthologies and on graduate reading lists—but rather a matter of . . . what, taste? A woman without a face is better than a woman writer with one? I've since discovered that these murals, in their various larger or smaller forms, occur in Barnes and Noble stores throughout the United States. In a New Orleans store, for instance, the mural dips back into the nineteenth century, incorporating thirteen white male writers, Mary Shelley, Emily Dickinson, and an unnamed aboriginal man (standing behind Melville) with tattoos, earrings, and a shell-necklace pipe, in addition to several other unnamed women and men.

I realize that I sound tiresomely obvious, offering a stale slice of the feminist enterprise of literary canon expansion that began in the 1970s. But such lists and murals and all they instill are cultural work. Their presence, and the work they do, argues that literature and literary study may now be of graver consequence to postmodern, transcultural feminist theorizing and activism than they have been understood to be.[12] Distrust of the literary and the narrative remains deeply embedded in the social sciences, and especially, as Barbara Christian has pointed out, in relation to the modes of theoretical discourse historically employed by people of color, which has often taken narrative forms. At the same time, though, theories developed through narrativity have been devalued within academic theoretical discourse that privileges abstract logic over the complexity and heterogeneity of narrative literatures ("Race for Theory" 336). In women's studies and cultural studies, for example, there is a continuing insistence that reading literature is somehow less a political enterprise than is reading empirical research in the social sciences—that the stories we read and our methods for reading them have little to do with how we live our lives. Large women's studies conferences often have only a few sessions on literature, which are usually not well attended.

Yet it has become commonplace to say that many women are writing to bring narrative space into a transformative relation with material reality. When my mother, Erin Clayton Pitner, sensed an oncoming sea change in her life in her midfifties, she began to write and publish poems she said were "set down between a rock and a hard place" (Pitner, preface). As Dorothy Allison says in her introduction to the short story collection *Trash,* "I write stories. I write fiction. I put on the page a third look at what I've seen in life—the condensed and reinvented experience of a cross-eyed working-class lesbian, addicted to violence, language, and hope, who has made the decision to live, is determined to live, on the page and on the street, for me and mine" (12).

Pitner's poetry and Allison's stories are about being between a rock and a hard place; tight spaces are their subject matter. Such texts shape the dynamic and incessant productions of ideology, as do our readings of them, and as do our readings of our own readings. To read literature with this awareness is not to view those stories as mirror images of feminist ideologies but rather to experience the workings of ideology, that is, the vast networks and systems of belief which inevitably engender and gender relations of power. To read is to participate in the workings of this production and reproduction.

At the same time, reading, as Moore notes in relation to "reading" space as text, may itself become complicit in maintaining the interests of dominant groups by limiting and controlling "the range of possible relationships between text and ideology," and thereby narrowing the field of interpretation (*Space, Text, and Gender* 89). Narrowing the field of interpretation—that is, limiting the range of possible relationships between the text and cultural production—historically has served important subversive purposes in literary study, a prominent example being Judith Fetterley's 1977 admonition to women to become "resisting readers" of the misogyny and androcentrism of white male American literature. As Johnson and others have argued, however, literature's importance to feminism lies in its resistance to delimitation. Literature travels.

Friedman stresses the importance of cultural encounter to feminist critical practice and offers film, art, and literature as meaningful examples of such encounter. My work here is to dramatize textual encounters in which narrative, space, and gender inscribe themselves on one another and their readers. Some stories are profoundly political, and in a dual sense. They give narrative frames—a sense of material relations—to women's very different but sometimes connected struggles. At the same time, though, they situate, complicate, and open gender as a category of analysis.

How are such texts related to the ideological processes that produce and are produced by them? How can one's own inevitably ideologically imbued reading open up, rather than close down, a text's spaces of production? The language and stories of some texts fuel our passions and imaginations in ways that are intense but difficult to describe. How do these texts and the way they move us bleed into the world? What is literature *for*?[13]

To contemplate space is to contemplate identity and relation. To read spatially is to enact identity and relation. In such contemplations and enactments, spatial strategies of reading can make possible travel between the many and varied locations and ideological spaces that encompass a complex world. These strategies need to take into account the complications of how both texts and readings produce and are produced by ideology. These are knotty issues, and it is significant that both Johnson (in *The Feminist Difference*) and Friedman (in *Mappings*) have worried about conflicts among feminists, both locally and globally, around issues of the ideological control of difference. I have my own story about this. Here is a story of a story and how it was read and not read.

In Albuquerque in 1992, a large group of feminists became engaged in a bitter battle over a short story published in *Frontiers: A Journal of Women's Studies,* then housed at the University of New Mexico. The story, "Crickets," by Nancy Gage, a white woman from a rural working-class background, includes an African American man who rapes a young white woman. The primary characters are white and working class (the rapist is in jail when the narrative begins), and some of the dialogue among these characters is intentionally racist and misogynist. Many readers, women of color and white women, believed the story to be racist in its characterization, language, and plot, while a minority, again some women of color and white women (most in literary studies), read the story as an exploration of the intersections of racism and misogyny, which was Gage's stated intent. The first group, who believed that the story should not have been published in a feminist journal, insisted that the second group recant what was perceived as a racist reading of a racist text. (Each group included varieties of subpositions.) Some did revise their initial readings of the story. Those who continued to advocate the possibility of multiple readings were publicly chastised as racists. The controversy quickly spread to the community, involving the local feminist newspaper and bookstore. Decades-long friendships were shattered. Coalitions dissolved in a torrent of bitterness and distrust. When months later "Crickets" was produced as a play at the local repertory theater, with an African American woman as director, some feminists and members of the NAACP picketed the theater and chanted so loudly during the performance that the audience was unable to hear.

The controversy itself became a text that was read by multiple audiences. Those readings were articulated in a number of polarities: "Racists" against "antiracists." "Good" white women against "racist" white women. "Real" women of color against "co-opted" women of color. "Academic elitists" against "women of the community." Those in favor of "censorship" against those opposed to "censorship." The question became one of authority and positionality: who was *authorized* to read this text "correctly"? Women of color? African American women? Women with black sons? Feminists who taught literature? Women who had been raped? African American men? "Antiracists"? The author? The issue of who held the authority to read "correctly" and the question of which women's texts were indeed "authorized" in feminist circles brought back for some in literary studies the ghosts of white male professors who had edited and published anthologies, controlled reading lists, and chosen their female students' dissertation topics. For some African American women, this was yet another case of white women's broken promises of acknowledgment and respect.[14]

Obviously, "The 'Crickets' Episode," as it is still referred to locally, reveals the dynamic shaping of feminist politics and its ideological contexts and contests, not to speak of the vulnerability of Patricinio Schweickart's suggestion that the validity of a feminist reading of a woman's text is "contingent on the agreement of others" within a feminist critical community (56). This story, its hotly debated readings, and the even more hotly debated question of the validity of multiple interpretations set into conflictual motion two ideological tenets commonly heralded in contemporary U.S. feminisms: the belief that racism is wrong and should be resisted and the belief that women's writing should be read and published. Schweickart also cites the necessity of keeping in mind the reader's responsibility to the woman writer and her contexts and of "reading the text as it was meant to be read" (54). Under some circumstances these three beliefs would have been happily sharing the same space rather than viewing that space as contested ground. Not here.

This episode also reflects Donna Haraway's assertion that readings of fiction are highly political practices which may themselves be read as "maps of possible modes of affinity and difference on the post-colonial terrain of women's liberatory discourses" (*Simians* 115). Haraway examines three different readings of Buchi Emecheta's fiction to show diverse mappings of women's consciousness and political agendas. Her reading of feminist readings leads her to consider the extent to which they are specifically and noninnocently positioned and how each text is "always already enmeshed in contending practices and hopes" (124). The "Crickets" issue reveals just how contentious those contending practices can become.

A similar and more recent case is that of Japanese American writer Lois-Ann Yamanaka, whose second novel, *Blu's Hanging,* won the 1998 fiction award from the Association of Asian American Studies. The AAAS then took back the award in response to complaints that the novel perpetuates racist stereotypes by presenting a minor Filipino character as a rapist and child molester. The controversy resulted in eighty-two letters of support from writers including Maxine Hong Kingston and Amy Tan and the resignation of many members of the organization (Foote 62; Shea 34).[15]

In such controversies around the question of reading, location and identity become what Yaeger calls "themed spaces" of consumption. This is worrisome, even, perhaps especially, when the product is oneself. In *Reading from the Heart,* a personal discussion of object relations theory and women's reading about (and for) love, Juhasz shows how the relationship of reader to text is one of mutual need: "I need to read the book, but the book needs me to read it. From the very start the situation displays the hallmarks of interdependence that make me feel that I am participating intensely in an activity with another" (270). Juhasz finds that women's stories can provide women readers with a feeling of plenitude and self-recognition ("the book recognizes me, and I recognize myself because of the book" [5]). For Juhasz, as the daughter of a difficult and inattentive mother, as another "reading girl" who devoured books from the public library, and as a voracious adult reader whose constant worry is that her library requests won't come in, reading was and is crucial to the development and maintenance of an identity in relation to others. She sees many books written by women, as well as their authors, as providing an approximation of maternal nurture for girls and women, "an environment for coming alive that is at once safe and challenging, supportive and guiding," an environment that has not been readily available for many females in the "real" world (9). Juhasz believes, then, that the reader may travel to fictional worlds to find and nurture none other than . . . herself.

Juhasz's argument, however, raises questions about the relations between identity and reading. "I" takes herself wherever she travels, but who "I" is can and does change. For most people, identity and positionality have been dependent on time and space.[16] When Maria Lugones contemplates the issue of separatism, she says she doesn't know to whom she would go back or what "pure" identity she has, nor does she wish for "separation into clean, tidy things and beings" ("Purity" 469).[17] This untidy quality of identity is what makes art possible. In the case of literature, the reader who travels—who is herself read, understood, and relocated at the same time she is reading, understanding, and locating a text—becomes text as well as reader. This doesn't mean donning the double lens of self and other to seek entry into an immobile text, to become a tourist looking for themed space. It is rather a mutual encounter that offers both strangeness and familiarity. Reader asks text questions; text asks reader questions. Reader travels text; text travels reader. Identity becomes not something one reads from, or even for, but a mode of readerly travel.

Travel is a problematic metaphor. As James Clifford points out in discussing cross-cultural studies in anthropology, "every focus excludes; there is no politically innocent methodology for intercultural interpretation" ("Traveling Cultures" 97). Moreover, inside and outside have permeated material reality and philosophical discourse in Western culture; as Gaston Bachelard has illustrated, the ideology of inside and outside forms a "dialectics of division" through which language develops its own dialectics of open and closed (211). More to the point, metaphors of travel in poststructural theory and cultural studies are far from being free from the ideological underpinnings of gender, race, or class bias. Women, Janet Wolff says, have never had the same access to the road as men. (Cynthia Enloe's *Bananas, Beaches, and Bases* makes the same point.) Simple metaphors of unrestrained mobility are problematic because "the already-gendered language of mobility marginalizes women who want to participate in cultural criticism" (Wolff 234). Citing Adrienne Rich's well-known insistence on "a politics of location," Wolff believes that any feminist destabilization of subjectivity and positionality must be "*situated*" in some "*place*" (235). bell hooks sees the metaphor of travel, especially when it is "playfully" evoked, as irretrievably tainted by imperialism ("Representing Whiteness" 344–46).[18]

I do not believe this has to be true, especially in regard to reading as imaginative travel.[19] Stories are not tourist sites to be entered by a privileged and mobile reader/traveler; like ghosts, stories do their own traveling. Stories are mysterious; they have agency of their own, gliding in and out of people's lives and thoughts, through confluences of imagination and identity.[20] Nancy K. Miller suggests that "the articulation of difference cannot be undertaken with old metaphors and familiar recipes" (*Getting Personal* 36). One way of thinking about confluences and divergences of difference is to think spatially, conceptualizing differences as fluid *spaces* of identity and relation that create their own stories, their own texts—that involve real people, who have their own specifically located and dislocated lives, who are always complicated, always in transit.

Many of these spaces are pain filled. Some are terrifying. For example, this passage from Dorothy Allison's novel *Bastard Out of Carolina:*

> My shoulder hit the doorjamb as he pushed me ahead of him into the bathroom. . . . He kept one hand on me while he pulled his belt out of its loops with the other. "Don't you say a word," he hissed at me. "Don't you dare."
>
> No, I thought. I won't. Not a word, not a scream, nothing this time.
>
> He pinned me between his hip and the sink, lifting me slightly and bending me over. I reached out and caught hold of the porcelain, trying not to grab at him, not to touch him. No. No. No. He was raging, spitting, the blows hitting the wall as often as they hit me. Beyond the door, Mama was screaming. Daddy Glen was grunting. I hated him. I hated him. The belt went up and came down. Fire along my thighs. Pain. . . . I would not scream. I would not, would not, would not scream. (234)

The space is the bathroom, the house, the father space. Allison draws it around me like a net. I as reader, as girl, as woman, am being pulled into a material and cultural space in which a young girl named Bone lives with a violent and sexually abusive stepfather in a poor white southern family. Bone describes that space in terms of an enduring chill, "something icy in Daddy Glen's houses that melted out of us when we were over at our aunts" (80). Bone and her sister, Reese, tiptoe around, stand in dark corners, know that the wrong gesture, the wrong word, the wrong silence will set Him off. Reading on becomes a claustrophobic experience in itself because I find myself in the space of the imprisoned. I become Bone.

As this stepfather loses job after job, the net woven by poverty and violence pulls tighter and tighter. Produced within this constricted space are the ideological workings of a dominant culture of white middle-class health professionals indifferent to Bone's suffering and her fear of speaking, and contemptuous of her mother's inability to stop the cycle of violence. In the end, when Bone is taken into the hospital (not for the first time) with multiple injuries from having been raped by her stepfather, the sheriff reminds her of "Daddy Glen in a uniform. The world was full of Daddy Glens" (296).

I can step back from Bone's story and say: *Bastard Out of Carolina* is a brilliant meditation on the interactions of class and gender oppression in southern culture and the violence that erupts as a result. I can say that this story draws us into the interlocking spaces of those interactions. It tells us what can happen when a man like Glen transforms economic despair into violence against a daughter.[21] Yes, but.

The truth is: Reading is personal. (In the next chapter of this book, for example, I will read this text again and differently.) I can choose not to read this book. But if I do read it, I am not outside looking into that bathroom. Nor am I really inside. But I am inside a textual space that reproduces material female space under siege from patriarchal violence—a space that, by the novel's end, will be violated by rape. A tiny bathroom. A locked door. A sweaty cursing man with belt. Cold porcelain. The slap of the belt. Things can only get worse.

And yet, Bone resists. She will not scream. Her resistance seeps out under the bathroom door and through the cracks of the wall. Her resistance produces new ideological categories, new spaces to read that not only keep her alive but contain the potential, through my attention to those spaces and their configurations, to reproduce themselves again and again.

Juhasz, as I discussed earlier, believes that certain texts create a kind of maternal space for the female reader. This novel works to the contrary for me: it requires me to become *both* daughter (I am in that bathroom; I know how the linoleum curls, the lavatory faucet drips) *and* mother (I want to comfort this girl; I want to take her into my lap and dry her tears, rock her to sleep, put salve on her welts, kick the husband out on the street; I want to call 911 and the state social worker to get us out of this mess).

When I travel this book's spaces, it requires of me that I remember who I was (a girl afraid) and that I become someone else (the good mother neither Bone nor I ever had, though surely they both must have tried; the good mother I've tried to be to my own daughter). What I must understand, I think, is that were I *really* Anney, Bone's mother, who at least once resorts to prostitution to feed her children, who is both afraid of and in love with Glen, who gave birth to Bone at age fifteen, I could not be the "good mother" I read for myself.

The social relation between Anney as fictional mother and myself as reader mother is the space I need to pay attention to. It lays bare my arrogance, my belief that, were I in this story, the ending would have turned out differently. The truth is: *I* would have turned out differently. Identity fluctuates in relation to the space of social relations it finds itself in and constructed by; my spatial reading of this book helps me understand this complexity by reading my own reading practice. "I" (and I) becomes the traveled text.

Is it possible, then, that the very process of reading allows a kind of absorption of the workings of cultural experience which is not possible except in very intimate relations? Again, though, one must ask how and under what conditions this blurring—this folding of space and time and identity—can occur. There has to be a cognitive lurch, a metaphor that propels.

> Skip, skip
> snake in your hips.
> wiggle around
> and break your lip. (Cisneros 51)

In and out spacings. The short sketches in Sandra Cisneros's *The House on Mango Street* contour the constriction of "house"—so many people, so little space. Cisneros has said that she structured her book around the metaphor of a house. Interestingly she was first compelled by the idea of a perfect house when, as a child, she read over and over Virginia Lee Burton's *The Little House.* Later, in a class discussion of Gaston Bachelard's book *The Poetics of Space* during her tenure at the Iowa Writers Workshop, Cisneros realized the power of the spatial metaphor of the house: "the metaphor of a house, *a house, a house,* it hit me. What did I know except third-floor flats" (in Olivares 465). As Julían Olivares notes, Cisneros "inverts Bachelard's nostalgic and privileged utopia" of "'felicitous space'" (465) to make tight stories about tight spaces in Chicago's Latino neighborhoods.[22]

But as tight as these stories and spaces are, there's play here. Creativity and a rich female culture inside these boundaries. Motion and expansiveness. Girls skip and hop. This space has a pressurized interior like an inflated balloon. Inside this house, this street, there's motion within compression, lively possibilities. To enter this space, this place, is to be swept into the rhythms of jump rope, song, giggles, running, play—a series of dexterous negotiations, by girls, of taut spaces. Subtle, refined, nimble motion within confinement and rigidity. Girl space, girl talk.

Then there's the squeeze. Girls grow up, get hips, get beaten, get raped. Get married.

The open space of the vacant lot—a garden where the girls used to play amid "sunflowers as big as flowers on Mars" and "dead cars [that] appeared overnight like mushrooms"—becomes dangerous ground (Cisneros 94–95). Boys take a pretty girl named Sally behind the cars, and Esperanza, the girl who tells these stories, can't find her. Sally, who was beaten by her father, ends up married to a marshmallow salesman who won't let her out of the house. Esperanza gets out, but not before she is raped by a man with a sour mouth and dirty fingernails who calls her his "Spanish girl" (100). She/we are still in border space, the in-and-out space of the jump rope. The space where resistance fights with itself. A misstep, a stumble can mean disaster.

Esperanza sees her life as a negotiation of the spaces between Mango Street and the rest of the world. She wants her own house: "Not a flat. Not an apartment in back. Not a man's house. Not a daddy's. A house all my own" (108). Such spaces are created at a cost. Esperanza knows that although she may leave the house on Mango Street, she will come back to it again and again as a site of memory and longing. Location, in the metaphor of "the house," both stabilizes and destabilizes, producing some voices and silencing others. Cisneros's text becomes her house: "That's precisely what I chose to write: about third-floor flats, and fear of rats, and drunk husbands sending rocks through windows, anything as far from the poetic as possible. And this is when I discovered the voice I'd been suppressing all along without realizing it" (in Olivares 465).

When I read about Cisneros's house, I do not feel I am traveling a long distance. I think of the Houston apartment complex where I lived when I was six, seven, and eight. The children there were not brown but rather very pale, with white paper skin you could almost see through. The boys were skinny and mean. When someone cut off the tails of a litter of puppies, the boys dug them out of the dumpster and chased me for hours with bloody bits of fur dripping from their fingers. What I remember is having nowhere to go, no space to breathe. What I wanted more than anything was to get back to my grandparents' pleasant, cool house on a green streetcorner in a small town in Mississippi. I wanted to climb the round staircase and go up to my own room that overlooked the mimosa and pecan trees in the back yard. I would dream I was a bird and could fly back home. What I actually did was thumb through my worn Uncle Wiggily books, much, perhaps, as young Sandra would do a few years later with her Little House book. I was thinking about airships.

Although I might ask Esperanza, and Cisneros, about the yearning for assimilation into a comfortable middle class (a yearning I obviously shared), Esperanza's story leads me to think more about how original home space holds us, no matter what other houses/texts we create for ourselves to live in. Esperanza takes me into her house, and Cisneros's text travels to inhabit me. This dual spatial move, this back-and-forthness between Esperanza's house on Mango Street and my apartment complex in Houston—this is how we ("she" and "I") keep traveling, negotiating, moving the rope back and forth. It is for me a deeply personal relation.

Our cultural homes obviously differ. Cisneros describes herself as the daughter of a Mexican father and a Mexican American mother,[23] and

Esperanza's home girls are from Mango Street, not Church Street, where my grandparents' house still sits on its solid corner. Cisneros's border spaces are geographical and, as in the case of Anzaldúa and other Chicana writers, linguistic. But readers of *The House on Mango Street* likely share this negotiation between leaving and coming home and the way home itself becomes transformed in this process of travel. Home becomes what one can imagine behind the lighted window of another house, another apartment, another life.

One thing these texts share is their representations of home as spatial production. As I'll discuss more fully later, New Zealand writer Keri Hulme creates an isolated woman artist in *The Bone People* who is always leaving and returning home, moving between her Maori and Pakeha heritages, and who eventually remakes home as something else altogether, as a traveling text. Arundhati Roy's *The God of Small Things* opens with Rahel coming back to Ayemenem, her home in India, a place in which the magical Kathakali Man, with his painted mask and swirling skirts, performs his stories for tourists lounging around resort swimming pools who "mock him with their lolling nakedness and their imported attention spans." Instead of being "the most beautiful of men" whose "body is his soul," he is colonized (because he does not want to starve) into "a Regional Flavor" (219). After such truncated performances, he collects his money, gets drunk or smokes a joint, and goes to the temple to "dance to ask pardon of the gods" (219–20). This back-and-forthness of home space that such narratives convey brings the necessity of time to space and makes us pay attention to history. Such stories evoke the motion of the imagination to put us in transit and make us heed those social relations within time that create the abyss between, for example, a dance at the swimming pool and one at the temple—like Esperanza, skipping from one side of the rope to the other, and back again.

The rope that Esperanza skips back and forth over is indeed a kind of text of her life of intense spatial negotiation. It generates a specific kind of power through her motion over and around it. It is also a common ground of gendered experience which is molded in precise ways by class, ethnicity, and location. This experience of becoming "Esperanza" has spatial embodiment. There is *that* wall, *that* curve, *that* edge. That house on Mango Street, that dark alley, that side of the jump rope.

There has been much discussion about the tensions between being home and not being home, the necessity of leaving home, and feminism as home.[24] Until recently, however, home has remained a fairly stable concept in feminist discourse, and the possibilities involved in imagining home as containing elements of mobility and travel have remained largely unexplored. Caren Kaplan's and Friedman's books, which build in part on the works of such writers as Anzaldúa, Spivak, Said, Clifford, and others, have undertaken the theoretical work of considering how, in a world of migration, travel, and diasporic experiences, home and elsewhere have become unhinged from their oppositional relationship and more complexly conceptualized as being superimposed and overlapping.

How far can home travel? In her memoir *Refuge: An Unnatural History of Family and Place,* Terry Tempest Williams, a Mormon and naturalist, faces this question directly and painfully. Williams's narrative is concerned with the constrictions and fluctuations of space and history as she tells the story of her mother's illness and death by a cancer almost certainly brought on by fallout from nuclear testing. Both of Williams's grandmothers and her aunts also developed cancer. She is from "a clan of one-breasted women." Her mother, both grandmothers, and six aunts have had mastectomies. Seven are dead. She tells us that she herself has already had two biopsies of suspicious tissue.

As Williams tells the story of her mother's illness and death, she also recounts the record rise of the Great Salt Lake in the spring of 1983—a historical fluctuation which resulted in the death of many species of wildlife and the destruction of their habitats. Her book is about natural and unnatural fluctuations of space, and in a dramatic ending in which she herself trespasses the spaces allowed her by crossing the line at the Nevada Test Site, she recognizes that she must "leave home"—that is, her Mormon heritage; its history of travel, settlement, and motion; its adherence to authority; its constructions of ethnicity, gender, and class—to continue to expand her spaces of resistance in the present. As she has watched the women in her family die, one by one, shadows of themselves and in great pain, she finds that "the price of obedience has become too high." After her mother's death she writes that she is "drowning" in questions about the effects of the 1957 bomb tests at the Nevada Test Site, a tragic convergence of space and time for her people: "What I do know, however, is that as a Mormon woman of the fifth generation of Latter-Day Saints, I must question everything, even if it means losing my faith, even if it means becoming a member of a border tribe among my own people" (285–86).

The spaces that this book pulls me into—the geographies I travel here—are transitional and fluctuating: I move between life and death as Williams helps her mother breathe herself into death; between the spiritual and physical realms as Williams erases the difference between the two; between rising water and receding land, dream and reality, belief and doubt, the precancerous and the malignant; between daughter and mother. At the end of her narrative Williams moves outside history to recount her dreams of women—mothers—who have come to reclaim the desert for their children. She also tells the story of actually crossing the line at the Nevada Test Site to protest continued nuclear testing and about the power that her transgression conveyed. After their arrest, she writes, the ten trespassing women were left out in the desert. But the desert is their space; like Jacobs's garret, it is their location of power: "The officials thought it was a cruel joke to leave us stranded in the desert with no way to get home. What they didn't realize was that we were home, soul-centered and strong, women who recognized the sweet smell of sage as fuel for our spirits" (290).

Rejecting the patriarchal nationalism of a culture of death and a religion of limitation for women, Williams's writing makes home travel as she describes how she tries remake her own identity at a deep level of ecological and emotional soundness. She connects her own body and the body of her mother to the world's body. Several days after her mother's death, she takes the short dark hairs from her mother's hairbrush and spreads them over the tips of young cottonwood trees for the birds to make their nests in the spring. She creates a habitat in motion, a home that can take flight.

To conclude this first chapter, I want to try to describe a few of the ways that space travels in Toni Morrison's *Beloved.* From the first lines of the novel, we are drawn into tight, tight space of spiteful 124, where we remain until Beloved is released to wander the vast expanse of history and memory. Like Harriet Jacobs's garret, like African American experience during and since the Middle Passage, this is a painfully compressed yet powerfully negotiated space of social relations.[25] This sense of constricted narrative space as a reflection of constricted cultural space is everywhere in *Beloved*—from the bodies, dead and alive, packed onto slave ships, to Sethe's impossible predicament when she and her children are discovered after their miraculous escape North, to the claustrophobia of 124. Much of the novel, in fact, has to do with attempts, sometimes successful, sometimes not, at keeping psyche and body pieced together in the face of the fragmentation that occurs from the implosion of identity brought about by annihilation and dehumanization of slaves for capitalistic exploitation.

Yet Morrison's statements about reading "helplessly" reflect the mysterious sense of invitational opening and inward pull that *Beloved* transmits and the complex shifting of identities among author, readers, and characters. This is a story not to pass on in either sense of that term; it is one whose spaces draw us in, travel us relentlessly. For example, the space of Sethe's kitchen.

Paul D has just told Sethe that, years ago on the Sweet Home farm, her husband, Halle, whom she has not seen since her escape to Ohio, was trapped in the loft the day she was molested in the barn by her master's nephews. Halle lost his mind after seeing what he saw. Sethe contemplates how much her own mind can hold:

> I am full God damn it of two boys with mossy teeth, one sucking on my breast the other holding me down, their book-reading teacher watching and writing it up. I am still full of that, God damn it, I can't go back and add more. Add my husband to it, watching, above me in the loft—hiding close by—the one place he thought no one would look for him, looking down on what I couldn't look at all. And not stopping them—looking and letting it happen. But my greedy brain says, Oh thanks, I'd love more—so I add more. And no sooner than I do, there is no stopping. There is also my husband squatting by the churn smearing the butter as well as its clabber all over his face because the milk they took is on his mind. (*Beloved* 70)

Sethe is wondering how tight spaces must become before the psyche implodes. As the two of them sit there, Paul D tells Sethe what it was like to be restrained by a bit and chains and watch a rooster named Mister sit freely on a tub in the sun. Sethe rubs Paul D's knee, trying to calm them both, trying to stop him from telling too much because "saying more might push them both to a place they couldn't get back from" (72). Her gesture is "like kneading bread in the half-light of the restaurant kitchen. Before the cook arrived when she stood in a space no wider than a bench is long, back behind and to the left of the milk cans. Working dough. Working, working dough. Nothing better than that to start the day's serious work of beating back the past" (73). What a narrow material space to be in—"No wider than a bench is long." Behind the milk cans. A dark corner in half-light. Again and again in *Beloved,* Morrison squeezes space—material, psychic, and cultural—by packing it so full that it becomes almost intolerable. I remember how, when I first read this book, I read it in bits and pieces. (This, I realized as I did it, was too easy.) I read it slowly because I could not read too much at one time. Now there are still the mossy teeth, tug of bit pulling back the lips, flattened tongue on fire, husband watching, rooster crowing, hands kneading what is not to be remembered and what cannot be forgotten. I want to get out of this place, this story, this space and this history. But I enter helplessly because Morrison brings us to the task of imagining unimaginable constraint, the tightest of spaces, and somehow I knew that, when I opened the cover of this book and began to read, this became my job. *This is my job.*[26]

The motion of the imagination, the language that sets the imagination into flight: these make it possible for me to do my job and know this story. Not know it in the sense of having lived it or anything like it, but know it through its spectral presence, its hauntings. Know it the way I know my own heart, through its beating.

Now, after I have read and taught Morrison's novel many times, Beloved's footsteps unaccountably roam my mind. She travels my world—in and out, in and out—"the rustle of a skirt," "the knuckles brushing a cheek in sleep" (275). Time does not keep her away. Our differences do not keep her away. I do not think she will ever stop traveling here. "Down by the stream in back of 124 her footprints come and go, come and go. They are so familiar. Should a child, an adult place his feet in them, they will fit" (275).

But this is not my whole story of reading *Beloved.* In the spring of 1999 I taught a crowded upper-level course in Toni Morrison at the University of New Mexico. One of the students in the class was Manuel-Julian Rudolpho Montoya, from Mora, New Mexico, a primarily Hispano community of around five hundred people. Manuel Montoya's father was shot to death when Manuel was a young boy; he, along with his brothers, was reared by their mother. By the time Montoya took my course, he was a graduating senior, a Truman scholar, a Rhodes scholar, and a lover of literature. During the spring semester he was named valedictorian for his graduating class and earned highest honors on his undergraduate thesis. One day in class, as we were discussing *Beloved* and questions about the function of such literature, he brought the class of forty-five students to silence when he suddenly burst out, putting his hands on his chest: "I love Toni Morrison. I take her to my heart and I will carry her there wherever I go. She will be with me as long as I live." Many others nodded. Some fought back tears.

Where has Morrison taken these readers? Where will they continue to travel? I do not know, but something has happened: journeys with destinations unknown are underway; Morrison's texts are being folded into the world.

At graduation I sat several rows from the back in a crowded gymnasium. The audience of parents and well-wishers included many working-class people from New Mexico—from small Hispano communities like the one my student had come from, several Indian pueblos across the state, the industrialized Albuquerque West Side, whose younger generations were beginning to go to college—not a well-to-do or particularly elite group, not the kind of people you'd find at a Harvard graduation or even at most other public university graduations. I had come to hear Manuel Montoya speak. He had asked me to come, saying that *Beloved* had helped him in writing his speech.

When he rose to the podium, his resonant voice startled the audience, which had become accustomed to the barely audible platitudes of the occasion. Instead, Manuel Montoya began an exhortation. He exhorted his audience to peace and self-examination. He exhorted us to love our lives and live lives of love. He exhorted us to take care of one another. He exhorted us to find beauty and joy within ourselves and in the world around us. As he uttered his message in both English and Spanish, I suddenly realized that I was hearing something familiar. I was hearing translated through his ringing bilingual exhortation to his own people of New Mexico Baby Suggs's message to her people to love themselves: "Love it. Love it hard. . . . that the only grace they could have was the grace they could imagine. That if they could not see it, they would not have it" (Morrison, *Beloved* 88). Similarly, Manuel Montoya called his audience to the motion of the imagination—to dance, cry, shout—"to love the greatness of this day" and "celebrate the world that lives alive and well within us," to "cry in honor of your suffering."

Where does this translated Baby Suggs go? How far can she reach? Manuel Montoya's audience of thousands rose almost in one motion during his final exhortation. We cheered and clapped as if our lives depended on it. Newspapers in Albuquerque and Santa Fe printed a text of the speech. Most of the people who heard Manuel Montoya that Saturday in mid-May will never know they have heard Baby Suggs's voice, but they know they heard something that folds them into the world in a new way.

As readers we may often find ourselves visitors in a different land, perhaps a strange land; we learn its dimensions as we travel through, not by any maps we have constructed prior to reading.[27] What, if anything, does it mean that I can imagine being Laura in the wheelchair and Laura can imagine flying? That Cisneros can read about a perfect house and make us imagine one less than perfect but big enough for us all to gather in and around? That students in a classroom can create a tiny garret and imagine being inside it for seven years? That a young Rhodes scholar from Mora, New Mexico, can bring thousands of listeners to their feet with an exhortation Baby Suggs might have delivered in the clearing?

Reading works of the imagination can shape an interior world in which laden questions of identity, location, and cultural productions of gender can be imaginatively thought. Reading can shape an exterior world in which such imaginings can be put to the service of large and complex issues, such as justice and social responsibility. Reading can even take us into dangerous woods where, despite our deepest desires and strangest dreams—perhaps because of them—irrevocable mutations take place.

Reading is a journey we embark on, helplessly.

2 *Nonfelicitous Space and Survivor Discourse: Reading Father-Daughter Incest*

The second part of this book will be an effort to locate the story of father-daughter incest within the material and textual spaces of certain texts of contemporary fiction, mark its place on the cultural maps of U.S. feminist history and contemporary survivor discourse, and trace the dimensions of the nexus at which these spaces converge and overlap. These convergences do not illuminate the nonfelicitous space of father-daughter incestuous abuse so much as they pluralize it and make it more enigmatic. I do not believe that writing or reading these stories creates "safe space," as both acts have been purported to do. To the contrary: one travels here at one's own peril. Such texts enact the lack of female safety; danger is always lurking and is almost always transparent. Moreover, such dangers and their multiple genderings can travel, appearing suddenly where least expected, perhaps even popping up within a themed space of "victimhood."

In Toni Morrison's book *The Bluest Eye,* Claudia McTeer, the narrator, begins to tell the story of young Pecola Breedlove's rape and impregnation by her father thusly: "There is really nothing more to say—except why. But since why is difficult to handle, one must take refuge in how" (9). The whys and hows of these stories, and my readings of them, are slippery. On the one hand, I don't want my readings to furbish this fictional survivor discourse as a comfortably liberatory home where to find one's voice is to solve all problems and miraculously be transformed from victim to survivor. Any kind of recovery from intense trauma is always partial and problematically contingent, and the boundaries between survivor and victim are less distinct than the discourse employing these two terms indicates. The whole notion of breaking silence and telling "it"—whatever "it" is—is not liberatory in and of itself. On the other hand, however, I don't want to be blind to the transparency of the cultural spaces that produce many varieties of Pecola Breedlove, a victim, someone Morrison herself called "that dead girl."[1]

Is it possible to enter such texts "*helplessly*"? To move through these stories is difficult and risky. They are specific, local, grounded in a gritty reality; they open to gendered constructions of social relations. They are littered with dead girls who sometimes come back to life and sometimes don't. Gender in these stories does travel, in the sense that one is forced to imagine the consequences of gender again and again. That these travels are arduous goes without saying; that these books travel their readers in disturbing ways needs to be said again and again.

I am in the university library looking for books about incest. I find dozens listed on the library computer, but when I climb the two flights of stairs to the social science floor, I find the HQ 71 and 72 shelves virtually bare. I sit down on the floor and survey the shelves for the call numbers I have scrawled on a sheet of paper. There are lines of dust on the shelves where most of the incest books should be. Most of the collection is checked out. Ironically, what I find on the same shelf and the one below it is a large group of books on homosexuality, many of them old, tattered and outdated, several of them marked with swastikas and messages proclaiming, "God will punish you."[2] Apparently books on queers have been shelved alongside the incest and child abuse books under the umbrella category "sexual deviancy." This should not come as a surprise, but it does. I sit on the floor facing the shelves empty of incest books and think about how spacious a word like *deviancy* has to be to hold, say, a lesbian who adopts a child and goes to swim meets and soccer games and a father who regularly rapes his daughter or son.

Two weeks later the books on incest I've requested come straggling (reluctantly, it seems) back to the library. When I pick them up the first thing I notice is that they are in terrible condition. The 1981 volume *Father-Daughter Incest*, by Judith Lewis Herman with Lisa Hirschman, has threads hanging off its edges. The binding has been partly secured with plastic tape. Diane Russell's *The Secret Trauma* and Karin Meiselman's *Resolving the Trauma of Incest*, published in 1986 and 1990, respectively, aren't in much better shape. These books, I see from the date cards inside their front covers, have been checked out many times. Their pages are stained and ragged. What is most striking about all three books is how worn the paths through them have become. Many readers have traveled these pages. In librarian terminology, these books have been badly defaced, although not with defamatory intent, as in the case of the books on homosexuality. Instead there are not only the underlinings, checks, and stars that one finds in an often used library book; there are also written responses in the margins and between the printed lines.

In Herman and Hirschman's book exclamation marks flank statements such as "Ensnared by the charms of a small temptress, or driven to her arms by a frigid, unloving wife, Poor Father can hardly help himself, or so his defenders would have us believe" (36). "Of course!" is written in the margin next to such findings as "Sixty percent (25) of the incest victims [interviewed by Herman and Hirschman] complained of major depressive symptoms in adult life" (99). Someone with more practical intent has written "use this" over and over in the margins of Meiselman's book. Others argue or embellish from the margins some of the assertions made in the books and in other marginalia; for example, in *The Secret Trauma* Russell says that, despite the imbalance in power between abuser and abused, "many children are extraordinarily brave and resourceful in implementing strategies to end the abuse" (123), to which a scrawled note between the printed lines responds poignantly, "Some can't." Yet another reader has placed this response under the first: "But what choice is there?"

These particular books on incest—the ones in my university library, though I'm certain that copies in other places have similar marginalia—are not only being well traveled but are themselves becoming material sites of conversation between writers and readers. Readers, and I can't help but believe that most of these are women, are engaging in a marginal (in both senses of the term) discourse of incestuous abuse with intense interest and passion, some obviously from the perspectives of victims and survivors. Others, such as myself, occupy a perspective outside the experience of incestuous abuse. I believe, in fact, that such lines need to be drawn; otherwise the experience of being inside becomes trivialized. On this point I disagree with scholars such as Janet Jacobs, who in *Victimized Daughters* argues that the cultural framework of male entitlement in the patriarchal family may at least partly close the gap between women who have been sexually traumatized in childhood and women who have grown up under patriarchal dominance (11). In *Interrogating Incest: Feminism, Foucault and the Law,* Vikki Bell makes a similar point, suggesting that "normal sexuality, normal power relations and the normal family are implicated in incestuous abuse. The men who are known to have abused children are not perverted, but 'normal,' everyday men" who inhabit a cultural space in which normality in male sexuality is tied to dominance and violence (82).

My work in this chapter is to trace the convergences of material, textual, and cultural spaces in contemporary U.S. women's fiction about father-daughter incest.[3] Such convergences become sites where gendering is both located and dislocated. This is not to imply that I see these three kinds of spaces as being distinct or noncontiguous. By material space I mean physical structures, landscapes, geographies, locations that are represented within a text—the places in which the story of incest or part of it unfolds (for instance, the parlor in Lee Smith's *Black Mountain Breakdown*). But a location such as these, as Michel de Certeau says, becomes a "practiced place" that is "composed of intersections of mobile elements" (117), a mobile field of social relations. Within these stories certain material spaces are linked, often ironically, to certain practices of location and dislocation in which gender itself can travel. The Breedlove kitchen in *The Bluest Eye,* for example, the site of Cholly's rape of his eleven-year-old daughter, merges in space-time with the southern woods of Cholly's remembered youth, where, in the midst of his first sexual experience, he himself was sexually victimized by white men. His act of sexual violence toward his daughter is haunted by his own victimization as "daughter."

Such hauntings are palimpsestically created by complicated and intricate openings and closures constructed by and within language, narrative, and silence. All of these texts evoke the divide between certain kinds of constriction and certain kinds of expansion. These textual spaces both merge with and exceed representations of materiality. They often fall between words that are hard to say and within stories that are hard to tell; they are there and not there. It is difficult to travel such spaces (for instance, the narrator's silences about her father's sexual advances in Kaye Gibbons's *Ellen Foster* or the mother's withdrawal from the abused daughter in *Bastard Out of Carolina*) because they are evasive, slippery, difficult to map. The moment when Ginny suddenly remembers her father's sexual abuse in Jane Smiley's novel *A Thousand Acres,* which occurs about two-thirds of the way through the book, still takes me quite by surprise, though I have read the book several times. It is a moment specifically located in her old room, in her father's house, in a landscape of prime midwestern farmland precisely mapped in the first chapter of the book. Yet Ginny's memory slashes across land and home and farm, all that "seemed secure and good" (5), to travel toward another reality, something far away and long ago which still bleeds into the present, flooding everything in its path, obliterating all maps of surface geography while excavating what has been long buried and haunts the land and the sisters who grew up on it.

This body of literature is thickly entangled in contemporary discourses around gender, race, class, sexuality, and nation. Cultural space, with its permutations of the dynamic and incessant workings of ideology, layers all narrative, but it is particularly foregrounded in these stories. In a carefully balanced article entitled "Not in This House: Incest, Denial, and Doubt in the White Middle-Class Family," Elizabeth Wilson focuses on the way U.S. cultural space has shaped and been reshaped by the recent outpouring of incest stories and the controversies they have generated in such arenas as "repressed memory." Wilson believes that contemporary debates around the issue of incest center on "the official domestic ideology" that children should be protected from early exposure to sexuality and that incest does not happen in the white, middle-class, heterosexual family. Instead the sexual abuse of children within the family is perceived as "a vice of class and racial others who lack the rationality necessary to control their impulses." Moreover, the notion that such "others" practice incest with children has "long been part of the arsenal of moral prejudice that has been used to justify the social and political hegemony of the white middle class" (38). The white, middle-class family thus defines itself as that entity which does *not* engage in incestuous abuse, a "practiced place" of purity and safety. Finally, as I hope to show in the analysis of southern U.S. fiction that makes up part of this chapter, the geographic frame of region is also an important component of cultural space, leaving ubiquitous traces of certain other distinctive interactions of gender with race and class in women's stories of incestuous abuse in southern families.

Together these spatial dynamics of fiction may be seen as creating a mutation of "survivor discourse," a term that in this country has come to mean the large body of autobiographical stories and commentary—oral and written—of those who have survived, physically and emotionally, rape, incest, and sexual assault (Alcoff and Gray 261). I have chosen to write about fiction specifically because I believe we need to expand our notions of survivor discourse beyond the boundaries of "the factual," whatever that term has come to mean; I have selected certain novels over others because they raise significant questions about how and under what circumstances such discourse can emerge and mutate.[4] I hope that reading these literary texts in terms of the way they both articulate and complicate contemporary discourse around incest may be helpful in analyzing the disturbingly mixed messages about sexual abuse we find in popular culture in the United States.

Writing about autobiographical narratives of father-daughter incest, Janice Williamson says: "To write a body in pain, a particular historical body that has suffered particularly damaging abuse, is to articulate one of our culture's unspeakable secrets. To read a daughter's interpretive account of incestuous relations with her father is to experience how feminist writing rattles canonical and textual borders" (133). The "survivor discourse" of women's fiction about incest is more complicated. It reflects and refracts the cultural prohibitions that shape the volatile act of speaking out about incest. It, too, rattles borders, but it also traces their foundations, mapping cultural constructions of home and family that are multiple, layered, and highly contested. Most important, it turns us back to the source of survivorship, which is imagination, being able to imagine one's life differently.

In her discussion of the relationship between the incest-recovery movement and white, middle-class ideology, Elizabeth Wilson points to the fact that contemporary debates around incest and repressed memory are "taking place largely within a middle class that has a deep, long-standing investment in denying that incestuous abuse can take place within its class boundaries" (52). There are other, specifically racialized boundaries to the incest story. For marginalized groups revelations of incest may be translated as being disloyal to the family and community. In her introduction to *Crossing the Boundary: Black Women Surviving Incest,* Melba Wilson expresses her fear that telling about her sexual relationship with her father will be frowned on and misconstrued by "many in our black communities," some of whom "may feel that I have breached an even greater taboo, crossed a bigger boundary (in their eyes) than incest" (1). Trudier Harris has pointed out that artistic writing among blacks has also avoided the subject of incest because, "in a country where blackness is maligned even in its purest, most innocent states, imagine how much more viciously it would be maligned if the writers chose to show something as debased as incest" ("Tiptoeing" 495–96). Much of the controversy encircling *The Color Purple* emerges from its treatment of incest.

Such prohibitions do not necessarily mean that survivor discourse, whether fictional or autobiographical, is liberatory or that the reader's or critic's work in reading these narratives should always be "emancipatory" or "recuperative," to use Carla Kaplan's terms (57). Citing such texts as Harriet Jacobs's *Incidents in the Life of a Slave Girl,* Kaplan, as I discussed earlier, finds that, even though the recuperative enterprise in feminist literary criticism has been extremely important in locating and reading the work of marginalized writers, its methods having shown us how to read the gaps and silences in their texts, it has nevertheless "also fostered a sentimentalization of the marginal, the oppositional, and the subversive, not to mention a very particular privileging of writing and narrative as subversive and oppositional practices" (53). Given how manifestations of survival discourse have traveled popular culture, textual agency is much more ambiguous and contradictory than the term "breaking silence" would indicate. One thing is certain: the discourses that have emerged around the issue of father-daughter incestuous abuse are laden with other discourses: psychoanalysis, feminism, health care, social science, education, and perhaps most important, entertainment and its themed spaces. Similarly, women's contemporary fiction about incest is compressed by layers of complexity as seemingly impenetrable as the obsidian shard of Smiley's *A Thousand Acres;* the survival discourse of these texts, situated in the mass market of transnational capitalism in which selling a book is often contingent on manipulating desire in a variety of directions, is thick with the strata and geographies of loss and desire, victimization and manipulation.

How does such fiction about incest function in a discursive environment so heavily invested in fact? Discussing father-daughter incest in African American fiction, Hortense Spillers maintains that, because the incest taboo is so strong, "fictions about incest provide an enclosure, a sort of confessional space for and between postures of the absolute, and in a very real sense it is only in fiction—from the psychoanalytic session to the fictive rendering—that incest as dramatic enactment and sexual economy can take place at all" (128). In a similar vein, James Twitchell believes that "we are drawn to contemplate, for reasons ranging from titillation to revulsion, sexual acts in fiction which we would abhor, or at least avoid, or profess to avoid, in reality" (31). Twitchell's analysis seems to distance the manipulation of the incest taboo in the popular culture industry from what really happens in the family—a questionable premise. Similarly Spillers argues for the borders between literary depictions of incest and its reality: "Whether or not father-daughter incest actually happens and with what frequency is not a problem for literary interpretation. For good or ill, it belongs to the precincts of the local police department (and the 'cat' should go to jail)" (128).

Such statements lead to what are for me disquieting questions concerning the readership of the voluminous material about incest. One question one might ask concerns the identity of Twitchell's "we." Is this the readership whose traces I found in the margins of my library books, readers who obviously have a personal stake in the story of incest? Or readers of pornography who like to be titillated? Twitchell seems to suggest that there may well be a "we" between these two possibilities, and, if so, I find this a disturbing idea. Is it possible to disengage the reading of fiction about father-daughter incest from its reality (which is usually kept comfortably *outside* the precincts of the local police department and remains the secret inside the house)? Or disentangle either writing or reading about incest from the ideological productions of the everyday world?

Such questions lead me to the hip and witty remonstrances of James Kincaid's book *Erotic Innocence: The Culture of Child Molesting.* Kincaid also creates a "we," which he defines in terms more of a discursive environment than of personhood or community: "the commonality formed by a set of cultural and historically specific stories that we are told and tell, quite earnestly, without recognizing their source or their consequences . . . the we watching *60 Minutes,* protecting our children, chemically castrating 'sexual predators'"(5). He believes that we have been telling the wrong story about children—a gothic story that we cannot resist because of our own desires, a narrative that victimizes the very children we claim to "protect." This is a story of monsters, repressed memory, and sexual abuse behind every door and around every corner that bleaches away difference and makes questions about race, class, and gender almost invisible: "There is but one erotic child, and its name is Purity: without color, station, or gender" (20). Kincaid believes that most adults are erotically drawn to children and the childlike (the photographs in his book show seductive poses by adult sex stars mimicking those of children), that eroticism of various sorts is a part of life and that to deny such feelings, displacing and projecting them as outrage, does not serve children well and makes escape from the entrapping circle of "porn-speak" impossible (25). This is a story "we" love to tell and hear because it allows us to displace such desires even as we titillate ourselves with them:

> The story of recovered memory has, one way or another, kept the erotic scapegoating story of child sexuality tantalizingly before us for a long time now. So eager are we for that story that books parading their own naivete sell millions of copies. For instance, the mammothly successful *Courage to Heal*[5] offers a circus of appeal to anecdote, reasoning from "raw experience," a disdain for theory . . . [,] a serene disregard for com-

> plexity, an inability to imagine other explanations for the phenomena the authors observe, and a reckless imprecision stemming from an addiction to their own nostrums. (244)

Kincaid is hardily indignant at all this and calls on us to exert common sense and quit scaring kids to death; *of course* we have erotic feelings for children: "Denial does nobody any good and drives the desire into the lying, scapegoating babble, where it thrives and does terrible harm. Erotic feelings are not rape" (288). He goes on to give directions: we should keep hugging, bathing, and photographing kids. One might perhaps follow Kincaid to this point, but he continues: "If you find yourself getting too excited, going too far, wanting to incite or not to stop—then stop. If you are hard-pressed, then indulge in voyeurism, which is child abuse only by elastic standards and seems to many children at least as funny as it is invasive" (289).

"Hard-pressed"? I have quoted and discussed Kincaid's ideas at some length because it is easy to lambaste such a book, in which tone and subject matter seem greatly at odds (Hey, lighten up; it's only sex abuse—there's not nearly as much of it as we think, and we'd all like to try it). What interests me most about Kincaid's argument is his seeming disregard for the gendered dynamics of child sexual abuse and the problematics his argument sets up for reading women's fiction about father-daughter incest.

Fiction, autobiography, and even biography all invoke quite similar spatial dynamics of reading: one is drawn into a life experience of another; one travels. In terms of Kincaid's argument, this could mean that we could be displacing our erotic desires even further by becoming participants in such fiction, but this, of course, depends on who's doing the reading. I am reminded of an annual Faulkner conference more than a dozen years ago during which a male professor gave a paper on reader participation in the corncob rape of Temple Drake in *Sanctuary,* arguing that we all participate in the rape through our own voyeurism as readers—after which an elementary school teacher from California, a small woman who had ridden a Greyhound bus across the country for this conference, rose from the audience of five hundred or so and responded in a quiet but penetrating voice, "But doesn't it depend on who the reader *is*?" One effect of these narratives of incest, whether fictional or autobiographical (and I don't want to draw too fine a distinction between the two), is to propel me into a complexly unsettling consideration of, on the one hand, patriarchal power carried to its most egregious form and, on the other, the daughter's submission and/or resistance to that power.[6]

A central question, which Kincaid's analysis ignores and Jacobs's answers a bit too quickly, is how the traumatizing relation between the incestuous father and the victimized daughter may be read as a cultural text. Like autobiographical narratives, father-daughter incest fiction removes the transparency from gendered power relations within the family. Because it is not laden with exigencies of literal and specific truth claims, as narratives of incest purported to be autobiographical have been, one might argue that such fiction is better equipped to tell the cultural story of father-daughter sexual abuse. However, it is clearly the relation of such fiction to the cold hard facts of many girls' lives—its own location in contemporary cultural space—that equips it to perform such a function.

Like other forms of survivor discourse, these texts expose in a general sense what Christine Froula has called "the hysterical cultural script: the cultural text that dictates to males and females alike the necessity of silencing woman's speech when it threatens the father's power."[7] This silencing, which Froula believes has configurations similar to those surrounding the daughter's silence about incestuous abuse, "insures that the cultural daughter remains a daughter, her power suppressed and muted; while the father, his power protected, makes culture and history in his own image" (623).[8] Yet, the novels I take up in this chapter,[9] while revealing the exploitative power of the father or at least *a* father, whether a biological father, stepfather, or father figure, also function in more complex ways. Make no mistake: these are stories of the father's power, and if this is the case, what do such stories convey? We can cheer on the daughter's survival, if there is a survival, or mourn the lack thereof, but there is a troubling feel to all of these texts (as there is in the highly disturbing novel *Find Him!* which I discuss in chapter 3) and a suspicion we take from them that, in the so-called "postfeminist" era, "the father" isn't really dead. He may simply be sleeping, or playing computer games, or out having a round of golf; he may be so much a part of our own constructions of home that, while we cannot live with him, neither can we live without him.

My concern with respect to these stories is primarily how the formation of the victim's/survivor's fictional identity occurs in relation to the material spaces of incest and the cultural spaces that in turn encircle and form that materiality. Being in space is indeed not easy, nor is it uncomplicated when the fictional subject/object is the daughter enclosed by the father's desire and perhaps also by her own desire for his love, whatever forms it may take.

These spaces are overlapping and multilayered. In the United States of the 1980s and 1990s, the story of father-daughter incest has been told across a cultural backdrop on which, as Jacobs puts it, "victimization has become a media event" and sexual abuse has increasingly become a commodity that sells advertising slots (ix). Significantly, several of the texts I will be writing about here offer critiques of capitalism and show how capitalist economy drives the father's abuse of the daughter as owned property (just as, interestingly enough, the incest taboo is also driven by the right of property for certain males). These texts are located at complicated intersections of race and class. Often such fiction reveals how the father's power in the family is produced within, and itself reproduces, a cultural space that has historically emphasized property ownership and built up an institutionalized system of the containment and usage of specific women's bodies to those ends. The wealthy white father of *A Thousand Acres* feels that he owns his daughters in the same way that he owns his farm. Legal historian Patricia Williams, following Angela Davis and other scholars of African American history, has pointed to the relation of white male dominance, property ownership, and the control of black women's (and black men's) bodies under capitalism (from southern slavocracy to contemporary transnational economic systems), particularly to the presence or threat of violence which undergirds that economy. Thus the white patriarchal family and its containment of all sorts of female bodies for the purpose of holding and expanding property claims and economic interests, both a part of a specifically institutionalized ideology of dominance, have historically far-reaching repercussions for familial dynamics and father-daughter relations in U.S. culture. Gayl Jones's novel *Corregidora* tells this story by tracing the lives of several generations of African American women, the descendants of a Portuguese slave trader who "fathered his own breed" by raping his daughters; this heritage is passed down, as one of the women says, "from generation to generation so we'd never forget" (9).

The various cultural spaces of fiction about father-daughter sexual abuse and its ideological origins and productions also reflect male disempowerment at the hands of other men. The fiction I discuss shows clearly how the father's disempowerment, whether based on race and/or class, is visited on the daughter; in texts such as *Bastard Out of Carolina* and *The Bluest Eye* race and class oppression are translated into gender oppression. The positions of "father" and "daughter" can travel. Spillers argues that both *father* and *daughter* are terms contingent on patriarchal privilege and hence do not "suffice for occupied or captive persons and communities in which the rites and rights of gender function have been exploded historically into gender neutralities" (129). Yet black "fathers" in *The Bluest Eye* and Alice Walker's *The Color Purple* do exert physical and psychological power over their "daughters." This is not to say that their power is not complicated and caused by historical and material contravention. Their own disempowerment, however, does not render them powerless over their daughters but rather complicates the limits of their empowerment in other arenas. As Morrison shows in *The Bluest Eye,* a novel set in the North but with its roots of violence still implanted in southern soil, the southern white man's violence against the black man can be reproduced with devastating effects on the black man's family. Walker's novel similarly shows a black stepfather (thought by the daughter to be her father) reproducing white patriarchal ownership of the daughter's body: raping Celie repeatedly, giving away her two children and telling her they are dead, and offering her services to another man in marriage. The narrator-survivor of Allison's novel is most in danger when her stepfather loses a job and thrusts the poor white family into economic crisis (which he does frequently).

Judith Herman writes: "It is not possible to write dispassionately about incest. The subject is entirely enmeshed not only in myth and folklore, but also in ideology" (3). Moreover, as I said in the previous chapter, just as are texts ideologically constructed, so are their readings. These narratives of incest are intensely disturbing. They turn around unerringly to read the ideologies of patriarchal power and dominance—stories of "romance" and "love"—that make father-daughter incest culturally inevitable. At the same time these stories, no matter what else they are (often they are also stories of great courage and insight), present the sometimes unsuccessful struggle for female agency under patriarchy. Directly or indirectly they draw many readers into the space of the daughter who is abused.[10] What can these books tell us about cultural narratives of gender as such narratives are figured both historically and spatially? Can their stories lead to reimaginings of home? I am most interested in their silences, the places where language or story may break down and a haunting silence is only thing left to be read and imagined.

How, indeed, does one read such texts helplessly? I am hoping that my writing about them bears some resemblance, at least in tone, to the marginalia in my library's social science books. These narratives deserve that kind of vehemence, that gut reaction, that embodied reading practice. Nevertheless, I have been careful about how I travel these spaces, and how they travel me. (Today I finished reading *A Thousand Acres* for the fourth or fifth time and realized anew just how devastating and haunting a novel it is and how difficult to speak or write about. I feel that the most appropriate response to it is to sit for days and weep for daughters everywhere.)

In the preceding chapter I argued for reading as a way of traveling between worlds, and the transformative effects of those worlds on identity and social relations. While writing this chapter I came to wonder why so much has been said within feminism on the subject of writing about incest and so little about reading incest narratives, or more specifically, about the relations of feminist literary criticism to incest narratives. Published from 1970 (*The Bluest Eye*) to 1992 (*Bastard Out of Carolina*), the novels I am reading span a period that has experienced an explosion of women's writing and speaking about incestuous abuse, particularly father-daughter incest. During this period of a little more than two decades, a whole discursive system has been built on the postulate of breaking what Sandra Butler called in 1978 "a conspiracy of silence" surrounding the issue of incestuous abuse, "a vastly elaborated intellectual tradition which served the purpose of suppressing the truth about incest" (9). As Herman has pointed out, this was a tradition of silencing the victim: "a tenacious prejudice, still shared by professionals and laymen alike, that children lie about sexual abuse" (11). Herman argues that the twentieth-century suppression of the reality of father-daughter incest originates in the work of Freud, who first acknowledged "seduction by the father" as the "essential point" in hysteria and then later repudiated his own seduction theory. This silence about father-daughter incestuous abuse configured a variety of psychiatric and legal studies and texts from Freud up to the 1970s. Studies pointing to the prevalence of incest, such as the work of S. Kirson Weiberg (published in 1955), were virtually ignored and quietly went out of print (Herman 9–18).

As Herman's research shows generally, this "conspiracy of silence" about father-daughter incest was still strong in 1978, when one study showed that approximately one million American women had been victimized as girls in incestuous relations with their fathers and that some 16,000 new cases were occurring each year (Herman 14). Diane Russell's *Secret Trauma* published research in 1986 showing that 2 percent of women raised by a biological father had been sexually abused by him before the age of fourteen; the abuse rate rose to 17 percent for those actively raised by a stepfather (83). Russell adds that the conviction rate in her survey (1 out of 187 cases) shows the extent of this conspiracy: "If talking about incest is taboo, it is evident from our survey that reporting it to the police and pressing charges against the perpetrators are even more taboo" (91).

These figures, as almost all researchers have been quick to point out, are merely the tip of a huge iceberg of unreported cases. (Kincaid has vehemently argued that, to the contrary, the numbers of child sexual abuse are blown out of proportion, especially when compared to other forms of abuse.) Russell's sample of 930 women included 648 cases of some type of child sexual abuse before the age of eighteen; of these only 30 cases had been reported to authorities, and only 4 of those were cases of incestuous abuse (85). Russell's research also shows that incestuous abuse and, to a larger degree, child abuse in general have been on the rise over the past few decades (4). In her 1995 study Jacobs's intensive interviews with 50 abuse survivors disclose the devastating psychological toll on identity development that fathers' sexual abuse extracts from daughters: the damaged development of an empathetic self, the severing of the mother-daughter bond, and the dissociation of mind from body.

When analyzing the discourse around father-daughter incestuous abuse, it is important to note that, on the cusp of the millennium in an atmosphere of revelation ("I was abused"), leading to backlash ("The therapist put such ideas in her head"), leading to counterbacklash, the daughter's silences and the daughter's revelations seem to have become equally onerous. Jacobs expresses dismay about current backlash that denies sexual victimization within families. Kincaid argues that the "look-alike indignation" of *both* backlash and counterbacklash serves merely to enhance images and desires circulating around child sexuality, adding that the children are the losers in this argument (260–62). Jacobs believes that "as the concerns over credibility become the focus of the public discourse on sexual violence, we risk becoming a culture where denial obscures the need for protection and revictimizes those who have already suffered far too much" (x).

Breaking this second taboo and opening survivor discourse, both in this country and abroad, were largely the work of feminism; as Russell notes, "it is a terrible indictment of both researchers and clinicians that credit for the public attention now focused on these serious and longstanding societal problems must be given not to themselves but to a political movement that was willing to provide validation and support for victims with the courage to tell the truth about their experiences" (5). If, however, the feminist movement can be credited with unleashing the tremendous wave of women's grief and anger about father-daughter incest that has flooded books, art, and the airwaves, then the question becomes not so much a matter of the validation of this profusion of material but one of analysis—how carefully and well have we read these texts of incest, and how precise, scrupulous, and sustained have our responses been?

A 1996 collection of women's writing entitled *Nature's Ban: Women's Incest Literature* comes close to defining incest out of existence for the purposes of inclusiveness; its editor, Karen Jacobsen McLennan, chose selections to reflect a definition of incest as "the expropriation of a child's body through transgressions of the parental role," as well as "the oppressive and inappropriate parental authority over a daughter's marriage or her right to grow into her own sexuality" (9–10). This multipurpose definition fits quite a few of the anthology's inclusions, which most readers would not by any stretch of imagination consider to be incest literature. There are, for instance, excerpts from *Incidents in the Life of a Slave Girl,* Harriet Jacobs's story of her owner, Dr. Flint, an infamous sexual predator but certainly not her father. (Gayl Jones's *Corregidora* would have fit well but is not included.) Some poems included in the volume, McLennan writes, "elude a strict definition of incest but express a resistance to patriarchy in the language of incest trauma. The economic, political, or spiritual world is described in the terms of feminine violation" (10). Such poems (presumably) include "I never lost as much but twice" and three other poems by Emily Dickinson and Sharon Olds's "The Blue Dress," none of which seems to be about incest. These are for me troubling matters related to locating and marking literature by women as incest literature. There is a need for restraint and rigor in this undertaking if we are to be able say quite particularly and specifically: "*This* is incest literature; this is a body of work that is somehow different because of location, relation, and history." We need to read such texts very carefully for *what they do* because they can show us things we don't yet know about gender and reading.

Despite the expansiveness of its title, Rosaria Champagne's *The Politics of Survivorship: Incest, Women's Literature, and Feminist Theory* (1996) is limited to psychoanalytic readings of a few texts yet diffuse in its multiple interests in all forms of incest, incestuous desire, and their aftereffects. Although Champagne is interested in how reading and politics coincide, her reliance on psychoanalysis circumscribes their encounter. Melba Wilson's *Crossing the Boundary: Black Women Survive Incest* (1993) offers one chapter about her own responses to black women's writing about incest.

Two books from 1998, Brenda Daly's *Authoring a Life: A Woman's Survival in and through Literary Studies* and Tomoko Kuribayashi and Julie Tharp's collection of essays entitled *Creating Safe Space: Violence and Women's Writing,* take incest as a partial subject in the sense that both books have a wider range of purpose. The collection includes several essays on incest in women's writing but mainly addresses the larger subject of violence against women. Daly's book draws on her personal experiences as both an incest survivor and a feminist professor to illustrate dramatic parallels between patriarchal oppression in the home and the academy. The scope of Daly's intentions—to help student survivors, to promote canon revision and collaborative scholarship, to analyze her own feelings about being part of a community of feminist scholars, and to write autobiographically about the tabooed subject of incest—works against detailed analysis of the incest literature she brings to the forefront, despite her enactment of some interesting reading strategies involving conversations between her and her students about such texts.

These books do mark some movement toward more serious consideration of incest in women's literature. Nonetheless, despite compelling single essays about women's incest and sexual abuse narratives and several books about incest in certain texts, such as Shakespeare's plays, feminist literary criticism in the United States does not seem to have developed comprehensive strategies for reading the huge quantity of contemporary incest narratives, fictional or autobiographical, that the past two decades have produced.[11] Take, for example, six major U.S. anthologies of feminist criticism and theory published between 1985 and 1993, a period in which incest narratives were everywhere: *The New Feminist Criticism: Essays on Women, Literature, and Theory,* edited by Elaine Showalter (1985); *Gender and Reading: Essays on Readers, Texts, and Contexts,* edited by Elizabeth A. Flynn and Patrocinio P. Schweickart (1986); *Feminist Issues in Literary Scholarship,* edited by Shari Benstock (1987); *Feminisms: An Anthology of Literary Theory and Criticism,* edited by Robyn Warhol and Diana Price Herndl (1991); *De/Colonizing the Subject: The Politics of Gender in Women's Autobiography,* edited by Sidonie Smith and Julia Watson (1992); and *The Intimate Critique: Autobiographical Literary Criticism,* edited by Diane Freedman, Olivia Frey, and Frances Murphy Zauhar (1993). Of the dozens and dozens of essays in the volumes—essays that offer readings of and critical paradigms for all kinds of women's texts, from African American slave narratives to contemporary lesbian poetry, and for a wide variety of topics, from postcolonial subjectivity to erotic triangles—*not one* deals with reading women's narratives of incest or childhood sexual abuse.

This is surprising since, during the same period, not only were more and more women's narratives of incest and child sexual abuse being published in the Unites States and abroad, but feminist scholars, physicians, and psychologists were vigorously addressing the subject, producing literally hundreds of books and articles, both popular and scholarly.[12] Although there is inevitably a lag between the publication of categories of writing and their critical and theoretical acknowledgment, one must wonder about this hiatus in U.S. feminist literary criticism and theory and its inevitable, if inadvertent, perpetuation of an ideology of silence surrounding the issue of incestuous abuse of girls and young women, particularly at a time when the "strategic metaphor of 'breaking the silence' is virtually ubiquitous" through the survivors' movement (Alcoff and Gray 261).

There are complex reasons for this gap, with work now underway to fill it.[13] Jacobs reflects on the similarities between the psychology of survivors and female psychology in general and argues that her study of identity development in survivors may teach us how female personality "is shaped by the forces of male domination and the power relations of a gender-stratified society" (12). For some feminist readers to confront the daughters in these stories, fictional or actual, is in part to confront the unsettling specter of women's exploitation. Nor is it necessarily true that all survivors of incest want to read incest narratives, autobiographical or fictional. Recently I told a childhood friend about Allison's *Bastard Out of Carolina,* the story of a poor white southern girl who is repeatedly beaten and sexually abused by her stepfather. My friend replied: "I don't need to read a novel about *that.* I know the real thing, and it's bad enough." In terms of my arguments about reading, such women may *not* want to travel or be traveled by these texts. The space between father and daughter becomes anathema, hardly seductive—definitely not felicitous.

For those readers who have not been sexually abused as children, narratives of father-daughter incestuous abuse may dramatize uncomfortable truths about the relations of power and dominance at work within the ideologically constructed space of home. Herman points out that in terms of a gendered analysis, father-daughter incest "represents a paradigm of female sexual victimization. The relationship between father and daughter, adult male and female child, is one of the most unequal relationships imaginable. It is no accident that incest occurs more often precisely in the relationship where the female is most powerless" (4). Discussing the corrosive effects of racism and poverty in two texts of incest by African Americans—Morrison's *The Bluest Eye* and Maya Angelou's autobiographical *I Know Why the Caged Bird Sings*—Cheryl A. Wall writes: "In a society ordered by hierarchies of power based on race, class, and gender, no one is more powerless, hence more vulnerable, than a poor black girl. In these texts, such characters anchor the critique of social ideology" (3). In short, these stories, no matter what else they are (often they are also stories of great courage and insight and, as Wall notes, texts of social critique), to some extent narrate female powerlessness. This is still not a story many of us want to hear or tell, and in its face, liberatory modes of reading may break down.

As Alcoff and Gray discuss at great length, however, there are other troubling issues surrounding survivor discourse and its functions within the discursive perimeters of 1990s popular culture. I have noted how vulnerable incest stories are to co-optation as themed space. This co-optation occurs in complicated ways. Kincaid is right in noting the complexities of cultural responses to stories of sexual abuse and the fact that such stories fill many needs. Themselves both survivors of incest, Alcoff and Gray, unlike Kincaid, argue from a feminist perspective that, although survival speech "has great transgressive potential" to disrupt dominant discourses that protect and enhance male power, those dominant discourses can and often do "subsume survivor speech in such a way as to disempower it and diminish its disruptive appeal" (270).

This process is complicated by the fact that such speech has been prohibited and excluded from cultural discourse (Alcoff and Gray 265). Although it is to be hoped that survivor speech educates society and empowers victims, in reality "the speaking out of survivors has been sensationalized and exploited by the mass media," such as TV talk shows and programs with news-as-entertainment formats. Survivors are often eroticized, and discussions of sexual violence are used to titillate and expand audiences (262); moreover, the confessional structure of survivor speech and its mediation by "experts," in addition to the speaker's own internalization of dominant ideas ("It was my fault"), often force such speech into conformity with dominant ideology. Thusly, Alcoff and Gray argue, the transgressive challenge that survivor speech poses to dominant ideology is lost or greatly diminished when such speech about incestuous abuse, speech that has been and still is taboo, becomes a titillating media commodity objectifying the survivor, stripping her of authority and agency, and thereby deflecting attention away from the perpetrator and from societal responsibility for child abuse. Instead of engaging readerly travel, such texts promise something more like a cheap and titillating tour. Numerous shows, whether hosted by Phil Donahue, Geraldo Rivera, or (to a lesser degree) Oprah Winfrey, among others, produce such effects (273–80).

Furthermore, mediation of those experiences by "experts," whose theories or therapies dominate a survivor discourse conceptualized as "nontheoretical," displaces survivors as authorities on the subject of incest. What is needed, Alcoff and Gray insist, is a survivor discourse that is both experiential and theoretical, that does not "retreat from bringing sexual violence into discourse, but, rather, . . . create[s] new discursive forms and spaces in which to gain autonomy within this process" (287).[14] Alcoff and Gray urge survivors to seize control of survivor discourse and make that discourse transgressive. Interestingly, then, the issue of control of survivor discourse parallels the issue of control of the daughter's body.

My project here is not to suggest that we need to take control of these literary texts about incest; such texts always resist such impulses (which I admit I often bring to my readings of them). I suggest instead that we pay more attention to the way we read women's fiction about incest, both for what it can tell us about cultural narratives of gender and for its important and compounded contributions to the contemporary discursive network about incest in this country. Spatial strategies of reading such texts of women writers, for whom space—material and metaphoric—is an integral and conflictual domain, not only can set these texts into discursive circulation in new contexts but also may reveal the extent to which the subject of father-daughter incest still holds us hostage as writers and as readers.[15]

My intention is not to become an outside "expert" who seeks to validate or theorize from this fiction. Nor am I attempting to transpose these narratives into a feminist liberatory themed space in which a safe home is miraculously restored. I suggest instead that traveling the material, textual, and cultural spaces of these women's fictional narratives about the sexual abuse of girls by their fathers or father figures can be part of an imaginative transgressiveness which creates more space for incest to be spoken, and heard, in all its equivocal and disquieting cadences. It is indeed instructive, though, that in a discourse riddled with metaphors of breaking silence, silence is, more often than not, what we are left with.

"Hereisthehouse": Cultural Spaces of Incest in The Bluest Eye

> And always in our daydreams, the house is a large cradle. . . . Life begins well, it begins enclosed, protected, all warm in the bosom of the house.
>
> —Gaston Bachelard, *The Poetics of Space*

> These questions, which have engaged so many, have troubled all of my work. How to be both free and situated; how to convert a racist house into a race-specific home. How to

> enunciate race while depriving it of its lethal cling? These are questions of concept, of language, of trajectory, of habitation, of occupation, and, although my engagement with them has been fierce, fitful, and constantly (I think) evolving, they remain in my thoughts as aesthetically and politically unresolved.
>
> —Toni Morrison, "Home"

Gaston Bachelard argues that we do not know ourselves in time but rather in space. Houses contain our memories of ourselves at certain times, but these memories are quickened by material images of familiar spaces that return us to ourselves again and again. These images are of what Bachelard calls *felicitous space*—space that is protective and maternal, "the space that we love" (xxxi).[16] This space is both expansive and nostalgic. "The house," he says, "constitutes a body of images that give mankind proofs or illusions of stability" (17). The "normal unconscious" is "well and happily housed, in the space of its happiness," and "knows how to make itself at home everywhere" (10). Admitting that he ignores "hostile space" in the belief that "the space of hatred and combat can only be studied in the context of impassioned subject matter and apocalyptic images" (xxxii), Bachelard constructs the felicitous space of the house as a stable order that protects and the unconscious as happy, healthy, and secure in its right to belong anywhere. His house has many rooms and several floors; it has delicious nooks and crannies; it is both spacious and cozy.

Notably absent from Bachelard's widely cited and highly evocative depictions of material and emotional space are questions of power. Who owns "the house"? Who rules the roost? And who offers stability, security, and protection? Who can live in this house? Bachelard's notion of the house as a conflation of felicitous material and psychic spaces also parallels the ideological construction of home as a place of comfort and safety. In recent years, however, contemporary discussions of incestuous abuse have challenged such a construction of home. Alcoff and Gray believe, for example, that "the notion that the 'home' signals safety and protection is a claim that is not only wrong but complicitous with sexual violence" (276). Its implicit reinforcement of the patriarchal construction of home space as felicitous for everyone makes it more difficult for women and children to name their fathers or father-figures as attackers and thereby diminishes the credibility of survivor speech. (Adrienne Rich, in her poetic sequence *Sources*, in *Your Native Land, Your Life,* calls the family home "that most dangerous place" [poem 6, l. 14] and "that dangerous place" [poem 13, l. 9]). Assigning to the house the characteristics of maternal nurturance (as he puts it, "the maternal features of the house" [7]) makes Bachelard's claims for the efficacy of felicitous (home) space even more questionable, particularly when he also defines inhabited space as "the non-I [gendered female?] that protects the I [gendered male?]" (5). Given such a frame, it isn't surprising that Bachelard does not explore the dark corners of the house he loves.

What happens when the space of "home" becomes nonfelicitous? The space of the unspeakable? What happens when the unspeakable is spoken? When the house's ideology of purity is contaminated by another story?

Written in the mid-1960s and published in 1970, before the contemporary explosion of incest narratives in the United States, Toni Morrison's first novel, *The Bluest Eye,* complicates these questions in a story of incest that shows how the father's physical and psychological power over the daughter derives from his own disempowerment through historical and material contravention. In the Breedlove kitchen of Morrison's novel, for example, the father's violence—Cholly Breedlove's rape of his daughter—is enacted against the backdrop of what in another house might have been a nurturing domestic space for eating and talking. Pecola is engaged in an everyday task when the rape occurs: she is at the sink doing the dishes. The consequences of the father's race and class disempowerment are thus visited on the daughter; the positions of "father" and "daughter" implode, causing the "house" to collapse upon itself; and the text turns a highly critical eye toward any analysis of incestuous abuse that insists on the purity of gender as a category.

And yet, although this implosion of gender stems from Cholly Breedlove's own mistreatment as a poor black youth in the South, I do not believe that Cholly does not exert power over his daughter, as might be inferred from Hortense Spillers's more general argument that both *father* and *daughter* are terms contingent on patriarchal privilege and hence do not "suffice for occupied or captive persons and communities in which the rites and rights of gender function have been exploded historically into gender neutralities" (129). It cannot be overlooked that, however disempowered he is and has been in other spaces, in the house, specifically in the kitchen, Cholly feels empowered enough to rape his daughter.

Here is the house. It is green and white.
It has a red door. It is very pretty. Here
is the family. Mother, Father, Dick, and Jane

> live in the green-and-white house. They are
> very happy. See Jane. She has a red dress.
> She wants to play. Who will play with Jane?
> See the cat. It goes meow-meow. Come and
> play. Come play with Jane. The kitten will
> not play. See Mother. Mother is very nice.
> Mother, will you play with Jane? Mother laughs.
> Laugh, Mother, laugh. See Father. He is big
> and strong. Father, will you play with Jane?
> Father is smiling. Smile, Father, smile. See
> the dog. Bowwow goes the dog. Do you want to
> play with Jane? See the dog run. Run, dog, run.
> Look, look. Here comes a friend. The friend will
> play with Jane. They will play a good game.
> Play, Jane, play. (*Bluest Eye* 7)

Morrison begins *The Bluest Eye* with this Bachelardian description of a house's felicitous spaces containing and protecting a happy white, economically secure, heterosexual family. The irony of this story of home from the familiar narrative of the Dick and Jane reading primer is given particular valence as the passage or portions thereof are repeated in typographies that become smaller and more squeezed together, with the boundaries of punctuation erased. Morrison makes metaphoric space material. Home becomes a tight squeeze, marked by the erasure and exclusion of difference as this passage is repeated twice in diminished type and without punctuation before the narrative of Pecola's rape begins. Many of the chapters also begin by repeating segments of the Dick and Jane narrative with claustrophobic typography and spacing, as well as the slashing of certain words (such as, in the following example, *father*); for example, the story of Cholly Breedlove, a man who rapes his daughter, has as an epigram:

> SEEFATHERHEISBIGANDSTRONGFATH
> ERWILLYOUPLAYWITHJANEFATHER
> ISSMILINGSMILEFATHERSMILESMILE. (105)

The Bluest Eye is itself thoroughly devoted to subverting—within the overlapping cultural spaces marked by blackness and whiteness, wealth and poverty—the happy middle-class, white home in which Dick and Jane can be safe: "the moral self-representation of the middle-class family as the biological unit of reproduction that nurtures rather than exploits its offspring" (E. Wilson 52). With its multiple narratives of abuse, this novel tells us that the contiguity of multiple oppressions is a treacherous space indeed, one in which the dangers of being inside are actually worse than those of being cast out, which seems for those in this economically unstable community the worst that can happen because it *does* happen. Even as children, Pecola's friend Claudia McTeer, the narrator of the novel, and her sister Frieda realize:

> There is a difference between being put *out* and being put out*doors*. If you are put out, you go somewhere else; if you are outdoors, there is no place to go. The distinction was subtle but final. Outdoors was the end of something, an irrevocable, physical fact, defining and complementing our metaphysical condition. Being a minority in both caste and class, we moved about anyway on the hem of life, struggling to consolidate our weaknesses and hang on, or to creep singly up into the major folds of the garment. (18)

Cholly Breedlove has been put outdoors. From his abandonment by his mother—he is thrown away like garbage—and denial by his father to the violence of being forced by white men to have intercourse with a young black girl in the woods while they shine a spotlight on him, Cholly's own virtual rape by white men and disempowerment as a black man have tragically spiraling consequences. Time collapses into the space of those social productions that make Cholly the father-abuser. As Vanessa Dickerson notes, Pecola's rape "is the culmination of Cholly's own deflowered life, his own weakness and powerlessness, his own nakedness" (121). The gendering of Cholly's own debasement places him in the position of "daughter." All these events in his life combine to constrict his cultural space so radically that they lead unerringly to a Saturday afternoon "in the thin light of spring" when "he staggered home reeling drunk and saw his daughter in the kitchen" (127).

In this sense the book's gender travels counter any uncomplicated impulse to blame Cholly for raping his daughter and instead insist on the perpetrator's own repeated victimization, that which makes him "love" Pecola. The novel's depiction of incest is further complicated, as Michael Awkward has noted, by Morrison's interest in revising certain cultural and literary narratives, not only her ironic use of the Dick and Jane primer in *The Bluest Eye* but also her revision of another story of father-daughter incest within the black community, the widely discussed Trueblood episode in Ralph Ellison's *Invisible Man.* Awkward believes that "Morrison writes her way into the Afro-American literary tradition by bringing to the foreground the effects of incest for female victims in direct response to Ellison's refusal to consider them seriously" (66).

One of Morrison's primary preoccupations throughout her fiction, from *The Bluest Eye,* her first book, to *Paradise,* published in 1997, is the matter (following Judith Butler, I use that term in a complicated sense) of purity. For Morrison, there are no pure spaces, no felicity untouched by danger; in this novel love is only as good as the lover, nor is rape purely bad. Each is complicated by the other, and each is complicated by what moves on the outside of their relational space. Claudia, the narrator, insists: "Cholly loved her. I'm sure he did. He, at any rate, was the one who loved her enough to touch her, envelop her, give something of himself to her. But his touch was fatal, and the something he gave her filled the matrix of her agony with death. Love is never any better than the lover" (159). Pecola's rape therefore seems to be perpetuated by forces outside the father's control and becomes a grotesque repetition of the encounter in the woods in which white men forced Cholly to perform what became, under their scrutiny, a contrived sex act. This text of father-daughter incest emerges from a space in which both father and daughter are victimized, directly and indirectly, by the whiteness that encircles them both.[17]

From its depictions of the white men in the woods to the selfish, insensitive white women who employ Pecola's mother, *The Bluest Eye* casts an accusatory stare at the privilege of whiteness as well as black characters' aspirations to whiteness exemplified in the southern-born Geraldine, who knows the difference between "colored people," who are "neat and clean," and "niggers," who are "dirty and loud" (71), and the pedophile Soaphead Church, who construes his own blackness as filth. Like Claudia, who in childhood dismembers her golden-haired, blue-eyed dolls but later admits to being seduced by Shirley Temple, the novel makes visible the transparency of the white space that squeezes the Breedloves into a house in which there is no comfort, no felicity, no play. We see the force field of whiteness exert itself in the black community. In this sense whiteness becomes the abusive father.

The salience of this space of whiteness surrounding the story of a black family and community in Lorain, Ohio, is made manifest at every turn, especially in the colonization of Pecola's mother, Pauline, who loves the "beauty, order, cleanliness, and praise" in the white house where she works under the name of "Polly" but stops trying to keep her own house or take care of her own children, who call her "Mrs. Breedlove." Although many of the cruelties Pecola endures are perpetrated by various members of the African American community, which in the end symbolically puts her "outdoors" because she is pregnant with her father's child, the space of whiteness that encloses those actions also molds them. *The Bluest Eye* itself scrutinizes the culturally unexamined, unmarked violence of this white space.[18] The incest story of the novel, then, reverses the positions of text and reading eye. The text itself becomes the critical "reader," both of the culture that produces the familial "house" of the ironically named Breedloves and of any analysis of incestuous abuse that insists on the purity of gender as a category.[19]

The front cover of my first copy of *The Bluest Eye,* a 1972 Pocket Books edition, has a color photograph of an African American girl wearing ribbons in her hair and holding a white doll with a rouged porcelain face, platinum blond hair, and blue eyes. The girl's deep brown eyes are looking down, not at the doll, but at something beyond it. The girl's dark hand contrasts sharply with the doll's white face. The entire photo is boxed into a rectangle by a thin white space bounded by a black line. The rest of the cover surrounding the photo is white, except for black lettering. There is a wooden, framed quality to this girl on the cover. Throughout the novel Pecola is similarly framed in various kinds of claustrophobic spaces—cultural (she is a poor black girl within white-dominated patriarchal capitalism), material (her house, neither pleasant nor safe, is an empty frame of capitalism, an abandoned storefront), emotional and physical (she has been raped by her father and rejected by mother and community)—their concentricity squeezing her tighter and tighter until finally she goes mad.[20] Those spaces interlock to frame, then compress, then destroy her. Interestingly enough in the light of her later work, particularly *Beloved,* Morrison does not admit us into those spaces until the end of the novel, when we are privy to a conversation between Pecola's fragmented identities.[21] There is a reason for this. More often we are positioned as readers on the outside watching helplessly as a black girl becomes nothing but blue eyes intent on blinding themselves to what little in life there is left to see. Morrison's project in this book—and I believe it to be a book deeply concerned with the power dynamics of incest, the act to which everything leads and from which everything derives[22]—is not so much to draw us into the space of the victim, as other novels I'll discuss do, but to have us examine the architectonics of the multiple spaces in which Pecola has her material reality, spaces that ultimately disassemble her identity and implicate *readers* (the "we") in her destruction. In her afterword to the 1994 edition of the novel, Morrison says as much: "One problem was centering: the weight of the novel's inquiry on so delicate and vulnerable a character could smash her and lead readers into the comfort of pitying her rather than into an interrogation of themselves for the smashing" (Afterword 211).

And so Pecola is not smashed, but slowly and surely pressed into invisibility, framed and reframed into categories of "poor," "black," "ugly," "nasty," and so on, always under threat of expulsion, eventually pushed outdoors. ("Get out," Geraldine tells her. "You nasty little black bitch. Get out of my house" [75]). The storekeeper Mr. Yacobowski "does not see her" with his bleary blue eyes because, for him, "there is nothing to see" (41–42). The question she asks Claudia and Frieda in the first chapter—"how do you get somebody to love you?" (29)—echoes poignantly throughout the book as she moves from place to place, "never know[ing] her beauty," seeing "only what there was to see: the eyes of other people" (40).

Pecola is never safe, and she is seldom, it seems, comfortable. Perhaps the most felicitous space she ever inhabits is the McTeer house, where she is placed temporarily after Cholly burns down the Breedlove dwelling and "everybody, as a result, [is] outdoors" (17). After arriving with absolutely nothing, Pecola sleeps between Claudia and Frieda. The girls' mother, Mrs. McTeer, complains loudly about the amount of milk Pecola consumes but takes care of the girl when she begins to menstruate for the first time. Mrs. McTeer's maternal presence warms the "old, cold, and green" house and makes it seem alive. This is only a temporary haven, however, and one in which Pecola's outsider status is always a part of the family's discourse.

"HEREISTHEHOUSEITISGREENANDWH" (30): In contrast to the McTeer house, where the girls are safe and cared for, the Breedloves' dwelling in an abandoned store is a dismal, lifeless place where "joylessness stank, pervading everything" and the only living thing is the coal stove, which in the mornings "always saw fit to die" (33). There are three rooms: the front room, which houses two sofas, one already torn when it was delivered new from the store, and a dusty Christmas tree that has been up for two years; the bedroom, with three beds, one narrow iron bed for eleven-year-old Pecola, another for her fourteen-year-old brother, Sammy, and a double bed for their parents; and the kitchen in which Pecola is eventually raped.

"HEREISTHEFAMILYMOTHERFATHER/DICKANDJANE" (34): The Breedloves live in this house "because they were poor and black, and they stayed there because they believed they were ugly" (34). It is here that Cholly and Pauline fight viciously, often coming close to killing each other. In this squeezed material space, Pecola tries to make herself shrink into nothingness: "Little parts of her body faded away. Now slowly, now with a rush. Slowly again. Her fingers went, one by one; then her arms disappeared all the way to the elbow. Her feet now. Yes, that was good. The legs all at once. It was hardest above the thighs. She had to be real still and pull. Her stomach would not go. But finally it, too, went away. Then her chest, her neck. The face was hard, too. Almost done, almost. Only her tight, tight eyes were left. They were always left" (39).

Although the three prostitutes—China, Poland, and Miss Marie—who live above the Breedloves envelop Pecola with their joking stories about sex and love and make her welcome in their apartment, both the outside world and her home continue to constrict and displace her in a series of devastating events and scenes. Every material space she enters becomes dangerous. At school she is encircled by boys who jeer at her dark complexion. After school she is lured into "the pretty gold-and-green house" of Geraldine, "the pretty milk brown lady," who sees in Pecola everything she has tried to escape. When Pecola visits her mother's place of employment, a "big white house with the wheelbarrow full of flowers" (82), and knocks over a blueberry cobbler in the kitchen, burning her legs, her mother slaps her to the floor and tells her to get out (86–87). Toward the end of the story, twelve years old, pregnant by her father, and still yearning for blue eyes, she enters the apartment of the pedophile Soaphead Church and, as a result, journeys further into the space of madness through her belief in his promise to fulfill her request.

In the end, her baby dead, she is symbolically put "outdoors," living in a little brown house on the edge of town with her mother, who never speaks to her. Her father has died and her brother is long gone. Seeing her more as a perpetrator of the incest than as a rape victim, the black community has put up boundaries against her, and she has become a grotesque liminal figure wandering its periphery. No one will look at her. All of her efforts are focused on transporting herself to another place, on trying to fly away. Claudia relates: "The damage done was total. She spent her days, her tendril, sap-green days, walking up and down, up and down, her head jerking to the beat of a drummer so distant only she could hear. Elbows bent, hands on shoulders, she flailed her arms like a bird in an eternal, grotesquely futile effort to fly. Beating the air, a winged but grounded bird, intent on the blue void it could not reach—could not even see—but which filled the valleys of the mind" (158).

"LOOKLOOKHERECOMESAFRIEND" (150): The space that Pecola now inhabits is the fracture. The fracture is what lies between Bachelard's house and her house. Elizabeth Wilson, as I said, argues that the white, middle-class, heterosexual family depends for its very existence on the displacement of the incest story elsewhere. Likewise, the maintenance of Bachelard's house depends on Pecola's being put outdoors. In the conversation between "her" and "her friend," whose voice reveals the gash in Pecola's psyche, what emerges is the deepest of longings. The revelation by Pecola's "friend" that there has been "a second time" of intercourse with Cholly, a time not in the kitchen but on the couch, raises the strong implication that Pecola either sought the encounter or did not resist it out of the desire for closeness, attention, love.

> *And you don't have to be afraid of Cholly coming at you anymore.*
> No.
> *That was horrible, wasn't it?*
> Yes.
> *The second time too?*
> Yes.
> *Really? The second time too?*
> Leave me alone! You better leave me alone. (156)

Writing out of personal experiences as sexually abused daughters, both Melba Wilson and Maya Angelou have described this troubling relation between the father's or father-figure's sexual abuse and the daughter's desire for love and comfort. Angelou writes of how, out of loneliness, she would initiate encounters with her mother's lover. Wilson says that she felt protective of her father when he and her mother fought and thus became receptive to his sexual advances (28). Christine Courtois has pointed out that the victim often sees the perpetrator as good to protect herself from the disillusionment of viewing him as bad and sees herself as the bad one who provoked the behavior (35). Most professional therapists point to the fact that, as Meiselman puts it, "child victims tend to blame themselves, and if they enjoyed or benefited from any aspect of the incest situation, their guilt is exacerbated. If their disclosure has precipitated dissolution of the family, their guilt may be further intensified" (42). Pecola's disclosure to her mother and the girl's pregnancy have completely destroyed the love-hate relationship with Cholly that sustained Mrs. Breedlove. The girl's guilt is obvious in the conversation between "Pecola" and her imaginary "friend," in which "they" decide that Mrs. Breedlove's silence results from the fact that "*she doesn't feel too good since Cholly's gone*" (153).

But such desire as Pecola's is also racialized, as Morrison shows again and again. After all is said and done, what Pecola desperately wanted and what she has now convinced herself that she has are blue eyes. Produced and reproduced in white space, black space, father space, mother space, home space, and outdoor space, "Pecola" herself has by the novel's end become a spatial text. "She" becomes those beautiful bluest eyes, which gaze without blinking, without seeing, from this book's white margins . . . to mirror what? The father's own unseeing, his most deleterious desires, yes. But, as daughter, Pecola also becomes a text of gender relations so thickly complicated by race and class as to become almost indecipherable. In this regard, *The Bluest Eye* is surely one of Morrison's most unresolved engagements with the concepts of habitation, politics, and aesthetics: with home.

We see the transparency of the blue eyes' gaze—their blueness must be seen as white space—how that transparency hides its power to delimit what stories can be told about father and daughter. The freezing of Pecola into social text is so solidified at this point that we wonder indeed whether there is anything one might call, in contemporary terminology, "survival discourse" still alive in this text. Then Claudia McTeer's voice, with its cadences of grief and guilt, ambiguity and anxiety, resonates from the final pages of this book of sorrow. At the end of the last chapter, Claudia's voice emerges without a break from the dialogue between fragmented identities, and so seems grafted onto the engorged spatial text that "Pecola" has become. Claudia breaks through the space of madness and silence to insist on "the damage done" and to tell the story of a daughter who became a wounded bird and could never fly away. Although (and perhaps because) she is not a victim, Claudia generates the survivor discourse of this particular story of incest, when, for the daughter, "it's much, much, much too late" (160). At the same time Claudia claims authority not only to reproduce this text but also to explicate it. She seizes the narrative and theoretical productions of the story of Pecola's multiple victimizations and, in so doing, shows us how to read it.

Like Pecola's silence, her mad gesticulations, Claudia's furious, guilty, loving words haunt the landscape of this text, and, more importantly, travel the world outside it. As a member of the black community, she admits culpability: "All of us—all who knew her—felt so wholesome after we cleaned ourselves on her. We were so beautiful when we stood astride her ugliness" (159). But who is included in this "we"? Who is *responsible* for the loss of this girl among, as Claudia says, "all the waste and beauty of the world—which is what she herself was" (159)? Not just Cholly who victimized and, Claudia believes, loved Pecola, but "all of us" who inhabit and perpetuate a culture that "acquiesce[s] and say[s] the victim had no right to live" (160), a cultural space that produces the Chollys of the world who inevitably must come home to their daughters and bring the violence of outside into the house.

In the end Claudia pries this text open and releases it to travel the space of "we." She insists that, whoever we are, we belong inside this story's spaces, however much we may wish to position ourselves outside, however much we do not want to be the "we" of whom and to whom she speaks.

The Space of the Ellipsis: Southern Stories of Incest

I want to circle back to a specific contour shaping this book: that textual spaces reveal and reflect the workings of ideology, and are themselves ideological productions, as also are their readings. At a rudimentary level the first such space one usually encounters in reading a particular book is its cover, which promotes and, one might say, "themes," for the purposes of sale, the book's interior textual spaces. As Alcoff and Gray have noted, the commodification of survivor discourse has become perilous ground for survivors to negotiate in a media-driven capitalistic culture that exploits both sexual abuse and violence. The covers and cover materials of books of fiction by southern women I'll be reading in this section are relevatory in this regard. This external information/advertising is part of what Diane P. Freedman has called a book's "borders—its packaging, format, and the contexts in which it is read and published [that are] inseparable from its more apparent content" (31). Does the marketing of fiction that relates stories of father-daughter incest reflect and reproduce the dominant ideological productions which have shaped the daughter's story and harnessed survival discourse to consumer desire? How is the patriarchal secret protected, and under what conditions is it revealed? Of all the books discussed in this chapter, Morrison's (interestingly enough, the earliest) is the only text whose cover (at least in the edition I own) reveals the novel's story line of father-daughter incestuous abuse.[23] In fact, one may wonder whether the original reception of *The Bluest Eye* suffered because of its forthrightness about its taboo subject matter. In a 1994 reissue of the book Morrison states in an afterword: "With very few exceptions, the initial publication of *The Bluest Eye* was like Pecola's life: dismissed, trivialized, misread. And it has taken twenty-five years to gain for her the respectful publication this edition is" (215). A 1970 review by Haskel Frankel in the *New York Times Book Review* is a case in point: Frankel relegates Pecola's abuse to a phrase, "pregnant by her father," and faults Morrison for, among other things, "the fuzziness born of flights of poetic imagery," getting "lost in her construction," and yielding "center stage to Frieda and Claudia . . . [, who] serve little purpose beyond distraction" (20). It is significant, I think, that the cover materials of my editions of the four southern novels (I will discuss *A Thousand Acres* in a section following this one) lack any words such as *incest, rape,* or *sexual abuse.*

The cover of a 1993 paperback edition of Lee Smith's *Black Mountain Breakdown,* originally published in 1980, bears this incongruous quotation from the *Washington Star:* "*Black Mountain Breakdown* has a jaunty charm that is entirely infectious. . . . Reading it is a genuine pleasure." Above the quotation is a Norman Rockwell–like drawing of several white clapboard houses standing in a row with grayish mountains behind them. Nothing on the cover of this edition, either commentary or summary, indicates that the book focuses primarily on the way incestuous rape affects the victim (like Pecola Breedlove, Crystal Spangler is not a survivor). To the contrary, the summary of *Black Mountain Breakdown* reads as follows:

> Crystal Spangler lives in rural Appalachia. She's the apple of her mother's eye—not beautiful yet, but she will be. She's the most popular girl at Black Rock High. She makes cheerleader, gets good grades, and is elected beauty queen. Crystal discovers God, goes to college, and falls in love. When she comes home, she's disheveled and confused. Crystal becomes a wealthy politician's wife. But there's something calling her, drawing her back to where it all began, in the shadow of Black Mountain . . .

The ellipsis at the end of the last sentence, like the description, is obviously designed to sell the book in a mass market. Its lacuna leaves readers with the sense that this is another exciting mystery with a beautiful woman at its center—a Cinderella story with an unusual, perhaps thrilling twist left to the imagination by the open-ended ellipsis.

The cover of the original 1987 hardcover edition of Kaye Gibbons's *Ellen Foster* has a picture of a white iron bed with what look like remnants of small bare branches on the white, rumpled pillows. On the back, one of the many laudatory quotations is from Alfred Kazin. It reads: "A captivating, often hilarious mix of Victorian fairy tale and fresh American lingo, told by an eleven-year-old orphan driven to desperation by the wickedest relatives in literature since *King Lear.* She saves herself and enchants the reader by recounting her story, line by line, in a style primitive, *saucy,* and exhilarating" (my emphasis). Reading this description, we are left with the impression that this is a picaresque tale about a young damsel in distress whose "saucy" style of story-telling is enchantingly seductive. Nothing is mentioned of that wicked relative, the father, and the kind of abuse encountered by Ellen.

When I open my 1982 paperback edition of *The Color Purple* to the first page, I see that the text has nine parallel lines marked through the third paragraph. This is because my daughter chose this passage for a dramatic reading in her tenth-grade drama class. Her teacher agreed to the reading but marked through the third paragraph, which she forbade my daughter to read as part of her dramatic presentation. The passage is the story of the rape by the man Celie believed to be her father: "He never had a kine word to say to me. Just say You gonna do what your mammy wouldn't. First he put his thing up against my hip and sort of wiggle it around. Then he grab hold my titties. Then he push his thing inside my pussy. When that hurt, I cry. He start to choke me, saying You better shut up and git used to it" (11). My daughter decided to read from another book for her presentation. She didn't know how to read the story without the erased passage because nothing made sense without it.

The front cover of this edition has a drawing of a small white house by the side of a road. On the back cover the description reads:

> Life wasn't easy for Celie. But she knew how to survive, needing little to get by.
>
> Then her husband's lover, a flamboyant blues singer, barreled into her world and gave Celie the courage to ask for more—to laugh, to play, and finally—to love.

Again, this description, like my daughter's teacher, censors certain parts of Celie's story (no, life surely wasn't easy for Celie) and downplays others (yes, Shug does teach Celie to love). It is part of the network of censorship surrounding and theming the novel. In response to other efforts at censorship stemming from Celie's graphic description of her sexual abuse, Walker herself has said:

> I remember actually trying to censor this passage in Celie's voice even as I wrote it. Even I found it almost impossible to let her say what had happened to her as *she* perceived it, without euphemizing it a little. And why? Because once you strip away the lie that rape is pleasant, that rapists have anything at all attractive about them, that children are not permanently damaged by sexual pain . . . [,] you are left with the positive horror of the lives of thousands of children . . . who have been sexually abused and who have never been permitted in their own language to tell about it. ("Finding Celie's Voice" 71)

The front cover of the 1992 original hardcover edition of *Bastard Out of Carolina* is a black-and-white photograph of a young white girl pressing against a barbed-wire fence in the foreground. Behind her a woman, one assumes her mother, stands in the background of a bare yard, one hand shading her eyes as she looks at her daughter, whose hands make fists on the barbed wire. There is no man, no father in this picture, and no indication in the cover materials that this is a book about a stepfather's escalating violence, which culminates in a particularly brutal rape, described in minute detail, as well as the ruinous effect that violence has on the daughter's obvious alienation from her mother. The lengthy blurb on the book jacket describes the stepfather as follows: "At first infinitely gentle with Bone, Daddy Glen becomes steadily colder and more furious—until their final, harrowing encounter, from which there can be no turning back."

What are the obviating gaps here, and how do we read them? Although incestuous abuse is by no means the central focus of two of these novels (*The Color Purple* and *Ellen Foster*), they all have the incestuous rape of a young girl as a significant topic. What does this particular form of silence in marketing these books tell us about the cultural enclosure of survivor discourse and the ideological terrain these books inhabit? Unlike the marketing strategies Alcoff and Gray describe as manipulating survivor discourse for entertainment purposes, the omitted information and the tone of these cover descriptions keep what Herman calls "the incest secret" secret (12), and something of a titillating one at that. Twitchell points out that, as long as incest is hidden by the mantle of secrecy, as long as it remains unspeakable, it will continue to have excessive potency (32). These silences are particularly ironic in regard to *Black Mountain Breakdown* and *Bastard Out of Carolina,* both of which, in different ways, focus on the way silence about incest, domestic violence, and that dangerous place called home can endanger the victim. Like *The Bluest Eye,* each of these four books explores the ideological construction of home as a space of female entrapment and sometimes (but not always) suggest that home can be reconstructed as a site of empowerment and survivorship for women.

Helen Levy has shown how many women writers of the South and other regions of the United States have subverted masculinist systems by creating a "home place" (24), and Ann Romines argues that in some American women's writing, "the story of housekeeping, the 'home plot,' has generated forms and continuities very different from those of the patriarchal American canon" (17). In incest narratives written by southern women—also stories of home—the disruption of father-rule carries a particular insistence. This disruption occurs in part because of the connection in southern culture between geography, material place (in these novels the house, which in many cases isn't really the father's but the landlord's and in some isn't really a house either) and identity (in these novels, the female's identity as daughter in the house). The equation of place and identity therefore becomes compoundly conflictual because, in the daughter's predicament, place/identity equals powerlessness.

This conflictual relation of place and identity has a haunting and peculiar resonance in southern women's writing. In general, women's writing and life experiences, so often vexed with a sense of constricted material and cultural spaces because of gender and perhaps class, race, and sexuality as well, share certain borders with southern culture and literature, with their attention to place and the evocative nature of place in the formation of identity. As Lewis P. Simpson puts it, the South has been traditionally "both an emotional entity and a geographical place" (9)—a relation between identity and place that continues to be reflected in the writing of southerners. The relation of place and identity is multiply complicated in these narratives of father-daughter incest in that they are located within the material spaces and ideological networks of southern rural geographies where land and its ownership and use are tied to distinctive historical interventions, most notably slavery. (This sets them apart from Jane Smiley's novel *A Thousand Acres,* set in rural Iowa.)

Moreover, narratives of incest have long circulated in southern popular culture, and narratives of incest in the South have circulated in popular culture generally. Such narratives have been especially directed toward poor white Appalachian culture and the cultures of other sparsely populated areas of the South (consider, for example, the joke about the only ten-year-old virgin in Redneck/Hillbilly County—she's the one who can run fast or whose daddy and brothers are in wheelchairs—or stories about *Deliverance*-style offspring resulting from sexual activity among relatives).[24] The theme of incest from the point of view of the white male also has been the subject of southern male writers, particularly the contemporary South's literary father, William Faulkner, whose white male characters have had incestuous relations with a black daughter (*Go Down, Moses*) or desired a white sister (*Sanctuary, Flags in the Dust, The Sound and the Fury,* and *Absalom, Absalom!*). What Allison, Gibbons, Smith, and Walker do that Faulkner does not is to dramatize the effects of incestuous abuse on the daughter *from her perspective.*

This is not to deny that these texts handle the topic in importantly different ways. The instances of incestuous abuse in *The Color Purple* and *Ellen Foster* are relegated to few words (although quite explicit ones in the former), but their results are multifarious. Situated in one claustrophobic space after another, *Bastard Out of Carolina* moves in excruciating fashion *toward* the particularly brutal rape, which looms larger and larger as it becomes inevitable. *Black Mountain Breakdown* is a study of the devastating effects of a rape that cannot be remembered until many years later. The first three novels are primarily about survivorship, even though all three depict scenes of brutality. *Black Mountain Breakdown,* the only one of these books not told from the victim/survivor's point of view, is about Crystal Spangler's devastating psychic enclosure. The first three narratives are primarily about poor rural people—African American and white—whereas Smith's novel focuses on a family of white, middle-class, small-town Virginians. The father figure in three of these texts is not biologically related to the victim. Celie's father turns out not to be her father after all but her stepfather. Bone's attacker in *Bastard Out of Carolina* is her stepfather, Daddy Glen. Crystal's rapist is her mentally disabled uncle, Devere, who, I will argue, carries out her father's incestuous desire. Only Ellen suffers sexual abuse from her biological father, and the depiction of it is oblique and limited to a few sentences. As in contemporary autobiographical narratives of survivors, the spaces of father-daughter incestuous abuse in these fictional texts obviously have their own silences, their own blank spots, and, at the same time, their own transgressive politics.

In part their transgressiveness involves reversing the play of power between father and daughter through the act of telling the story of incest and thus revising a dominant cultural narrative of the father's power and the daughter's obeisance. This master narrative, as Lynda Zwinger has observed, has represented "normative" heterosexual desire within fiction that sentimentalizes women as desiring daughters whose "fathers" are innocent of any but culturally sanctioned designs on them. These representations "ground the system of cultural constructs and prescriptions that we have learned to think of as heterosexual desire" (5). Such stories, Zwinger points out, are always about power, and often the coercion of the father's "seduction" of the daughter is veiled: "The daughter's need for love and approval is glossed as complicity or even mutuality, while her vulnerability increases the titillation always encoded by virtue in distress" (9). As Gallop shows in *The Daughter's Seduction: Feminism and Psychoanalysis,* unveiling the father's seductive power requires interrogating and sabotaging dominant narratives of gender identity and relations (46).

These four narratives of father-daughter incest undertake this task with complex variations, through confrontation and indirection, by "home" breaking and "home" making, in language and silence. By conflating the seductive father with his "retarded" rapist brother, who "looks so much like [her father] that it sometimes makes Crystal cry to see him" (29), the earliest of these novels, Lee Smith's *Black Mountain Breakdown,* ambiguously masks and unmasks the father's power in a series of steps and countersteps leading in and out of certain spatial dimensions. It begins with an opposition of the beauty of motion and threat of enclosure. Crystal is catching lightning bugs in Mason jars; a lightning bug emerges magically, making Crystal forget her mission: "It is so close she can breathe on it and see the whirring, tiny wings. Crystal doesn't move. She could catch it, but she doesn't" (3).

This is a complicated book that itself holds secrets. The openly sinister space inhabited by her father's doppelgänger brother, Devere, overlays what appears to be Grant Spangler's intense but innocent attachment to his loving and obedient daughter. Grant is a white middle-class father who is both ailing and alcoholic. He has withdrawn from the world and, at the beginning of the novel, inhabits his wife's front parlor, which now "smells like old smoke, like liquor, like Grant himself, yet the combination is not unpleasant really and Crystal loves it" (15). This is clearly a place apart: "Behind the door is another room, another world almost" (14).

In an early scene of the book set in the parlor, Grant reads to his adoring twelve-year-old daughter, who loves the passages he chooses, and her friend Agnes, who says she doesn't like them. He particularly likes to read poetry and stories that either are about death ("Little Boy Blue") and reduce Crystal to "huge racking sobs" (17) or are very frightening, such as "The Spider and the Fly." Moreover, his choice of reading material seems keyed to younger children, and Crystal's response seems strangely immature for her age, as if he has been ritualistically reading her these texts since she was very young. I have argued throughout this book that reading is seductive in its appeal to imaginative encounter; here reading is used to seduce, but there is a disturbing element to the seduction:

> Grant makes his voice deep and full of cunning malice as he begins, "'Will you walk into my parlor?' said the spider to the fly; ''Tis the prettiest little parlor that ever you did spy.'"
>
> When the fly answers, Grant's voice is high and innocent.
>
> "'O no, no,' said the little fly, 'for I've often heard it said
> They *never wake* again, who sleep upon your bed.'"
>
> Unconscious of what she's doing, Crystal twists the hem of her father's robe into a hard tight ball and bites it. (18)

During this highly seductive reading of a story of dangerous seduction, "Crystal sits close to [her father] on the floor, holding on to his knee under the old blue silk robe he always wears" (15). Earlier she is both horrified and titillated by his reading of "Little Boy Blue," the poem about a child's death: "it's hard to tell by the tone of her voice whether she's delighted or upset . . . [;] her usually dreaming face is wholly alive" (17). As Grant finishes reading "The Spider and the Fly," Crystal "shivers and lets all her breath out in one long shuddering sight" at the same moment that her mother, Lorene, flings open the door and exclaims to her husband, "You ought to be ashamed of yourself!" (19). There are obvious erotic implications to this scene—the seductive story, the father's seductive reading, the daughter's fear and pleasure, the marked difference between her response to the stories and her friend's, the mother's outrage. As the novel progresses Grant demands Crystal's presence in the parlor more and more often. We are told that when he calls "Honey?" it isn't clear whether he is calling his wife, from whom he has withdrawn almost completely, or his daughter: "Maybe her but more likely Crystal; he wants Crystal all the time now. Lorene shuts the door before he has a chance to see her" (24). (The last pronoun is left ambiguous; we are not certain whether Lorene is hiding herself or their daughter.)

Parks Lanier Jr. has argued that after Crystal's rape by her uncle and the death of her father (which occur within a twenty-four-hour period), the image of the dreadful parlor becomes Crystal's psychic space, a space from which she never escapes (63). I want to suggest instead that Smith succeeds in bringing about a narrative enclosure of Crystal that operates textually at the level of plot and character. (At the end of the novel, twenty years later, she is back in the family house, hysterically paralyzed and enclosed in her own room.) This incremental enclosure also transpires in the relation of reader to character. At the end of the book, Crystal, now thirty-two, lies unmoving in her bed like an old woman staring at nothing "as outside her window the seasons come and go and the colors change on the mountain" (240). The reader attends this paralysis, but there is nothing, no one, here to read. Like Crystal's friend Agnes, who sits on the edge of that bed talking to herself, the reader must create a story out of Crystal's silence. Crystal's memory contains and blanks out the rape for many years; her memory of it at the end of the book is anything but liberating.

So finally the space of the victim becomes a frozen, bare, uninhabitable terrain—a psychic barrenness in the face of which the reader remains as helpless as anyone else. Is this survival? Crystal is like Pecola in that she curls around her self and becomes a transparent container, a kind of sealed Mason jar that can be seen through. Crystal's enclosure may be read in terms of the daughter's transparent cultural space, which requires her, as Zwinger points out, "to want what she doesn't want" (120), that is, to succumb to the desire of the father—in this case a failed southern father—and embed that desire with her own.[25] This is precisely Crystal's situation; she has learned to "read" from her father. Zwinger writes: "The production of a daughter with the right (that is, sympathetic to and complicitous with the father) reading perspective is an urgent patriarchal necessity. The one in the daughter's place is asked to agree to incite the very activity and instability she is constructed to disavow and also to repress any knowledge of the contradictions of her position. Essentially, this is the hysterical position" (122).

Except for short periods in her life, Crystal essentially remains in the hysterical position, which reaches its culmination at the end of the novel as she lies in bed, not speaking and not moving—not even looking out the window. Froula believes that the woman reader of a literary tradition that inscribes violence against women is like an abused daughter (Crystal in the parlor) and that, like physical abuse, "literary violence against women works to privilege the cultural father's voice and story over those of women, the cultural daughters, and indeed to silence women's voices" (633).

Can Smith's project in *Black Mountain Breakdown* be read as an attempt to expose the exploitative nature of that voice and the father's story as violent and destructive to the daughter? Crystal's rape by her uncle, which takes place in the toolshed at her father's family home, is textually enclosed between two scenes in the parlor with her father. In one Grant tells Crystal gruesome stories of murder and hanging, including a story about a man killing his own son (66–67). In the other she finds her father dead and has to be dragged away from his body and tranquilized. She also refuses to leave her father's graveside, feeling "there's no ground at all, nothing but empty space beneath her feet" (83). The night of her rape, remembering nothing, Crystal sleeps in the bed in her father's childhood room "with her father's initials on the windowsill, W.G.S., the room where she always stays, and she does not dream" (69). The positioning of the textual space of the rape by Crystal's blank-looking uncle, with "his deepset eyes, those Spangler eyes," in proximity to the material space of the parlor elides the rape in the toolshed with Grant's incestuous desire for his daughter, desire that can move beyond the parlor obliquely, that smears the text and the daughter.

In the years that follow her father's death, Crystal the good daughter continues to want what she does not want. She wins beauty contests. She becomes promiscuous. She tries to be saved. She becomes involved with an angst-ridden man who eventually hangs himself, leaving her to find his body. Finally, after being hospitalized with a breakdown, Crystal comes back to Black Rock as an adult and begins to teach. For the first time in her life she feels content and fulfilled. She is happier than she ever thought possible. She busies herself with her students and community activities. Then her former high-school boyfriend, Roger Lee Combs, who is married to another former classmate, appears at her door, declares his undying love for her, and persuades her to run off to Florida with him. When he kisses her breasts, "a feeling she has almost forgotten sweeps over her, closing her in" (209). The phrase "closing her in"—echoing the space of her rape and the claustrophobic parlor—is particularly apt here, for after Crystal runs off with Roger, her sense of well-being and purpose dissolves. As Anne Goodwyn Jones points out, she returns to passivity, to a state in which choices are made for her rather than by her (262).

In "The Second 'Rape' of Crystal Spangler," John D. Kalb argues that Crystal's enclosure within her marriage and Roger's seductions leading to it are a second rape. When Roger becomes more successful and runs for Congress, she finds she has nothing to do. She is campaigning for him by visiting a mental institution when one of the patients, a moon-faced man who reaches from his hospital bed for her hand, reminds her of Devere and triggers the memory of the rape. This encounter leads to a downward spiral back to her father and the enclosure of father space ("the way daddy said it was" [235]). In the end she goes home to her mother, lies down on the bed in her old room, and "paralyzes herself," becoming an uncanny double of her withdrawn invalid father and locating herself within the more narrow psychic space of the daughter-victim. To compound the father's seduction and the rape by her uncle, Crystal has been taught by Lorene to embrace femininity: frosted hair, a boyfriend at an early age, beauty contests. Her eventual enclosure of self in hysteria, then, is "simultaneously what a woman can do both to be feminine and to refuse femininity, within patriarchal discourse" (Mitchell 289). It is a last resort.

Is there a survivor in this novel, much less a "survivor discourse"? In *The Bluest Eye* Claudia speaks of "the damage done" and theorizes from a deep sense of what that damage is, both to Pecola and to the community. There is no character in *Black Mountain Breakdown* to serve such a function. Crystal's jealous friend Agnes is actually enjoying Crystal's paralysis and enclosure; Crystal's mother takes what comes and doesn't ask hard questions. The narrator's difference from and sympathy for Crystal's position are everywhere apparent, yet the narrator's position does not move into the arena of transgressive speech, except by indirection and implication. Material space (the parlor/toolshed), textual space (the blankness and silence of Crystal's hysteria), and cultural space (the white southern belle/failed father configuration) all move to enclose and silence the daughter. At the close of this novel I find myself drawn into a silent psychic space created by the narrator yet from which I as reader am led to create a form of transgressive speech. It's a space I'm unwilling to travel for long, and Crystal herself gives me no clues about how to live within it. She "just lies up there in that room every day, with her bed turned catty-corner so she could look out the window and see Lorene's climbing rambler rose in full bloom on the trellis and the mountain all green beyond the railroad track if she would turn her head" (238).

Crystal, I find myself saying, I want you to get out of that bed and let me show you the way out of here. Hey, girl, I want to take you *somewhere else.*

Look, I say, look outside your daddy's house. Look beyond your mama's roses. See the mountain all green.

Crystal, though, does not answer.

> Oh, Nettie, us have a house! A house big enough for us and our children, for your husband and Shug. Now you can come home cause you have a home to come to!
> Your loving sister,
> Celie
>
> —Alice Walker, *The Color Purple*

Crystal Spangler's victimization is figured in final enclosure within her father's house. In *The Color Purple, Ellen Foster,* and *Bastard Out of Carolina,* the recovery or renovation of home and its attendant restructuring of family makes female survivorship, in all its attendant contradictions, possible. I want to stress, though, that this process is both complicated and partial, especially when considering the very different spatial dynamics of these texts. Space is both metaphor and materiality in *The Color Purple,* in terms of home and text, although perhaps more interesting is the way often contentious readings of the novel have claimed it for highly contested themed spaces, such as "feminist literature," "lesbian literature," "black women's literary tradition," and seen it as an assault on others, for example, "the African American male" and "the black family." In the text itself, the process of creating home is at one level quite literal. Toward the end of the novel, when her stepfather, Alphonso, dies, Celie inherits his house, along with the land and a drygoods store adjacent to it. The property actually belonged to Celie's biological father and so was to be handed down to Celie and her sister, Nettie. Alphonso, whom Celie knew as "Pa" and believed to be her father for many years, is the father of her two children through repeated rapes when she was fourteen and fifteen; he also bartered her off to Albert before she turned twenty. Celie inherits the father's house and over time transforms it through concrete action—a kind of "housekeeping" or "homemaking." This process begins with Shug's smoking the house from attic to basement with cedar sticks, "chasing out all the evil and making a place for good" (217). Despite further hardships—Shug leaves her, and word comes that her sister is dead—Celie settles into her house and, in what has been a gradual transformation of identity, into someone who is in charge of home. She hires Sofia to help in the drygoods store. She realizes that she is at peace with herself and "can live content without Shug" (247). She accepts her own lesbianism and rejects a second marriage offer from Albert. For hours she and Albert sit on the porch and talk about the meaning of life. He makes shirts to go with her pants and even makes her a little purple frog perch for her mantelpiece—an implicit acceptance of her lesbianism. When Shug returns for a visit, Celie shows her the pink room she has selected for her and then Celie's own room: "purple and red cept the floor, that painted bright yellow" (248). Celie has remade home as "a practiced place," a space created through activity and encounter. The final scene, when Nettie and her family arrive, is for Celie a doubly resonant moment. She has a home to offer her sister and children; she has taken the father's house and transformed it into felicitous space.

Celie's claim to home depends on her creation of a textual space to gather and protect herself. It has become commonplace to say that Celie writes her way to a new sense of herself. Alison Light, for example, finds *The Color Purple* "a profoundly inspiring and contradictory text because it is finally *utopian:* it is a fantastic success story, offering its readers an imaginary resolution of political and personal conflicts" (105). In terms of Walker's rather determined drive toward resolution and restitution in this book—which has been both praised and dismissed as simplistic—it is interesting to see how Celie's letters mark on the page certain material shapes with borders, margins, and centered substance. These map the relation between metaphor and materiality. Like Cisneros's short sketches as they shape her textured house and Morrison's ironic use of the squeezed reading primer text, Celie's letters—their materiality, their placement on the page, their substantive and well-formed shapes—are specifically located in the space of social relations that bring them into being. They present the evolving field of Celie's reality, concretely locating her social relations over the decades. They are readerly, in the sense that they are highly invitational, while maintaining certain borders that distance them from the reader: distinctive salutations and closings, wide margins, and a sense of space between. The letters (space) mark both story (time) and geography (place), creating complex patterns of space-time that fold the decades into the fabric of Celie's life. They also, as Deborah McDowell notes, "offer a compelling model of the relationship Walker implies between herself and her readers, her own correspondents, her audience of 'kissin' friends' who enter by the 'intimate gate,' to borrow from Zora Neale Hurston. In choosing them as her auditors and their experiences as her story, she has made the private public, and in the process created a new literary space for the black and the female idiom against and with a traditional Eurocentric and androcentric literary history" ("'The Changing Same'" 298–99). But this is a highly contested space. One cannot help but note the startling similarities in the controversies of the 1980s surrounding the reception of *The Color Purple*—the novel and film—and contemporary discussions of incestuous abuse in the family. Steven Spielberg's glitzy, hanging-basket version of southern African American life provides an obvious comparison to the appropriation of survival discourse in contemporary popular culture. The film, as Gerald Early notes, is typical of Spielberg: "the experience of an exaggerated morality in an excessive spectacle," which Early believes to be, "not an experience of art, but an experience of the negation of art" (263). The novel enacts a disquieting convergence of cultural space and literary history that has not been fully discussed. The obvious similarities in structure, narrative trajectory, point of view, and theme to slave narratives of the nineteenth-century South insinuate that a dominant ideology of white patriarchal privilege, with its links to property, can become a pattern for the relations of father and daughter in the African American family.[26] Walker implies this in her statement that the character of Celie is based on Walker's own great-grandmother, a slave who, at age twelve, was raped by her master. Walker has said: "I liberated her from her own history. . . . I wanted her to be happy" (in Harris, "On *The Color Purple*" 157).

These convergences suggest the very Foucauldian way in which institutionalized systems of dominance, such as slavery and patriarchy, can reproduce themselves in socially mutated forms. In this sense *The Color Purple* clearly inhabits the terrain of contemporary survivor discourse, which, through disclosure of father-daughter incest, unmasks the production of patriarchal power at its very site, the home, and in its most extreme form. At the same time the act of father-daughter incest in the novel is tied to the institution of slavery in a disturbing way because it renders the black father not only as father but also as master. (This is also the case in Walker's story "The Child Who Favored Daughter," in which the father's incestuous desire drives him to cut off his daughter's breasts.) Celie speaks the unspeakable—"Then he push his thing inside my pussy" (11). This is a story of the father's invasion of the daughter's physical and psychic space that may also be read as a cultural narrative whose story of incestuous abuse interlocks with the racial dynamics of historical intervention, the white invasion of African American home space, whose "survivor discourse" became the slave narrative and its literary antecedents. The fact that *The Color Purple,* vexingly enough, resembles a slave narrative in form, subject matter, and trajectory unveils the incessant workings of power and domination that intersect and overlap in complicated networks that are never mutually exclusive.

Some readers have strenuously resisted the novel's unveiling of incestuous abuse in this southern African American family and the feminist message of Celie's survivor discourse. When incest is reported, the family may break apart, with the child removed from the family and placed with other relatives or in foster care. Often the child is not adequately protected from the father's or father figure's recrimination, and she feels her removal from the family as punishment.[27] It is not too much of a stretch to say that vociferous attacks on *The Color Purple* and its author from various "families," both inside and outside the black community, have reproduced this pattern of blaming and dislocating the victim. The controversies involving *The Color Purple* have included widespread efforts to ban the book from certain schools, libraries, and specific sites of reading (for example, my daughter's high school drama class). Certain responses to Walker's portrayal of Alphonso and the early Albert, and Celie's relations to them as father and husband, respectively, may also be related to the taboo described by Margaret Randall as "the speaking out, the telling" (Preface xi), a taboo punishable (by the family or by society, or both) by putting the one who speaks "outdoors." To some members of the African American community, as Melba Wilson indicates, disclosure of "the dirty linen" may be construed as a disloyalty carrying more reprobation than does incest itself (1).

In her compelling article "Reading Family Matters," McDowell shows how certain contemporary black women writers, especially Walker, have been most roundly criticized for violating the "story of the Black Family cum Black Community headed by the Black Male who does battle with an oppressive White world" (78). Such attacks are couched in what McDowell calls a "rhetoric of family" (79). A particularly egregious example of such punishing rhetoric is found in Philip R. Royster's critical article "In Search of Our Fathers' Arms: Alice Walker's Persona of the Alienated Darling" (also cited by McDowell), in which Royster accuses Walker of creating personae that act out the author's psychological compulsion to look "for father figures with whom to be a darling" and to portray "women with frustrated psychosexual attitudes towards men (Ruth toward Grange, Meridian towards both Eddie and Truman, and Celie towards both Alfonso [*sic*] and Albert)" (349). Royster claims that Walker's "alienation from black men influences her portrayal of them in fiction" and attributes this attitude to a childhood accident in which her brother shot her in the eye with a BB gun, which created a "disenchantment [that] sounds like that of a child who no longer feels like her father's darling" (363). Detailing what he sees as Walker's "hardheartedness towards her father" (364), Royster attempts to uproot Walker's narrative of male-female relations from its home in the black community by portraying her as an antimale, antiblack bundle of childhood neuroses. She is not a good daughter. (Interestingly, he does not mention her somewhat affectionate portrait of her own father in her essay "Father.") Royster also critically reproduces the all-too-familiar "blame the victim" syndrome by chiding Celie for being "too stupid to protect herself from Alfonso" and playing "the same game" with Albert (367).

This is not to say that some vehement critiques of *The Color Purple* have not contained more thoughtful arguments. Trudier Harris, in "On *The Color Purple,* Stereotypes, and Silence," recounts her readerly struggle as a African American woman critic with an intense dislike for the novel, which she feels has erroneously become "the quintessential statement on Afro-American women and a certain kind of black lifestyle in the United States" (155). Harris strenuously resists Walker's characterization of Celie as victim, which Harris believes does a grave disservice to the real lives of black women and southern black communities. She believes that the novel's popularity has created "a cadre of spectator readers" (155), which seems to mean white racist readers, and in so doing "gives validity to all the white racist's notions of pathology in black communities" (157). These spectator readers, "who do not identify with the characters and who do not feel the intensity of their pain, stand back and view the events of the novel as a circus of black human interactions that rivals anything Daniel Patrick Moynihan concocted" (155). Harris notes several times that in her discussions with white women who have read the novel, especially feminists such as Gloria Steinem, most have been quite vocal about their love for it, while many of the black women she has talked to display a "quiet strain of discomfort with it, a quiet tendency to criticize," but also an uneasiness with "the idea that to criticize a novel that had been so universally complimented was somehow a desertion of the race and the black woman writer" (155).

In her accusatory stance toward "spectator readers" of *The Color Purple,* of whom Steinem, a well-known white feminist, is held up as example, Harris presents an argument similar in certain ways to Kincaid's contention that the texts of personal narrative, literature, and film about incest and the sexual abuse of children are being greedily absorbed by a group of "readers" who use such texts to fulfill and displace certain less than scrupulous desires. Neither analysis considers the ways that complexly gendered locations might affect either writerly motivation or readerly empathy. Transgressing an ideological terrain in which certain forms of power are maintained by displacing the disempowered, *The Color Purple* thus occupies a dual position, as a text that tells Celie's story and as a textual configuration *about which* certain critical communities have told stories,[28] my "story" of the novel as a spatial text being no exception. These positions elide, disclosing and denaturalizing layered and multiple sites called "home" and "family," whether they be fictional or critical. So poised, Walker's novel, as narrative and as cultural artifact, establishes at once the necessity—and the cost—of speaking out about incest.

> When I was little I would think of ways to kill my daddy. I would figure out this or that way and run it down through my head until it got easy.
>
> —Kaye Gibbons, *Ellen Foster*

Because of its complex interchanges between gender and race, *Ellen Foster* is an interesting novel to follow a discussion of *The Color Purple* and its discursive community. Kaye Gibbons's book is the tale of a poor white girl's liberation from her father, but it is also a text that problematically figures both the father's incestuous abuse and the daughter's liberation from that abuse in terms of blackness. I'm reminded of Morrison's discussion of the way the Africanist narrative of bondage and freedom functions in white American literature as a means of providing "opportunities to contemplate limitation, suffering, rebellion, and to speculate on fate and destiny" (*Playing in the Dark* 53). Whereas Crystal Spangler is drawn into the spider's (father's) parlor, Ellen Foster imagines putting a poisonous spider in her father's bed: "It would bite him and he'd be dead and swollen up and I would shudder to find him so" (1). Ellen, who has taken the last name of "Foster" because her foster family is the only cohesive family she has ever had and she does not want her father's name, moves between present and past, safe and unsafe spaces—material, cultural, and textual—as she tells her story. Space-time is always traveling in this book. Safety lies in the present. Displaced again and again, Ellen now lives in a decent house with her "new mama" and foster family; her "new mama" washes her hair in the sink, makes curtains to match the bedspread for her room, takes her grocery shopping, and lets her invite her friends over to play. For Ellen, this is heaven: "I live in a clean brick house and mostly I am left to myself. When I start to carry an odor I take a bath and folks tell me how sweet I look. There is plenty to eat here and if we run out of something we just go to the store and get some more. I had me a egg sandwich for breakfast, mayonnaise on both sides. And I may fix me another one for lunch" (2).

Such passages in the first chapter of *Ellen Foster* alternate with another narrative: Ellen's own mother's return from the hospital and subsequent death and her father's severe abuse of both mother and daughter, resulting in her mother's suicide/murder. These narrative alternations between unsafe spaces of the earlier part of eleven-year-old Ellen's life (her multiple enclosures—the closet, the house, the material poverty of her life with her father) and safe spaces of the present (her pleasant house with a caring, responsible adult in charge) shape the delicate, vulnerable equilibrium between victimization and survivorship, the then and now of her short life. For Ellen, her story is too claustrophobic, too dangerous a textual space, to be in for long. Her story needs be told, but must be cut down to size, revealed in bits and pieces; otherwise it would engulf both victim and reader. In this sense Ellen, in her own way and within her own back-and-forth spatial paradigm, becomes what Froula has called "the cultural daughter" (633), whose telling of her own story is a tricky jump of the rope between past and present, silence and language.

The spatial dimensions of Ellen's narrative fluctuate through necessity. The more painful her history is, the more firmly it is located in the present. Like Ellen herself, her story is displaced again and again. For example, early in the book she relates how her mother took an overdose of heart medication (or at least so her father claimed); how her father, by holding a knife to both of them, prevented Ellen from helping her mother throw up or going for help; how she finally took her mother to bed and crawled in with her while she died. This story, however, is interrupted at the crucial point when Ellen relates taking her overdosed mother back to bed, saying, "We will rest some more. The day is early and we need some more rest" (10). Following that recollection, Ellen as narrator then beats a hasty retreat to the present. Her next sentences are "I always love to eat a good supper, brush my teeth and go to bed early. If I am not sleepy I can always find something to do" (10). Several paragraphs later Ellen moves from the safe space of her present social relations—she is in a comfortable bed and bedroom in which she is reading a novel about "men and women sneaking around in a big dark house with one all into the other's business"—back to her mother's deathbed:

> I always want to lay here. And she moves her arm up and I push my head down by her side. And I will crawl in and make room for myself. My heart can be the one that beats.
>
> And hers has stopped.
>
> Damn him to the bottom of hell damn him. (11)

Following the story of her mother's death, Ellen again reverts to the present—"Oh I wake up and have the day and what do I want to do with it? I will go catch a pony and ride it" (15)—only to return several paragraphs later to preparations for her mother's funeral and the funeral itself: "I do hate to sit in between folks in a car. Put me by the window so I can get some air and get out quick if I need to" (17). This contiguous reconfiguration of space-time between past unsafe space and present safe space reproduces itself throughout the novel as Ellen—"old Ellen," as she calls herself—tells the story of incestuous and violent abuse at the hands of her father, the indifference of other relatives and the court system, and hatred from her mother's mother, who can see in Ellen only her father's face.

At the interstices of safety and danger is Ellen's journey toward a construction of home as a material and psychic space in which she can read in bed at night and eat as many sandwiches as she can hold. In her new environment she begins to read books that take her somewhere else. Like the Breedloves, her family hardly fits the model of the books she dislikes reading at school. Such books feature safe travel and safe homes: "Cindy or Lou with the dog or cat. Always setting out on some adventure. They might meet a bandit or they might hop a freight but the policeman or the engineer always brings them home and they are still good children" (11). Instead, having gotten the help of a school librarian in her desire "to read everything of some count," Ellen finds a model for travel in Chaucer's "laughing Middle Ages lady that wore red boots . . . on a trip with a group of people swapping stories, carrying on, slapping each other on the back" (11).

Ellen's own journey is more harrowing. After her mother dies when Ellen is about eight or nine, she has to steal money that her uncles leave in the mailbox for her father, live on frozen dinners, and attempt to survive in a house with her drunken, violent, lecherous father and his friends. When he is gone, which is most of the time, including Christmas Eve and Day, she manages to keep herself fed and clothed, with some help from her black friend Starletta and her family:

> While he is gone I stay in the living room and watch the television. Whenever I hear him drive up the path I go to my room and stay until he leaves or I think of somewhere to go out the window.

> It is much better if he is gone. If nothing jumps out at you to do then you walk around until something looks good. (39)

When he is in the house, her material space shrinks to her room, which she tries to lock by placing a chair up to the door, and sometimes to her closet ("I became the champion of not breathing or blinking to be heard" [52]), outside of which her father stands and speaks obscenities.

Ellen allows her father's sexual abuse little space in her narrative. It is mentioned obliquely and tersely in such statements as "he got to me but I got him away from me pretty soon" (52), as if Ellen is trying to make him and his actions as insignificant as possible. By regulating her own text and maintaining carefully balanced fluctuations between horror and safety, she restricts her father's parameters, through dueling narrative strategies of remembrance and enclosure of remembrance. In the end she makes him very small indeed. One way she does this is to enclose him in blackness.

In the following passage both claustrophobic space and sexual abuse of young girls is figured in terms of "a whole pack of colored men" Ellen's drunken father brings home on New Year's Eve. These men eat up her precious food, drink more, and sing. Ellen, hiding in her room, recounts the following conversation between her father and one of the men:

> One tells my daddy this sure is a nice house. Shame for a man to live by his self. My daddy says he has a girl running around loose somewhere.
>
> That same colored man asked him how old is his girl.
>
> He says I am nine or ten.
>
> I married Delphi when she was thirteen, he tells my daddy. Yours is just about ripe. You gots to git em when they is still soff when you mashum. That is how that man said it.
>
> My daddy did not say anything back but the colored men laughed anyway. I bet he made a face. (44)

At this point Ellen, whose window is frozen shut, is so fearful that she gets into her closet. When the drunken men fall asleep on the floor, she tries to escape: "You pray to God they forget about you and the sweet young things that are soff when you mashum and how good one feels when she is pressed up by you. You get out get out before one can wake up from being passed out on your floor. You get out before they start to dream about the honey pie and the sugar plums. Step over the sleeping arms and legs of dark men in shadows on your floor" (44–45). It is at this point in her attempt to escape that her father emerges from the bodies of dark men to grab her:

> Get away from me he does not listen to me but touches his hands harder on me. That is not me. Oh no that was her name. Do not oh you do

> not say her name to me. That was her name. You know that now stop no not my name.
>
> I am Ellen.
>
> I am Ellen.
>
> He pulls the evil back into his self and Lord I run. Run down the road to Starletta. Now to the smoke coming out of the chimney against the dark sky I run. (45)

She runs to Starletta's "colored house" and begs Starletta's mother to let her in, offering her a dollar. Starletta's mother immediately knows that she is in trouble at home, tells her to put away her money, and lets the girl sleep in bed with her. This series of events thoroughly racializes Ellen's predicament. A southern white father's incestuous abuse of his daughter is figured on southern black men's talk and bodies, and a southern African American woman becomes the site of refuge.

When, after many difficulties, Ellen does finally find a home with her "new mama" and a group of foster children, she revises her sense of what home is. She begins to travel in her understanding of the complexity of social relations by realizing that her own racism and that of whites like her have made her black friend both victim and survivor, much like Ellen herself. In the final scene of the story she is lying in her own bed with Starletta, who is visiting for the weekend. Ellen, who had in her earlier days refused to eat and drink with Starletta's family, although they were the only ones to help her in her predicament with her father, admits that she always thought she was better than Starletta and her family, because, as she says, "when I thought about you I always felt glad for myself" (146).

Having been the difference within other people's houses, especially those of her own relatives who don't want her, Ellen realizes that home can be constructed not on the exclusion of difference but rather on inclusion and empowerment of the disempowered. Her identification with Starletta, developed under the worst of conditions, allows her to comprehend the restrictive dimensions of her African American friend's cultural space, to travel that space, and to see Starletta as a subject within Starletta's own world. As a result Ellen becomes another kind of reader whose reading of another's spatial text problematizes and alters her own identity. The text of Starletta's life as a black girl in the South becomes transformative when Ellen learns how to read it. In the final scene of the book, she watches her black friend resting on her shared bed and realizes:

> I came a long way to get here but when you think about it real hard you will see that old Starletta came even farther.
>
> And I watch her resting now because soon we'll all be eating supper

and maybe some cake tonight and I say low Starletta you sure have a right to rest.

And all this time I thought I had the hardest row to hoe.

That will always amaze me. (146)

Here Ellen ends her story. One can cheer her liberation and her entry into Starletta's space of social relations, as I have done. Yet my travels in this text have been troubled. Perhaps it is those dark men on the floor and the way the white father jumps out of their darkness. Perhaps it's the way Ellen looks at Starletta sleeping on the bed, as if the black girl were a text of Ellen's own life. Blackness in this novel figures the southern white daughter's bondage to and freedom from the abusive father. Gender pivots on race to tell its story of victimization and to create the rhetoric of its survivor discourse.

> "I'll give you what you really want," he said, and his whole weight came down hard.
>
> —Dorothy Allison, *Bastard Out of Carolina*

My earlier discussion of Allison's *Bastard Out of Carolina* focused on material and cultural spaces of victimization and resistance—the bathroom, the patriarchal family with another failed southern father, the enclosure of a southern "white-trash" girl within a disdainful, insensitive health care and social services system. It is tempting to conclude there and not discuss what I find most difficult to address about this novel: the disturbing link between pleasure and violence, not only for the perpetrator, but also for the victim. (Angelou and Melba Wilson both address this issue in discussions of their own abuse.) From early in her life, when her mother first marries her stepfather, Bone is eroticized through violence. Her stepfather, who considers Bone his property to do with what he will, is continually snatching her up and brutally rubbing her against him. Her beatings are obviously a sexual experience for him. She in turn masturbates to fantasies of the very violence that has victimized her, and she feels disgusted with herself for doing so ("I lived in a world of shame," she says [113]). This is not an uncommon experience. As Meiselman points out, for many victims "the humiliation and helplessness of their incest experience, along with premature sexual stimulation, can lead to attempts at mastery and reassertion of personal power in sexual ways" (49). Bone imagines herself being beaten by Daddy Glen with groups of acquaintances watching: "In my imagination I was proud and defiant. I'd stare back at him with my teeth set, making no sound at all, no shameful scream, no begging. Those who watched admired me and hated him. I pictured it that way and put my hands between my legs. It was scary, but it was thrilling too. It was as if I was being beaten for them. I was wonderful in their eyes" (112). Ann Cvetkovich sees Bone's fantasies as a complex way of salvaging both power and pleasure: "The shameful fantasy also provides her with the sense of self that is her way out, that gives her the strength, for example to renounce her mother" (370). These fantasies are fed by sexual violence but largely contrast to the reality of Bone's beatings: "There was no heroism possible in the real beatings. There was just being beaten until I was covered with snot and misery" (113).

In its unrelenting representations of violence and sexual abuse far exceeding those of other such novels, including *The Bluest Eye* and *A Thousand Acres,* Allison's novel walks the tightrope of survivor discourse: the necessity of graphic narration without having its detail appropriated and commodified to *contribute to* the ideology that perpetuates the father's power and violence in the first place. As Roseann Lloyd, one survivor writing in the anthology *She Who Was Lost Is Remembered,* acknowledges, this is not an easy balancing act: "The sexual details of abuse may seem to be a turn-on to the reader. Yet some explicit details *have to* be used . . . because the denial of abuse is so strong in our culture" (72). Allison herself has denounced "the pornography of victimization, commenting that "half of the incest books or family violence books sell on sexual voyeurism. . . . It's very hard not to titillate when you're working with this kind of material, because American culture is consumed with it" (in Bronski 3).

This tightrope becomes even more perilous in a fictional text that itself is a commodified object (as are all of these texts)—in the case of *Bastard Out of Carolina,* one both deeply disturbing in its subject matter and highly provocative in its ability to draw readers into its textual space. Allison describes writing as "an act that claims courage and meaning, and turns back denial, breaks open fear, and heals me as it makes possible some measure of healing for all those like me" (*Skin* 181). "True stories"—the "full, nasty, complicating lives" of the "queer and disenfranchised and female"—may well be "violent, distasteful, painful, stunning, and haunting" *because* they tell whole complicated truths (*Skin* 166) and create textual spaces to house those truths. And yet this novel derives its considerable power from its ability not only to reveal the horror of incestuous violence but also to keep readers reading by sustaining narrative suspense (and the reading pleasure that narrative suspense inevitably proffers) about the nature and extent of that violence. In doing so, it may be read as a troubling commentary on the relation between pleasure and violence in the act of reading itself. It may also be read as a manipulation of that relation.

The vicious father space of this novel becomes a black hole we as readers are sucked into at our own peril. Maternal space is more equivocal. Cvetkovich has argued that Allison transforms the dramatic structure that locates violence at the climax of the book by her focus on the mother-daughter relationship and therefore is able to weave "a much more complicated narrative of family and social structures, where loss and betrayal are not punctual events" (368). At times Bone's mother, Anney, tries to take direct action to save her daughter (she takes her to the hospital; she leaves her husband once; and she sends Bone to stay with her aunt); at other times and ultimately she chooses Glen over Bone. Allison writes: "By the time I taught myself the basics of storytelling on the page, I knew there was only one story that would haunt me until I understood how to tell it—the complicated, painful story of how my mama had, and had not, saved me as a girl" (*Skin* 34).[29]

Anney's story is that of a poor, working-class white woman in the South desperately trying to keep her family together and even more desperately in love with an abusive man—a woman who ultimately leaves her daughter to go with her man, whom she mothers more than she mothers her own children. Her decision to remain with Glen feels like a decision between *children* rather than between husband and child.[30]

Oddly, though, Bone, unlike many victimized daughters, does not ultimately blame or turn away from her mother.[31] At the end of the book her mother has left her, yet she still sees herself in relation to her mother and her mother's struggle. She wonders: "Who had Mama been, what had she wanted to be or do before I was born? Once I was born, her hopes had turned, and I had climbed up her life like a flower reaching for the sun. Fourteen and terrified, fifteen and a mother, just past twenty-one when she married Glen. Her life had folded into mine. What would I be like when I was fifteen, twenty, thirty? Would I be as strong as she had been, as hungry for love, as desperate, determined, and ashamed?" (309). In the final scene Bone is sitting on the front porch with her aunt Raylene. In her pocket is the birth certificate her mother gave her before leaving. Having defended her own physical space so many times in her young life, she now allows her aunt to enter that space: "When Raylene came to me, I let her touch my shoulder, let my head tilt to lean against her, trusting her arm and her love. I was who I was going to be, someone like her, like Mama, a Boatwright woman. I wrapped my fingers in Raylene's and watched the night close in around us" (309).

In these final words of the novel a spatial transmutation has occurred. The mother has left, but felicitous space lingers. It is the night that covers Bone like a blanket, the loving touch of her aunt, Bone's own fierce imagination. Bone is not yet thirteen. She has been raped by her stepfather and abandoned by her mother. Yet her eyes are dry. What she and this novel tell us is that survivorship may be a matter of the imagination: the daughter's dexterity in reshaping those alternate and necessary spaces of social relations in which identity can be reconceived and reborn. Yet in *Bastard Out of Carolina* the material that complexly sets the imagination in motion may well be sexual violence itself. And thus the question becomes not so much whether the father's tools rebuild the daughter's house but what manner of house emerges.

"The Gleaming Obsidian Shard": Compression/Expansion in A Thousand Acres

> If you raked your gaze from the silos to the house and barn, then back again, you would take in the immensity of the piece of land my father owned.
>
> —Jane Smiley, *A Thousand Acres*

Space is not what it seems in *A Thousand Acres.* In the first few paragraphs of Jane Smiley's novel, Virginia Cook Smith describes the flat vastness of her father's thousand-acre farm at the T intersection of County Road 686 and Cabot Street Road in Zebulon County, Iowa, and recalls how, as an eight year old riding over that road with her parents and sister Rose in her father's new Buick sedan over that road, "Our farm and our lives seemed secure and good" (5). Yet Ginny Smith's story of her father and family, which she begins to tell when she is thirty-six, quickly dispels this initial impression of a spacious geography and a spacious life. In an ironic inversion of *King Lear*—like Morrison, Smiley is interested in narrative revision and reversal—the novel draws us into the claustrophobic space of the two sisters, Ginny and Rose, whose lives were and are ruled by a father-despot, Larry Cook, who in his midsixties deeds his farm to them and then decides he wants it back. Rose, Ginny, and their families live on the farm property in houses adjacent to their father's. By the end of the story, about a year later, many things have happened:

— Ginny and Rose, both in their midthirties, have been estranged from their younger sister, Caroline, whom they brought up and protected from their father's possessiveness and sexual violence from the time of their mother's death, when the older sisters were respectively fourteen and twelve and Caroline was six, until she left home for college.

— Both Ginny and Rose have had an affair with a younger neighbor, and Ginny has (ineffectually) attempted to poison Rose with ground hemlock mixed in with some home-canned sausage and sauerkraut.

— Ginny has left her husband, Tyler, and her father's farm and gone to work in a truck stop restaurant in St. Paul.

— Rose and her husband, Pete, have died, she from breast cancer, he by a probable suicide.

— The sisters' father is also dead after becoming senile (or so it seems).

— The farm has gone bankrupt. Ginny's legacy from the property is half of a $34,000 tax bill, which she works overtime to pay.

— Ginny is rearing Rose's two daughters, Pam and Linda, whom she has always loved, perhaps in lieu of the children she desperately wanted and almost had but lost through miscarriage, most likely caused by the same substance that caused Rose's and their mother's breast cancers—nitrate-polluted well water on the farm property.

Before her death Rose, whose anger at their father has boiled over in numerous ways, tells Ginny that, after their mother died, their father sexually molested them repeatedly over a period of years, first Ginny at fifteen and then Rose at thirteen and throughout her teenage years. Rose remembers, but Ginny does not, until one day she enters her father's house looking for remnants of her dead mother's presence. Instead she finds, as she lies on her bed in her old yellow bedroom, the memory of her father's weight on her young body. In a devastating flashback she remembers looking down at the top of his balding head on her breast. For Ginny, who has spent much of her adulthood catering to her father's wishes and excused many of his more recent cruelties, this memory, which occurs about two-thirds of the way through the novel, changes everything.

In her thoughts years later at the end of the book are two images. The first is the jar of poisoned sausage she gave to Rose when her sister took her lover, Jess (and by implication, her father's love), away from her—the jar that the unsuspecting Rose stored in the dark recesses of her cellar but never ate. For Ginny, who loved her sister, the sausage "and the ability it confers, of remembering what you can't imagine" (370), mean confronting her own capacity for evil, for committing the unimaginable. The second image, in the final passage of the novel, is of her father. She says, "I can't say that I forgive my father, but now I can imagine what he probably chose never to remember—the goad of an unthinkable urge, pricking him, pressing him, wrapping him in an impenetrable fog of self that must have seemed, when he wandered around the house late at night after working and drinking, like the very darkness. This is the gleaming obsidian shard I safeguard above all the others" (371).

The spacious thousand acres of the opening of this narrative are thusly winnowed down, compacted, held aloft for contemplation at the novel's end: the gleaming obsidian shard Ginny safeguards. (Obsidian, an acid-resistant lustrous glass from compacted volcanic matter; shard, a fragment, usually of broken earthenware).[32] The productions of landscape, of earth, of mixture and fluctuation. A sharp thing, used for cutting, for surgery, in other times for spears and knives. That which is left after everything else is gone.

Yet what is left at the end of this story is not so much a shard of truth, one thing cut away from everything else, as the fluctuation between compression and expansion that renders one substance into another. The word *obsidian* evokes the archaic *obsidion* (related to the verb *obsess*), which carried the meaning of being under siege. Ginny Smith Cook's story is about the wrenching act of the self's spatial alteration under siege, under compression. At the novel's end she herself is a compression of others: her lover, Jess, who taught her that the land is poisoned; her five miscarried children, whom she imagines at varying ages on the street; her angry sister Rose; her husband, Ty, and his ordered world; and primarily her father, whose presence and body haunt her: "Remorse reminds me of Daddy, who had none, at least none for me. My body reminds me of Daddy, too, of what it feels like to resist without seeming to resist, to absent yourself while seeming respectful and attentive. Waking in the dark reminds me of Daddy, cooking reminds me of Daddy, the whole wide expanse of the mid-continental sky, which is where we look for signs of trouble—that, too, reminds me of Daddy" (370).[33]

By the end of the novel Ginny is a different person. Whereas she had been soft, malleable, willing, she has become hard, shiny, sharp: compressed. And yet that compression has its expansive points, extending beyond her father and his dominion, beyond her unborn children and failed marriage, beyond even her own desires. At the end of the book Ginny is making a home for Rose's two daughters in a small "garden apartment" in St. Paul while working overtime to serve food from someone else's kitchen to congenial strangers. She seems to have exceeded her own history while continuing to bear its story as her burden—a burden, it feels to me, that she places on the reader's shoulders as well as carries on her own.

As her story begins, it is clear that Ginny occupies highly compressed physical and psychic space. The consummate farm wife living on her father's land with her husband, she spends her mornings fixing three different breakfasts in three different kitchens, her own, her father's, and her ailing sister's. Her mornings at the stove, she tells us, start "before five and didn't end until eight-thirty" (7). She is cooking for her father, who still lives in the family home; all his meals have to be specific dishes at specific times on specific days (e.g., on Tuesday nights, "pork chops baked with tomatoes . . . , fried potatoes, a salad, and two or three different kinds of pickles" [47]). Besides feeding her father and taking care of his house, she helps her sister through her fight with breast cancer and cares for Rose's two daughters, Pam and Linda. At her own house she gardens, cleans, cans, and helps in the fields. She is the model farm wife. At the beginning of the story, her primary desire is to "carr[y] the darling child into shore" (27)—that is, have a baby. To this end she conceals from her husband that, against his wishes, she is continuing to work on what she calls "her pregnancy project" and buries the resulting miscarriage under the floor of the dairy barn.

The material space of Ginny's compression, and eventually her expansion, is primarily the kitchen, an equivocal space that historically has been physically, psychologically, and culturally confining for women, yet one which has often been the site of subversion, rebellion, pleasure, and creativity. One of Ginny's only memories of her childhood is of being eleven, losing her shoe after a Halloween party, and making her seething father wait in his pickup outside the school. When she gets home and enters the kitchen, the shoe is discovered missing. Over her mother's protests, her father begins to hit her with the flat of his hand. Ginny squeezes herself between the range and the window and refuses to come out. Her father insists that her mother call her out, and when Ginny obeys her mother's call, he pushes her against the doorway and straps her with a belt until she falls down. This memory of physical and psychological compression emerges in the present time of the book, interestingly enough, at a moment when her drunken father, now in his sixties, is cursing her as "a dried-up whore bitch" (181) in front of her family; it gives her an uncharacteristic courage to resist his abuse, replying, "Daddy, if you think this is bad, then you'd be amazed at what you really deserve. You don't deserve even the care we give you. As far as I'm concerned, from now on you're on your own" (183).

Earlier in the story, though, Ginny is far from rebellious. Coming in late (a bit past 6 A.M.) to her father's kitchen to fix his breakfast, she finds him surly and angry.

> He met me at the back door. "It's bright day." His tone was accusing. It meant, I'm hungry, you've made me wait, and also, you're behind, late, slow. I said, "I had a few things to do."
> "At six o'clock in the morning?'
> "I just picked up the house a little."
> "Hmp."
> "Sorry." (114)

As she picks up an apron from a hook, he says, "Nobody shopped over the weekend. There's no eggs." Ginny, who is also responsible for keeping her father's kitchen stocked, realizes she has a choice, "to keep him waiting or to fail to give him his eggs" (114). This is a choice, she realizes, that will show him something about her:

> either that I was selfish and inconsiderate (no eggs) or that I was incompetent (a flurry of activity where there should be organized procedure). I did it. I smiled foolishly, said I would be right back, and ran out the door and back down the road. The whole way I was conscious of my body—graceless and hurrying, unfit, panting, ridiculous in its very femininity. It seemed like my father could just look out of his big front window and see me naked, chest heaving, breasts, thighs, and buttocks juggling, dignity irretrievable. Later, after I had cooked the breakfast and he had eaten it, what I marveled at was that I hadn't just gone across the road and gotten some eggs from Rose, that he had given me the test, and I had taken it. (114–15)

Although this scene occurs before Ginny's memory of incestuous abuse, there is in this very self-conscious description a disturbing sense of her body on display for her father and her own dissociation from her body—a distanced, objectified viewing of it through her father's eyes.

I rehearse this scene at length because, like so many similar scenes in the novel, it carries a sense of disquieting and escalating pressure. Here the daughter is being enclosed within the father's house in her proper daughterly place, the kitchen. Here and elsewhere in *A Thousand Acres* the escalating sense of the daughter's spatial compaction is similar to that of *Bastard Out of Carolina.* In fact, it seems preferable for Ginny to run like a frightened rabbit back to her own house for eggs than for her to remain for another moment in that kitchen, under her father's silent glare. But escape is also compression, for in this scene at least, the father's gaze owns the daughter's body, even as she attempts to escape him and it. She carries him with her, feeling herself naked under his gaze. Her adult body is not her own, just as her teenage body was not. Even her memory of her body is not her own, for she later observes that she has only a single memory of her younger body, her pride in her slim legs: "One thing Daddy took from me when he came to me in my room at night was the memory of my body" (280). Clearly Ginny's bodied self has been compressed so dangerously by her father's abuse that her recourse, like that of many such victims, has been to leave her body behind, to dissociate herself from her body, to watch herself from afar, and in doing so to flee what Janet Jacobs has called "an unbearable reality" (129).

This compaction of identity is replicated within Ginny's marriage to Ty, who, because of his attachment to the farm, urges her throughout to acquiesce to her father's demands on her. In a later scene, however (also set in a kitchen, but this time her own), she, in the midst of cooking supper, walks out on her husband. This time the process is one of expansion: after an excruciating court hearing in which she ends up screaming at her (seemingly) senile father and the judge rules that the land belongs to her and her sister, she and Ty, who thoroughly disapproves of her actions, return home. Yet she feels immediately dissociated from her own kitchen space, remarking, "How strange and far from home I felt taking meat from my refrigerator and salting it with my old red plastic saltshaker and slapping it onto the broiler pan I'd used for seventeen years" (328). Preparing supper, she puts potatoes and brussels sprouts from her garden on the stove. As she puts the chops under the broiler, which she has done hundreds of times, Ty tells her he thinks she's "shown off plenty" (329). She tells him she needs a thousand dollars, he gives it to her in cash, and she walks out the door, leaving him, the burning food, and her kitchen forever.

When she does return to the farm months later, it is to the kitchen of her father's house where as an eleven year old she squeezed herself between the stove and window to avoid her father's belt. Rose and her daughters now occupy the patriarchal home, though Rose is in the hospital, dying. At her sister's request, Ginny, who now enjoys microwaving every meal she doesn't eat at the restaurant where she waits tables, makes a fried chicken meal for Pam and Linda. As she works at the stove, reassuring her nieces and cooking the meal, she finds the kitchen "arctic": "The blue gas flames of the burner fluttered coldly. The grease in the pan popped chillingly. When it spattered my hand, the burned dots felt frozen. I looked around, then took Rose's old beige sweater off the hook behind the door. I huddled into it, browning chicken and shivering. It seemed an impossible defeat that I was back in this kitchen, cooking" (348). As Ginny browns the chicken in the chill of her father's kitchen, she thinks longingly about the truck stop in St. Paul where she now works: "The restaurant would be filling up at this hour, each cheerfully lit table bright with menus and paper place mats. On the other side of the black windows of Rose's kitchen, though, there was only outer space, a lightless, soundless vacuum that on this thousand acres came right down to the ground" (348).

Does Ginny's love for her nieces transform this space, this "lightless, soundless vacuum" of outer space, this freezing kitchen? There seems to be little in the way of comfort here. The unopened jars of poisoned sausage lurk in the dark of her sister's cellar. In the kitchen there is only the chill. Ginny turns on the yard lights, but she doesn't "really believe them" (348). The food may warm the girls for whom it is cooked, girls who have been protected from their grandfather (Rose sent Pam and Linda off to boarding school so that they would be safe from her father). But it does not warm Ginny, who will live out her life with the cold, or Rose, who will die angry, bitter, and lonely. Nor will it warm the protected daughter, Caroline, who never knew the truth and so who loved her father and hated her sisters because they feared and loathed him. The obsidian shard remains; the unspeakable haunts the father's house. Compression still compresses. Ginny remains the daughter, and she carries the burden of the father wherever she goes. This is her story, which she delivers to us as onus. The survivor discourse, in this novel, seems to derive from the heaviness of that burden and Smiley's unwillingness to lighten the load.[34]

She hands us the gleaming obsidian shard. It is hard and heavy. It weighs more than we thought, and we labor to hold it.

Like Pecola, like Celie, like Crystal, like Ellen, like Bone, Ginny Smith tells the story of displacement. Angelika Bammer defines displacement in its cultural sense as the "separation of people from their native culture either through physical dislocation (as refugees, immigrants, migrants, exiles, or expatriates) or the colonizing imposition of a foreign culture" and calls it "one of the most formative experiences of our century," one marked by "the relationship between the experience of cultural displacement and the construction of cultural identity." Such a relationship is itself configured "by the tension of the historically vital double move between marking and recording absence and loss and inscribing presence" (xi–xiv). Bammer warns against the abstraction and metaphorization of displacement, yet I can't help but see displacement (always psychic but often physical and cultural) as being the situation of these fictionalized daughters, marking and recording absence and loss (displacement) even as they are attempting to inscribe presence. They are refuges from *home.*

Within these fictional tensions between displacement and loss and a repeated, stubborn insistence on presence, I have found myself compressed within the layers of material, cultural, textual spaces that crowd these daughters' stories, compacted into that obsidian shard and unable to do much more than display the pressures that led to its creation. I am wondering, in fact, whether this may well be the role of the feminist reader of the daughter's survival discourse within fiction. Simply that: bearing the story, reinscribing the text, carefully, laboriously, with the most meticulous of scripts, like the monks of the Middle Ages. In writing *Beloved* Morrison, whom I quoted previously, says she looked for the language not to compete with the story or to enhance it but only "to hold it." This, it seems to me, is what feminist readers/critics may need to do in writing about fictional or autobiographical depictions of father-daughter incestuous abuse. We need the language to hold it, to open a space for the daughter's complicated story, the equivocal discourses of victimization and survivorship. Where that language is, I don't know. We find it perhaps by not finding it, by relating the story as it is told to us—nothing more, nothing less. Perhaps this is enough.

What I do know as I end this chapter is that I am exhausted, although I have no right to be. I have traveled these spaces, but I have not lived in them; and as I hope I have indicated, I know the difference. Last night I dreamed I watched as, one by one, Pecola, Crystal, Celie, Ellen, Bone, Ginny, and Rose were sucked into a whirling watery vortex. They were struggling to swim, to get out, and I knelt on the edge trying to reach their desperate outstretched hands. But soon they all had disappeared.

In its early stages, and even midway through, this chapter began to take on a life of its own and tried to transform itself into a book. Certainly, as I've mentioned in my earlier footnotes, there are many more fictional texts about incest relating to fathers or father figures and their daughters: Kathy Acker's *Blood and Guts in High School,* much of Joyce Carol Oates's writing, Gayl Jones's *Corregidora,* Elaine Kraf's *Find Him!* Mona Simpson's haunting story "Lawns," Elizabeth Spencer's *The Snare,* and Kathyrn Harrison's *Exposure.* These are only a few. But the truth is that each day it has become more difficult to pause within these spaces and open myself to their travels, though to say this reveals limits to myself I'd rather not admit to: a fear of such travel, a desire for safety. A yearning for "home."

These unsettling yearnings and fears return me to the discussions of my first chapter: each of these stories of incest in its own way embodies Henrietta Moore's assertion that a text, be it a book or a living space, is not *representative* of ideology but is a *product* and *producer of* ideology, "of the 'lived' conditions of social reality" (87). To read these fictional narratives and others like them with this awareness is to experience the process of ideology at work, to enter into the workings of this production and reproduction, not only in the texts themselves, but within our/my readings of them.

This teaches us that the stories we tell ourselves about home—the places we come from and the places we make our own—are the means through which we undertake the excruciating, redeeming work of renegotiating identity. The produced representation of the material and cultural spaces of father-daughter incestuous abuse in these fictional texts, regardless of their geographies, interrogates the ideological construction of home—not just its felicity for girls and women when the father is in the house but how we remake it in our own images.

That interrogation exposes the blank spaces in the scripts we ourselves write about home and suggests that, for some daughters, home may be grounded not in place but in the *re*placement of the displaced self elsewhere, in an aptitude for travel. What such writing as this—and the type of readerly travel it demands—can do is to point to that other space, that "elsewhere," in which the daughter can begin to write her own cultural story, create her own felicity.

Call it home; call it travel. The way in and the way out.

3 *Gender Travels*

The final chapter of this book offers readings of three texts that enact certain kinds of encounters which dislocate "gender" and set gender in motion under duress. "Gender" is a slippery notion in these texts, taking on multiple embodiments and mutations. (Call it "queer." Call it "home." Call it "culture." Call it "reader.") These are not stories to be easily entered or easily left behind; their spaces are tight squeezes. Accommodation is required.

I choose these readings not because they are notably feminist—in some ways these novels stubbornly resist feminist analysis—but because they are especially interesting in the formidable challenges they pose to the act of reading space, gender, and their travels in the readerly imagination. In the introduction to this book, I described the paradoxical effect of constricted space in women's narrative. Like the other texts of this book, and perhaps in a more intensive and problematic way, these novels are about how the tightest of spaces (and the social relations that construct them and converge in their material manifestations, such as a prison, a house, or a geographical—or cultural—location) can unhinge and open in the strangest of ways and by the strangest of means. There is an inverse relation between the inward turning force of such spaces and the outward pressure of the imagination as it is multiply manifested in writer, reader, and character.

Each of these texts in its own way demands to be read yet resists the act of reading. Each is vexing in terms of those demands, and each relies heavily on violence. I read these books on their own terms, and those terms are exacting. It is no accident that these books, appearing within a decade of one another, have in common the fact that they are outsider novels, published (at least originally) by small, special-interest presses. Only one, Keri Hulme's postcolonial narrative *The Bone People,* has received anything resembling a broad readership or critical recognition. The other two, Madelyn Arnold's *Bird-eyes* and Elaine Kraf's *Find Him!* are virtually unknown in feminist or other literary circles.

What these texts have in common are their calculated efforts at dislocation; space is rendered, enacted, in bizarre and complicated ways involving both interior and exterior worlds. Body, identity, and social relations are put under intense pressure. Gender becomes the traveler in these texts; they insist on the motion of gender and the necessity of imaginative encounter with gender.

These texts travel gender and make "gender" travel. They are outlaw books, displacing normativity, moving in and out of the spatial demarcations of identity, sometimes leaving the traveling reader stranded without map, compass, or resting place.

The Incarceration of the Queer: Madelyn Arnold's Bird-eyes

> Don't know where this woman and I
> will find each other again,
> but I am grateful to her to something
> that feels like blessing
>
> that I am, in fact,
> *not* trapped
>
> which brings me to the question of prisons
> politics
> sex.
>
> —Cherríe Moraga, *Giving Up the Ghost*

Situated (ironically? aptly?) in the *Trends* section of the local newspaper, the headline catches my eye: "Activists angered by diagnosis of gay teens." The article begins with the story of Daphne Scholinski, who at the age of fourteen was diagnosed with "gender identity disorder," defined by the American Psychiatric Association as "the insistence that one is of the other sex" and a "persistent discomfort about one's assigned sex" (*Albuquerque Journal,* July 30, 1995, C8). This "disorder," according to some psychiatrists, "can lead to alienation, low self-esteem, out-of-control behavior at home, depression and even suicide, if untreated." Its devastating effects are said to be worse in boys than in girls. Treatment, according to these folks, is difficult "and involves intense therapy that can last up to three years" (C8). Not surprisingly, insurance companies don't want to pay for making boys who think they're girls back into boys and vice versa, but lots of private hospitals currently specialize in curing such "troubled youth" as Scholinski, and parents are paying big bucks to send their quasi-gendered offspring to these institutions for "conversion therapy."

As a girl, Scholinski, now about thirty, was institutionalized in three different midwestern mental hospitals and, besides being given Thorazine and other antipsychotic medications, was ordered to wear makeup and dresses and to curl her hair. She underwent what she now describes as four years of "psychological torture" after being locked up by her parents when she told them she was a lesbian. Dr. Anney Rothenberg, of the Children's Health Council in Palo Alto, California, offers the following rationale for getting such young people straight. These kids, she says, don't know what's best for them: "A young child's natural instinct might be to just eat salty or sugary food. But every parent knows that is bad for them. They'll have a healthier life if they have a balanced diet. And emotionally they'll have an easier life if they are heterosexual" (C5). The bases of this argument are as follows: binary productions of gender produce coherent subjectivity, and multiple productions do not; heterosexuality is being, and homosexuality is nonbeing. Nonbeing needs to be transformed into being or else confined away from being. It must be excluded, but not extinguished, because how else to determine being but by measuring its coherence against the incoherence of nonbeing?

All of this is ringing a bell. I turn to Foucault's *Madness and Civilization,* in which I find descriptions of ships of fools, barges that keep afloat their cargoes of "madmen" so that these individuals remain both absent and liminal, not here and not there, moving from port to port but never making landfall. Foucault writes of the huge network of workhouses for the mad that spread across Europe in the eighteenth century. To what purpose such confinement? To make both absent and present the otherness of the other, to make manifest the beingness of nonbeing. Ultimately, Foucault argues,

> the essence of confinement was not the exorcism of a danger. Confinement merely manifested what madness, in its essence, was: a manifestation of non-being; and by providing this manifestation, confinement thereby suppressed it, since it restored it to its truth as nothingness. Confinement is the practice which corresponds most exactly to madness experienced as unreason, that is, as the empty negativity of reason; by confinement, madness is acknowledged to be *nothing.* That is, . . . madness is immediately perceived as difference. (115–16)

In other words, certain spatial arrangements have to be made. Within such arrangements madness is itself an opaque space with distinct boundaries. It can be seen but cannot see. It must be what reason is not, or more precisely, it must *not* be what reason is.

To the good doctor previously quoted on unhealthy habits, gender "confusion" and homosexuality occupy the liminal, necessary space of nonbeing. Diagnosis thus transforms opacity into transparency. As Lefebvre suggests, this "transparent space tends toward homogeneity, toward a denial of difference" (28). Transparent space thus assumes that the world can be seen as it really is and that one can see that world and its objects clearly and truly. Transparent space does not cast a shadow. In the good doctor's terms, it is what is "healthy" or "natural." But what happens, one might ask, when the borders of this transparent space of the knowing subject are splintered by the object it thinks it knows? When the object begins to perform the ideological conditions of its necessary liminality?

One thing that happens is that, within the context just described, transparent space becomes visible as straight space or, as Judith Butler calls it, the "*heterosexual matrix*"—"that grid of cultural intelligibility through which bodies, genders, and desires are naturalized" (*Gender Trouble* 150n6). The denaturalizing of transparent space into straight space is, in Butlerian terms, the function of "gender trouble." Butler argues that gender identity is culturally constructed by "the regulatory fiction of heterosexuality" and that "gender trouble" may occur when the performative nature of gender is revealed, sometimes through parody, as in the case of drag and cross-dressing, or through any act that disrupts "the regulatory fiction" (*Gender Trouble* 136). Butler goes on to argue that, within the constraints of highly gendered regulatory models and institutions, even the materiality of the body is subject to the cultural enforcement of heterosexuality, and sexual difference is made to consolidate "the heterosexual imperative" (*Bodies* xi, 2). The unruly nature of desire is thus "deflected across the sexual divide to members of the opposite sex" (*Bodies* 99), and compulsory heterosexuality reigns.[1] This cultural production of acceptable genders, bodies, and desires requires "the simultaneous production of a domain of abject beings" who represent "uninhabitable" zones of social life—the queer outside that makes the inside normative (*Bodies* 3)—or, in the terms of my argument here, the nonbeing that makes being come alive. Put another way by Tucker Pamella Farley in her essay "Lesbianism and the Social Function of Taboo,"

> any system pretending to exclusiveness, like heterosexuality, uses scape-

> goats. *By definition heterosexuality denies homosexuality; but it both requires and suppresses the scapegoat. Her function is to be the unthinkable alternative,* the nonchoice of heterosexuality; to validate it by being a mistake; to preserve the system, the ideological construct and its material, institutionalized forms. To be wrong, so the other can be natural: to be Different. (270)

These material and institutionalized forms are "dividing practices," techniques of domination whose purposes are to objectify the social subject (Rabinow 8). They require space. Spatial arrangements enforce the zone of the unthinkable. In the case of queerness, the Daphne Scholinskis of the world must be put in the lockup, displaced into the discursive terrain of the abject. As Foucault's body of work has shown, though, the one in the constrained position nonetheless exerts certain forms of power despite, within, and even because of confinement or displacement. In certain literary texts, as Butler explains, these socially unsanctioned spaces of abjection and their exertions of power in performances of queerness have certain disruptive effects that may range from the subtle to the obvious. Thus such performative textual spaces of queerness enact a reversal by exposing the concealed spatial text of straightness. They mark and measure its ideological borders and divulge the violent policing that occurs at those borders. They make heterosexuality cast a shadow, lose its transparency.

Such texts perform spatially. They engage the embodied imaginations of their readers. They make us fumble within and recoil from the compression of the straight.

Nowhere is this sense of compression more acute than in Madelyn Arnold's excruciating, profoundly troubling novel *Bird-eyes*[2]—the story of a young lesbian who, like Daphne Scholinski, gets locked up in the loony bin to straighten her out. A narrative of how gender and sexuality can be and are spatially enforced, *Bird-eyes* is a spatial text that is violent and claustrophobic. Its most salient features are its textual performance of spatial enforcement and the linkage of normativity to the binary constructions of gender and sexuality. More than that, the novel forces us to travel the *process* of how straight space is created and enforced as we trace a winnowing, a narrowing, of already constricted spaces for the less-than-straight, the deviant. As we travel these primary highways of straightness, however, *Bird-eyes* often unexpectedly takes us on certain gender-troubled detours and byways and thereby remaps the terrain of the straight. This revised cartography reveals, above all, that straightness is a construction: the straight can never be truly straight.

> Once there was a space for you in everything but the space is now filled in and you don't fit there. It's filled in.
>
> —Latisha Earl Prentiss, in Madelyn Arnold, *Bird-eyes*

It is December 1964. Latisha Earl Prentiss, hooked on heroin, driven to the streets by a sexually abusive father ("*You're a wo-min now,* says my dad" [124]), and incarcerated as "incorrigible" at age sixteen, is "five-feet-four and 98 pounds soaking wet" (Arnold 138). Latisha inhabits "Women's D" ward at Eastern Central State Hospital in Chicago. ("I was stuck on a back ward as incorrigible. I wasn't sent to Juvenile Hall or one of the teen-age wards. Incorrigible is catching, like a basic social disease. I was stuck back there because I was infectious" [14].) It is her lesbianism, not her prostitution or drug use, that got her locked up. Latisha's predicament poses pressing questions: when your space has been foreclosed and filled in, where do you situate yourself? *Who* do you become? If space is practiced place, what practices can one perform to create space for oneself when the space that identity inhabits has been snatched away? What accommodations can one undertake, what interiorities can one plumb, what performances can one render to create psychic and physical space where there is none? Raising questions such as these, *Bird-eyes* links the policing of gender and sexuality with incarceration, enclosure, and claustrophobia. The paradox of the novel is that space is created as the practiced place of identity *out of* the articulation of displacement, what Angelika Bammer, as I've noted, has called "the tension" of the "double move between marking and recording absence and loss and inscribing presence" (xiv). Displaced by family, society, and lover, Latisha creates identity from the obsidian shard of displacement; she makes presence out of the inscriptions of absence and loss. Under the circumstances this is something akin to alchemy.

In the hospital and even prior to her being committed, the onslaught on Latisha's body and mind has been phenomenally violent and macabre. Her father fucked her when he could (her doctor in the hospital refers to this as her "temptation" [88]); her uncle set her dog on fire with lighter fluid (like Pecola Breedlove, she is a victim of the myth of the happy family); after she hits the streets, her lover, Tina, forces her to hustle, gets her hooked on hard drugs, and slaps her around when she feels like it. In the hospital Latisha is invaded sexually by men and women alike; her gay friend Brian, himself the victim of countless electroshock treatments and stomach-turning "aversion therapy" to "treat" his homosexuality, makes her pay for his guidance by burning her with cigarettes and setting her up with his friends; attendants watch and laugh when a deranged male inmate publicly beats her and almost rapes her during a movie. Sometimes she is put in the sideroom, "that teeny grey room [where] you could hear the tinny flat automatic Muzak. . . . The Muzak played the same tape over and over. And over. And over" (43). The sideroom is very cold, and Latisha, like other inmates who "misbehave," is put there naked. There are no windows, only a bucket and a canvas cot without a blanket. Attendants and other inmates peer through the glass on the door ("I felt like I had never known before that I was naked. And I didn't want them to know how well it worked. How cold it was" [44]).

When she is first committed, Latisha is taken in a straitjacket to the downtown Medical Center, shoved into an enormous room filled with people in white coats and taping equipment, and ordered to talk "about girls. About being attracted to girls, whatever made a person do that? About my sisters, about my mother, about my grandmother, about my father; have I ever screwed with my father?" (139–40). When she refuses, she is forcibly drugged. She remembers answering all their questions, "but not truthfully" (141). She remembers the taping equipment whirring and the way everyone, especially "the girls," blushed and leaned forward in their seats. What she learns from the experience is that "there's no end to what they can do to you" (141), that there's always something worse waiting around the bend if you don't appear to be cooperating.

To prevent further invasions, the street-smart Latisha quickly develops a cache of tricks; her battle is to stay sane until she is twenty-one and eligible for release: "It takes a lot of things to make you crazy; more than you think because you fight to save your home, and you live in your head" (33). She has learned early to sleep only on her back ("It's harder to be taken by surprise that way" [75]). She knows how to scoop up the disgusting mounds of hospital food on her plate and make them disappear on the plates of "the guys from the vegetable C ward," with whom the females from her ward are forced to socialize. She knows how to put her pills under her tongue, later spitting them out and bartering them on the institutional black market. She teaches her friend Anna, a deaf middle-aged farm woman who speaks only in sign, how to drink dozens of cups of coffee to counteract the sedatives being constantly pumped into the inmates' bodies. She knows the shower is the only place she can evade the constant assault of pills, Muzak, and regimentation on her body and mind, and she takes as many scalding showers a day as she can, rubbing green soap over the bones under her skin as the water gets hotter and hotter ("I *like* my bones. . . . they were my friends" [34]). She knows how to stab herself in the stomach again and again with jagged glass shards and how deaden herself to hot and cold.

Most of the time Latisha can displace her mind from her body—"crawl out the back of [her] head" (116)—when selling sex to men on the street or giving blow jobs to the hospital's recreational therapist ("Guys like Rec Therapy make me sick, but you need them" [125]; "take it from me, you can put anything in your mouth" [10]). She seduces Nurse Wykowski, not an unpleasant task, in hopes of getting good reports on her chart ("it's almost like I'm wanting her" [143]). Her material space is altered by the color of her passes, and she learns how to ask for the passes that will take her the farthest, first within the circumference of the hospital and eventually outside.

The linguistic dimensions of Latisha's accommodation and resistance to severe spatial foreclosure and invasiveness are especially interesting, not just because her use of language may reveal something about the discursive terrain of the abject (in this case the locked-up lesbian), but because they may offer insights about the complex relations among language, accommodation, and resistance. In recent decades feminism has generally held that accommodation and resistance are opposites, the former to be studiously avoided and the latter to be continually attempted. A disquieting yet provocative message of *Bird-eyes* is that accommodation and resistance may indeed be contiguous and sometimes overlapping, and that language oils their junctures.

In the end Latisha survives and escapes the institution. When a trucker tries to force her to give him a blow job, she stabs him in the groin; she has her first good meal since being committed; and she has decided to live (how, we don't know). Anna, whose resistance is pure, who (understandably, because of her deafness) has been considerably less successful in accommodating to restricted space, inhibited movement, and self-invasion, has in a frenzy of rage and grief killed an attendant, a black mother of ten, and as a result has disappeared into the bowels of the institution, presumably never to surface. What does language have to do with the difference between Latisha's and Anna's behaviors? Anna reads only with great difficulty, and she is forbidden the use of sign language, whereas a certain linguistic dexterity plays a part in Latisha's survival, as she herself realizes.

> I was adapting. Anna wasn't. . . . It could have been words, of course; she only had her eyes and her ideas. She didn't recognize many words on paper, and it's possible that all the ideas in the world were in her head, but the words—words I would know, words in English—were not there.

> And words would have helped her, that's what I think; words for ideas help you misinterpret things and that makes life much easier. . . . Words prettify ideas, screen events for you; help you stand your life. . . . And that mesh of words is what Anna did not have; not words for the same thing that feel different. For her, *girl, chick, bobby-soxer, missie, maid, babe, cherry, baby-kiss, virg', filly, gal, broad,* and *debutante* could all be said as *woman, young* or *woman, child*—and then she'd act out the way she wanted you to see this—hand on the hip, or blushing and embarrassed—never exactly the same twice; but in her head it wasn't different words, it wasn't different signs but different actions. . . . She could not blunt the way she saw, with words. I would have blunted things by reexplaining them for her so she'd have hope. (135–36)

However one feels about Latisha's questionable distinctions between verbal and sign language, her larger argument—that the contours of reality can be reshaped by the *accommodative* agency of language—is politically suggestive within the abject space of her queerness, the scapegoated queer body by which the straight world marks its straightness. I stress this point because one does not think of accommodation as radical resignification or oppositional discourse. Latisha's accommodations emerge from a linguistic performativity that makes gender and sexuality fluctuate not so much by *revealing* incorporative fantasies which work to stabilize them, as Butler would have it (*Bodies* 235), as by both obliging stabilizing norms (Latisha has no choice, really; she is, after all, locked up) and countering their power by mitigating them linguistically.

In this back-and-forth move, Latisha doesn't make gender *trouble* (too much trouble can put her in the sideroom or worse) so much as engage in gender *travel.* Reading this novel, one might wonder, in fact, if this can be one way that oppositional discourse can really work: by traversing certain terrains which have been seen as oppositional (male/female, gay/straight, Western/Eastern, black/white) and through the very act of traversal, of *crossing* (one meaning of *queer,* as Sedgwick points out),[3] which in turn may reveal the instability of their borders.

In *Bodies That Matter* Butler worries about the oppositional quality of discourses of resistance and echoes Foucault's belief that one is never not inside power. She asks, "How will we know the difference between the power we promote and the power we oppose? . . . For one is, as it were, in power even as one opposes it, formed by it as one reworks it, and it is this simultaneity that is at once the condition of our partiality, the measure of our political unknowingness, and also the condition of action itself" (241). Needless to say, Latisha Earl Prentiss knows that she is located within a powerful institution, the U.S. mental hospital of the 1960s in which, history now reveals, people of all sorts got lost and were never found. Located within an omnipotence she rebels against but which nevertheless holds her in thrall, she exploits language to accommodate to that power even as language rescues her from it. This simultaneity of accommodation and resistance—their coexistence, their fluctuations within the same space—enables Latisha to evade the fate of her friend Anna, whose mode of language is forbidden and who experiences reality primarily in terms of actions.

And yet, as many of us know, accommodation harbors pitfalls. One might appreciate Anna's inability or unwillingness to accommodate. Anna has principles; she isn't duplicitous; she doesn't use sex for privileges or money. She is stubborn, proud, and unwilling to adapt to the role of a mentally unbalanced person. In the end she sacrifices herself for Latisha. In the process she kills the kindest attendant on the ward, Miss Hart, who is herself a victim. Before this final act that seals Anna's fate, Latisha wants to teach her friend duplicity, to "look cooperation. Don't cooperate" (138): "I say you can adapt to anything; if everybody hates you, so can you and there you are, on the same side—no reason to feel left out. What's the problem. If I could only have said such clever things to Anna; but then it would have been a two-way street. Then I would have had to hear what she had to say, and I don't think I wanted that. I saw that in her eyes" (144). Latisha worries, though, that she herself has become a lie:

> There was nothing sincere, I decided, left inside me; I kept looking in a mirror at myself to see if I could catch it in my eyes; it's bound to show there; but I was never quite sure where it was in my face, if it was in my face; maybe I was too good at it. Sometimes I thought I'd caught it out. And Anna didn't have that look; she was far too kinesthetic; she was madder and more frustrated and she showed it; not like me; not an adaptive one. And I cared because she could read *lie* in my face; she read how my eyes were changing.
>
> And I couldn't see how she could stand the sight of me. (145)

If the space that Latisha has created as the space of identity is a lie, is she not displacing herself again, beyond her displacements from home (real and imagined), from love (the woman she loved sent her into the streets), from her own diminished body (ninety-eight pounds soaking wet)? Perhaps. And yet the question remains: how does one make a space—in the terms of the previous chapter, a home—for the displaced, the scapegoat, the abject, when one inscribes those identities?

Is it possible that *spatial* accommodation can be oppositional at the same time it is adaptive, exploratory as well as restricted, able to travel while remaining in one place? Latisha gives lessons on reimagining constricted material space and oneself within it:

> You can fight those walls away from yourself, with effort.
>
> When you come into a small room and that oppresses you, this is because what you are noticing is the smallness of the room. Notice otherwise. Sit on a chair, sit in a corner, climb up onto a table; look around you. After a while, you'll find that the room gets bigger. The more you look, the more you'll find to see.
>
> You see places into which you think you could fit yourself. Into the corner, maybe under that shelf. Turning sideways maybe, between two chairs. Where at first your eyes bang into the walls—something blocking you—where at first those stand in the way of the room, then you see the range. You see where you can go. . . . Look at the space, at the number of blocks inside it. Look at the cracks that circumscribe each block. Look how deep; see how wide. What could fit there. Is there anything in that crack on the top of the middle block. Is there a little hairline fracture within it, moisture creeping in. Little bugs. A little fine hairline; several of them, featherlike. A pin could fit there or several hairs. Several of yours; some of your eyelashes; some part of yourself. One of your fingernails. (186)

This is how tight spaces are turned inside out, how constriction can open into something largely imaginative, how the woman in the red dress may take flight in the mind. Here Latisha manages to retell the *story* of such spaces—to alter drastically the imaginative production of identity under intense spatial pressure.

Such accommodation is not superficial, and it comes at a cost. At the end of this passage, Latisha admits, "Looking outside after that can upset you" (186). It is not possible to remain unchanged by spatial accommodation, especially when one becomes smaller and smaller to adapt to smaller spaces. When Latisha finally escapes from the institution, she finds that, on the outside, accommodation is no longer easy. She is beginning to get too large for it. The trucker who picks her up is "a little runt" (195). When he lays his knife on the dashboard and starts to unzip his pants, Latisha grabs the knife and stabs him before thinking. At this moment of sheer resistance, everything explodes with largeness, including Latisha herself: "I was fastwalking and sometimes running across that great lot with stars firing in my head. Stars ablaze; my mind ablaze; in my head there was a 21-gun salute to me. Stars and rockets, sprays and bursts of bright-colored roostertail 4th of July explosions, my head pounding. Explosions in my head, lightning fireworks, striding *like King Kong*. And then that wore off and I was freezing" (196; my emphasis).

The fact that Latisha describes her own sensations of heat and cold indicates that she is returning to life. She has spent much of her time deadening herself to feeling, hot or cold, happy or sad, pain or pleasure. As she walks away from the truck, she begins to feel not only cold but also hungry. When she comes on a restaurant and stands at the window longing for food, an old couple, a man and woman, approach her and offer to buy her a meal. She eats with gusto for the first time since being institutionalized: "I eat a meat-thing, covered with orange cheese. I eat a red sweet dough thing that is like plastic stuffed with sugar. What does it matter. I drink an orange shake and a cup of coffee and they watch me eat this stuff. And more coffee. Do I want more. I drink coffee" (199). Driven into a panic because of the kindness of the old couple, who offer her a ride, Latisha jumps out of the backseat of their car and begins slashing her palm, making herself stand the pain, as she has done most of her life. Yet at that point, as she stands in the freezing rain pushing the knife across her palm, the narrative takes still another turn. She thinks, "I have to stop. Because it *hurts*. . . . Anna; because of Anna. Anna" (200). This is an expansive moment. Has something opened up? A space, perhaps, for the practice of living?

How Latisha engages in that practice we never know. The epilogue to the book indicates that she lives with fear that "it may still happen," that she may, without warning, find herself back within the space of the abject, the scapegoat (200–201).

> One of the best things you can have is a bad memory. But if you've been in a place like that, if you've seen these things, you can't always keep that forgotten. It will come sometimes . . . when you're in a crowd and suddenly everyone around you pulls back and there you are, very sudden, in the middle of a strand of strangers with an old bag lady jabbering about her devils or what not; and in the strangers' eyes you see the *Insanity That Doesn't Happen to Us*; the *Way No Real Person (ME) Could Become*. That those people have a superior ability to misidentify what really happens; that maybe it never could happen to them, but it happened to people you knew; it happened to you. Or almost did—it was only a matter of time. It may still happen. (200–201)

Our last glimpse of Latisha is on the street. She is walking fast, evading those "who grab at your coat," not asking for anything.

What does Latisha tell us about space travel, spatial accommodation, as she darts by? At the beginning of this section, I suggested that *Birdeyes* teaches us something about straight space: that "straightness" can be queered, as seen in the African American nurse and mother of ten, Miss Hart, who is homophobic but a comparatively sympathetic health care worker, and, moreover, that deviant sexuality can be straighter than straight, as seen in the lesbian Nurse Wykowski, who, in her crisp white uniform, preys on Latisha. There is no positivist essentialization of identity or experience here. This is a book about the incarceration of people who don't fit, with tragic results in mental and physical torment for its victims, many of whom never recover. Yet the novel also is a spatial text, both in the sense of enclosure and release it offers and especially in its disturbing commentary on the spatial processes of identity formation. *Bird-eyes* tells us just how dependent identity is on space, how hard we will work to make the linguistic practice that creates space for ourselves or, more problematically, that accommodates *us* to the spaces we find ourselves in—that whittles us down to fit the siderooms, the ships of fools, created by those who want more and purer space for themselves.

This is not to say that the "we" I write here is not also part of "those." Released from the narrative spaces—the "hairline fractures"—Arnold has created in this book, I find myself, like Latisha, walking quickly away, evading the crazy bag lady who looks a lot like me.

Not looking back.

Lost in Space: Find This Book!

> You can never be certain of anything; but I don't have to teach you that. I learned it from Oliver and he learned it from you—this business of doors, of leaving through the rectangular space, of going away without a word.
>
> —Elaine Kraf, *Find Him!*

Find Him!—Elaine Kraf's brilliant spatial meditation on the "making" of the abstract machine of femininity—is lost. Published in 1977 by the Fiction Collective, a nonprofit publisher of highly experimental, primarily urban fiction,[4] *Find Him!* cannot itself be found, at least not in bookstores or from distributors. It is no longer in print and, to my knowledge, very much displaced from the terrain of contemporary feminist fiction. Even when it was in print, this novel remained outside the province of trade press, university press, or even feminist press consumer networks. This is unfortunate although appropriate: *Find Him!* resists categorization and interpretation, displacing whatever expectations or desires we may bring to the novel.

If Kraf's book can be located within any literary or artistic tradition, it is that rather amorphous body of creative work, which emerged in the United States in the 1970s and 1980s, by urban, avant-garde writers, visual artists, rockers, and performance artists, including women with potent, albeit nonconformist, feminist bents (for example, Kathy Acker, Lynne Tillman, Laurie Anderson, Cindy Sherman). In those two decades of deepening conservatism and further expansion of transnational megabusiness capitalism, such writers and artists produced gritty multimedia, in-your-face texts, art, and performance art that have been aptly called "suburban ambush" in that they powerfully resist and challenge bourgeois values of conspicuous consumption and normativity, which during the 1990s came to be called "family values"; the result, observes Robert Siegle in his aptly named *Suburban Ambush: Downtown Writing and the Fiction of Insurgency,* was a body of artistic labor engaged in a "guerrilla campaign against the imminent transformation of American consciousness into a shopping mall" (2).

Siegle's title comes from a poem by Ron Kolm, with graphics showing a military plane firebombing suburbia, that reads as follows:

> They firebombed
> the dinner table
> taking us completely
> by surprise.
>
> We evacuated
> our casualties
> from the patio—
> tracers skittering
> across the summer
> sky.
>
> Dad is a memory
> we're trying to keep
> alive. (Siegle, iii)

Interestingly, such writing, performance, and art, with their attacks on patriarchal capitalism and the normative family, are strongly insurgent but at the same time deeply skeptical of liberationist politics. The spatial dynamics of this writing are complicated, both ontologically and culturally. According to Siegle, this body of literary work, much of it fiction, "opens space—mentally, psychological, semiotically—where simulation, repression, and convention have converged to predetermine our Being. It shakes up reified relations—roles, genders, social structures—so that at least momentary experiences of various sorts of Other might take place before the great culture machine swallows it up again" (3).[5]

Although two decades later the great culture machine has swallowed up *Find Him!* I insist—certainly stubbornly, perhaps imprudently—on writing about this book, just as I persist in teaching it, despite the fact that students must trudge to the university library to read copies I've placed on reserve and despite the fact that you, my readers, probably haven't even heard of it. (You will certainly not find *Find Him!* in the 1998 *Books in Print,* where it should be, right after the optimistic title *Find Happiness in Everything You Do.* A World Cat search in 1999 using the terms "Find Him!" resulted in 130 titles, including many religious books, such as *Stepping Christward: The Way to Heaven and How to Find It* and *Why God Matters,* with the alternative title *If God Is So Big, How Come I Can't Find Him?*) I now own three copies and am looking for more; I will send you a photocopy if you promise not to turn me in to the authorities. I hope you would not be so inclined. After all, *Find Him!* begins with the inscription, "To You."

For now I will have to tell you the story, and I run the risk of boring you with an analysis assembled from the shards of a deeply inadequate and highly selective plot summary. This will spoil the story for you should you ever find *Find Him!* Moreover, it is impossible for me to tell you the whole story or even to give you a full sense of it. It is too complicated, too excessive. Just to give you a taste: there are drawings of a mad giraffe (see the illustration, p. 132); titled musical compositions (which one of my students played on the piano and taped for the class); a questionnaire for the reader ("*you*") and a blank space so you can draw the despicable male character, Oliver; a strange series of letters to Oliver supposedly from Hitler, Van Gogh, Napoléon, and Darwin; nebulous dream sequences; childish compositions that show the narrator's early struggle with language; and much more. Sometimes what happens in this text happens spatially on the page. So you can see how this is a risky business, trying to sum it all up or even tell you a little of it.

I know it's tricky, but I can't not look for *Find Him!* because, more than any other text I've been paying attention to throughout the preceding chapters, it calls *you,* its reader, to a spatially situated reading process that provokes the imaginative resituation of identity. It invites you—no, it compels you—to become, at various points, everyone in the book. More than that, it shoves a toe into your own private thresholds and demands entry. It is nudgy; it has no respect for privacy; it takes you over by creating and recreating "*you*" again and again. It is indeed because of the tightness of the book's spaces that readerly imagination is compelled to press toward expansion. Just to keep reading *Find Him!* (and, remember that no one is forcing you to keep reading), you, reader, are required to make certain spatial accommodations with respect to your own identity. There is a slippage here between your sense of yourself as a subject, a feminist reader with certain choices and belief systems, and your growing sense of yourself as an object in a claustrophobic discourse that allows you only limited agency. (Need I say that, for many women, this is a space that feels uneasily *heimlich*—like home, like life?) You are required to travel and, at the same time, to allow yourself to become the terrain for travel.

As one student said, "You're never really the same after reading this book." She is right, and although I'm not altogether sure why (you never really get a handle on this book), I think it has much to do with this always insistent, sometimes playful deferral of readerly identity—a kind of *différance* of self—that is required. You, reader, must travel the spaces of a textual "*you*" who is both reader and character. The difference in Kraf's book and others in which one is usually drawn into the experience of characters is that the narrator of *Find Him!* doesn't give you a choice about either how far you want to go or who you become. Mostly, she puts you where you don't want to be.

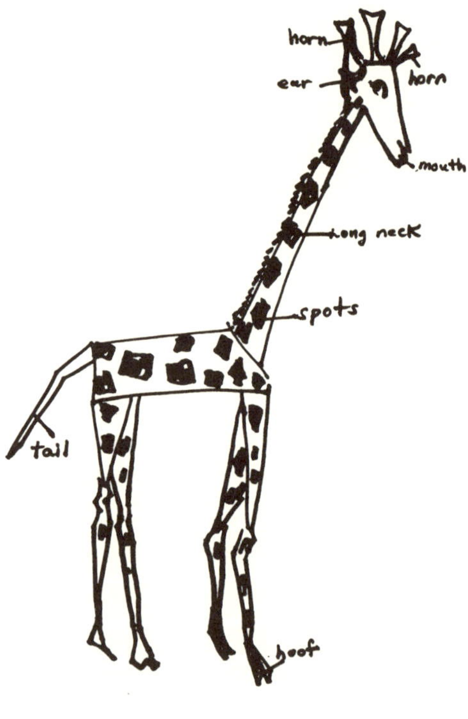

THE MAD GIRAFFE

Playfully (for small electric organ)

A QUESTIONNAIRE FOR YOU

1. Who do you like better, Oliver or me? ______________
2. Do you believe my story? (Yes, or No) ______________
3. Why did Edith leave Oliver? ______________
4. Why did Oliver teach me things? ______________
5. Who was most at fault? ______________
6. Why did Oliver leave? ______________
7. Where do you think he is? ______________

DRAW A PICTURE OF OLIVER IN THE EMPTY SPACE UNDERNEATH THIS

Although you probably haven't read *Find Him!* you may have already guessed that in these introductory remarks I am parodying it. *Find Him!* summons you to parody and performance, and I am trying to get you in the spirit. When I recently taught the novel in a graduate seminar, one student viewed the book as a parody of Victorian "Dear Reader" fiction; another just as persuasively called us to consider the novel as a parody of contemporary popular romance novels; and still another student, a medievalist, found in the grotesque male character Oliver a parody of the monstrous Grendel. The opportunities are apparently endless, but what I see happening in this book is that, like the various and pretty terrifying constructions of "woman" that occur therein, you, the woman reader (the narrator definitely genders you), find yourself under construction. "*You*" becomes a parody of you; you see yourself quite clearly as made. This, needless to say, is both interesting and disconcerting; despite your politics and way of living in the world, you see more clearly your "implicatedness"[6] in the narrative of patriarchal power. Inside this story, you see that you are neither innocent nor trustworthy.

It is for a feel of this disconcerting slippage of in and out that I urgently want you, my readers and witnesses to my reading of this novel, to know something about this book, although it has now, perhaps irrevocably, vanished. Let me continue to relate some of the story or, if I can, compel you to hear it for yourself from the unnamed narrator, a woman-girl whose hardly believable story, told years later, begins when she finds herself with no prior memories in a place she calls "Edith's house," whose claustrophic environs are anything but felicitious, with inside walls covered by heavy tapestries behind which there seem to be no windows or doors. (Later she will tell you: "Of course there was a door, fool; how do you think we ate?" [190].) "Edith," whose letters from a mental institution are part of the text, is not there (perhaps she never was, or perhaps, as you may begin to suspect, the unreliable narrator herself is a post-treatment [lobotomy? electric shock?] Edith). The "Him" of the house and the story—the man you are to find—is the ghastly Oliver, and as I tell you this story, you may rightly come to wonder why I didn't include this book in my previous chapter on father-daughter incest.

Oliver is the most disgusting man you can imagine. You come to know him much more intimately than you wish to ("If you have any prejudice against Oliver you must try to get rid of it," the narrator insists [91]). He is a very tall, very large man with a bulbous nose who expels foul breath and odors of sweat, moldy semen, and dried urine ("My Oliver has a large uncircumcised penis with blue booming veins running through it. He can cover the tip with that extra piece of skin or push it back. . . . It smells from unwashed smegma around the prepuce. You will be sure to notice that if I know you" [90]), and tufts of long black, red, and gray hairs protrude from his very large, forward-cupping ears, which contain "hard brownish orange wax" that he digs out periodically in bloody clumps. He has lost two joints on one finger, his toenails curve down like claws, and he tugs at his left earlobe ("I lie. . . . But I will never lie about Oliver. I will never change his name, soften his toenails, clean his ears, or keep his bottom lip from sticking out almost inside out very wet" [201]).

This quite graphic but thoroughly unreliable narrator, although physically postpubescent, has no prior memory of a life before entering this house. The solicitous Oliver teaches her how to chew, use the toilet, learn the words for things, and speak. (Indeed, Oliver may be seen as the grotesque embodiment of Lacan's phallus—the Name of the Father who ushers us into language. If so, it is an especially choice parody.) The narrator's first memory is of his hand with a spoon moving toward her mouth and his knocking her jaws together manually and holding her on his lap singing "'Chew,' while bouncing his knee in rhythm" (1). She first appears wearing a skirt of the familiar green tartan plaid worn by schoolgirls and a blue cotton blouse with a ruffle encircling the neck. Underneath she wears a tight camisole that deforms her large breasts into flat "pancake breasts." These "father" Oliver likes to fondle:

> From almost the beginning, Oliver was fascinated by my breasts, which I made no effort to hide. At any moment, when the camisole became too restricting, I might remove my clothes without self-consciousness. He held them and touched them quite often while he was helping me to eat or at other times. . . . I liked Oliver to touch my breasts. It was the perfect thing to do, considering my age and state. Had he seized me and raped me suddenly or had he ignored my woman's body, my development would have been slowed and possibly impaired. (13)

Isolated from the world outside ("your world," she calls it), the narrator becomes so dependent on Oliver that she lies outside his door when he shuts himself in his room; this is a feeling of deprivation she comes to know "in hundreds of variations before his final disappearance" (5). "I am a woman from another star," she tells you; "I came into existence with one man and had no contact with any society—knew only what I learned from him. He, Oliver, was *my* culture and *my* society" (3). Though he never gives her a name—an omission she eventually finds unforgivable—Oliver teaches the narrator language by putting signs on items in the house; the narrator's job is to match the proper sign to the proper item. When she doesn't understand and rearranges the signs improperly, Oliver flies into a rage: "Yelled words like 'No, no, stupid.' Red, he stamped his foot, banged his fist on the table, pulled his earlobe down. Worse, far worse, he ignored me. Though I tugged at him, whined, lay on the floor 'geeeeeech, geeeeeech,' he did not notice" (44). When the narrator, after much anxiety, accidentally pastes SINK on the sink, she receives from Oliver "the pleasure of a hasty coitus" (45); through this method of reward, she says, "I learned two languages with only one purpose: that Oliver would embrace me or say a kind word. He did. But the nakedness of my need made him stingy" (46). Oliver also beats and otherwise mistreats the narrator when he is displeased, but she will tell you about that later.

In the beginning the narrator loves Oliver unconditionally. She wants you to comprehend fully the nature and depth of her attachment: "Understand my beginning with Oliver. You will see that my love for him is not a romantic fantasy. Every bit of this love was formed from the reality of primary needs—ingestion, excretion, simple pleasure and pain" (3). More than three years later, as the narrator, now out in "*your* world" and working as a typist (although she's not telling you the whole truth about her present whereabouts), begins to tell her story, she explains that she is writing to "*you*" because she needs you to help find Oliver, who one day donned dark glasses, picked up the white cane of a blind person, stepped behind the tapestried walls of Edith's house to some unseen exit, and left the narrator alone. (The last lines of the book are "Please find him soon!" followed by a bar of musical notation and the final words "The End.")

Oliver's departure comes as a relief to the reader ("*you*"), who is forced to watch as he abuses the narrator in a variety of ways, including rape, beatings, emotional withdrawal, and mysterious punishments ("I was punished severely. I will not tell you how. It is no one's business. There are certain things you may not know about Oliver" [110]). During the third year, after measuring the narrator precisely inside and out ("making diagrams, pushing his fingers up into my vagina, wordlessly seeking entrance to the womb, finding my ovaries with some difficulty, and I—desperate, glad of any attention, not asking why or protesting, sensing a coldness about these manipulations" [165]), Oliver in a final creative burst of insanity constructs a fake woman ("Edith"), much as he has attempted (and partly succeeded) in constructing the narrator herself. Like a life-sized female figure assembled by photographer Cindy Sherman (whose aims are diametrically opposed to Oliver's), his construction is made from various objects and components. Oliver's "woman" has a utilitarian purpose, however, which involves various items: plastic and magnets; silk lingerie and perfume; pig's eyes, chicken gizzards and livers, and the formaldehyde necessary to keep them from rotting quickly; electric wires and dials for the simulation of motion. Secretively the narrator watches over the door transom as Oliver fucks "Edith." ("Edith's construction was perfect. I had learned to accept the fact that he preferred her to me, dressing her in detail from satin undergarments to pink fluffy gowns. She was always delicately perfumed and elaborately coiffed. I won't disclose to you the details of her anatomy—proof of my Oliver's ingenuity. I will never betray his deepest secrets. Let me state, although I may have stated it before, that every bit of her anatomy was as satisfying to a man as that of a real woman. Use your own imagination, but do not steal what was Oliver's" [192]).

This, then, is Oliver—woman builder, teacher, fucker, abuser, container. Patriarch par excellence. Maker of language and law. Sovereign of the hegemonic realm. Your job, the narrator insists, is to *find him!*

What is involved in finding this greasy-eared, semen-splattered, stinky, crazy, perverted creep? Who would want to find him, anyway? Clearly not the feminist reader. Not you. The *"you"* created by this text may have different ideas, though.

Let me return to the problem of implication. In *Feminism and the Politics of Reading* Lynne Pearce argues for reconfiguring the pleasure of reading as a far more emotionally complex and "implicated" relationship in which the reader's interactive response hinges on identification with a dialogic "textual other." Pearce's larger argument is that pleasure and politics often do not cohere in the reading experience. Obviously this other can take the form of a specific character in the text—"a humanistically defined, representational subject." A more interesting scenario occurs when the reader herself is constructed as a presence in the text—in terms of *Find Him!* how you as reader are "made."

As I've implied, there is an almost vibrating tension created in this text between you, the reader who lives in the world, and *"you,"* the reader who lives in this story. What *Find Him!* does is to displace the feminist reader from her aims and purposes; as *"you,"* you are not only seduced into looking for the patriarch (who in the end you learn is dead by the narrator's own hand—are you surprised?), but you are forced to acknowledge your intimacy with and implicatedness in his story. You are both seduced by *"you"*—I hope I've given you an idea of just how seductive our woman/girl narrator is—and repelled. You are compelled by the title's imperative; in the end, the narrator tells you that you can make Oliver live or make him die: it is your choice. Since Oliver is the story, you must kill the story if you kill him. Since you have been seduced by the story, it is hard to kill what you, like the narrator, have come (for your own reasons—I don't ask what they are) to love ("Oliver, Please don't go away [232]).

Pearce argues that "emotion and politics appear to tear apart from one another in most reading events" (132); as the "*you*" of *Find Him!* I find myself—and I'd venture to say you might well find yourself—entangled in a sticky web of emotion and politics. The space between requires certain accommodations and interchanges that you (I suspect) may be unprepared to make. The more you struggle the more stuck you become, the more you recognize the material space of "Edith's house" as a cultural space you cannot fully escape no matter how far you have traveled to escape it. This is not a story one can leave behind. *Find Him!* taxes you. More insidiously, as the epigraph to this section suggests, there is an eliding, perhaps even a reversal, of inside—the space of the narrator, Edith's house—and outside—the space of "your world," your house.

If you were to ask why *Find Him!* is so seductive, which is a question, if my summary has the limitations I expect it to, I would expect you to ask, my answer would be, in large part, its absolute and unwavering attentiveness to the reader. Not only is the novel dedicated "To *You*," but from the beginning you are welcomed into Edith's doorless, windowless house, into what the narrator calls "the community of we." To enter you must travel the distance between the narrator's world and yours. (It is only later that you will discover that this is not as far as you first imagined.) "I am inviting *YOU* to enter and eat the feast that Oliver and I created. In order to do this, you must abandon your world, at least temporarily. I hope that you will be able to understand what I am talking about. It will not be easy for you. I appreciate this because I have tried and failed to understand *your* world: *your* vocations, customs, societal divisions, politics and wristwatches" (3). Later the narrator, with elaborate precision, leads you into the space of the house, Edith's glass studio, the three bedrooms, kitchen, and eating area—a rather typically laid-out suburban house with a bizarre interior. Anxiously she asks, "Do you understand the relationship of room to room? Are you certain that you realize that the eating area was not enclosed and the breakfront with an upper ledge and three bottom drawers opened by tarnished keys was not hidden. Do not forget the patchwork walls" (113).

Throughout *Find Him!* the narrator's relationship to you and yours to her are vexed. She knows she needs you, not just as reader, but as the "*you*" who will fulfill the imperative. At the end of her story, she says: "If I understood everything, could figure it all out by myself, why then would I have called upon you to help? Do not expect a logical working out of everything from me. It is not as though I am telling you a story for the fun of it" (217). This "I" is wily and careful; she lies about some things (she admits it), she doesn't tell all of her story until the end, and she works hard to keep your interest, aware that, like Oliver, you could desert her at any given moment. She is afraid you "will go away just like Oliver did" if she doesn't show you "something interesting" (16), so she produces letters, questionnaires, dreams, and a considerable amount of suspense. Yet "I" is also a temperamental, impatient storyteller. On various occasions during the first section of the book she chastises you ("It is not for *you* to criticize," she says sharply on one occasion (55), later adding, "[Oliver] smells from urine, mildewed rags and strong soap and potato peel. I know you. You would think it loathsome. I know about that. Fuck you then!" [79]). She becomes angry and exasperated ("I like Oliver's toenails exactly as they are. So don't tell me to clip them or change his name. I would have every right to do that since he never gave *me* a name; I can't forgive him for that. But that is between Oliver and me—that is between Oliver and me and is none of your business!" [32]). She dissects the readerly psyche ("I am beginning to understand you and how you think. . . . Not by interest are you motivated, nor by compassion. I understand. Curiosity is everything—a watching wondering about everything point by point. Not child-like. You want to know everything. Gaps disturb you, make you suspicious" [40–41]). At certain times she is cajoling ("It is important to me that you respect Oliver" [41]); at others she insists on acquiescence ("*You* must love Oliver. He came out of his room with his huge smile—the smile Oliver still smiled sometimes then, tomatosweet" [53]).

For this "I," you are confidant, foil, voyeur, secret sharer, sexual object for Oliver, witness, attorney, life giver, murderer, and more. Whatever "I" makes you, your identity remains a highly unstable construction of your readerly relation to the text. For example, at the end of the first section of the book, "I" barrages "*you*" with a page or so of insistent questions demanding an analysis of the text thus far. Under the demanding tone is a parody of certain kinds of critical analysis, especially psychoanalysis. "Well, what do you think so far? I wish you could write to me, or that you were standing right here so I could explain things or clarify them if they are wrong. You know psychology. Do you think Oliver is a latent homosexual? Does he have masturbatory guilt? Was he guilty about sex? . . . do you think Oliver likes to fuck girls or people who act like girls and then gets tired if they grow up?" (83).

Such volleys of questions pressure you further, sometimes again blending the identities of narrator, Oliver, and *"you"* in disconcerting ways:

> Am I being a pest with you like I was with Oliver? Do you hate me? Would you have left also if someone loved you and annoyed you so much? . . . Do you think I have a father fixation or a mother fixation? Or penis envy? It is your world. I am waiting for you to tell me. . . . Do you think I am trying to seduce you and manipulate you like some other writers do? Should I have left you out of it and just told the story? Is the burden too much for you? Is that what you are so mad about? Am I stepping out of line? . . . Did I really know what Oliver was doing? How did he do it? Is that what you want to know? What do you want to know? (83–84)

The force and insistence—the sheer peskiness—of these questions irritate me. No, I *don't* want to be dragged into this weird story about this stupid woman and this repulsive man. But the last question of the section, followed by two pages of white space, does linger. *What do I want to know?*

In the white space I produce my own set of (feminist) questions: How can she not know that he is using sex ("coitus") as reward and punishment? That she is being craftily manipulated? How can she not know what intercourse *is*? The first few sentences of the second section startle me because they read my mind: "Yes. It is possible to have sexual relations with someone without knowing what it is. . . (87). "I" has invaded "your" mind; she knows what you are thinking. "No one knows I think these things except you," "I" writes to you (204), but it works the other way around, too. Here, as in many other moments of this text, a cloying, unwanted intimacy has been created. Moreover, in this same passage about the narrator's experience of sexual intercourse with Oliver, there is a switch of pronouns; suddenly it is *"you"* who is having sex with Oliver: "whoosh plop of water sounds, pah egg yellow stabbed shining on top of my eyes. 'Oom. oom.' Not knowing if it is enjoyable, particularly if you have never learned the word 'enjoy.' I never did. Only sensed it behind things sometimes or in the rhythm of the breathing and the heartbeat. Possible, yes—to want something you don't understand, not separating it from anything. Something I didn't know. Surrounding us not knowing who was who. Yes" (87).

Just as the identities of "I" (narrator) and *"you"* (reader) converge in this section (as they do in many other parts of the book), the narrator is herself awash with Oliver, particularly in her early experience with him ("Don't forget that his unconscious was mine" [149]). Add to these confluences the *"you"* that Kraf creates as the identity of the reader becoming troubled by and laden with the character of the despicable Oliver. This also occurs at a syntactic level when the narrator speaks both to Oliver and the reader, aligning the two "yous": "When you [Oliver] wiped my eyes I assume it was simply to blot up the wetness. Now when I cry in another room it takes me so long to associate it with something that has upset me. To name the event itself is often impossible. . . . But I have a method which I am proud to tell you, Oliver, or *you,* that I invented myself. When I cry I say, 'I am crying. It is wet. Babies cry, dogs cry, maybe Oliver cries'" (69). In another scene the narrator takes it upon herself to instruct the reader on how to behave sexually "if you are a woman and Oliver happens to be in your house" (222). The rule, of course, is unequivocal passivity:

> You must never make the first advances to Oliver. He will not like it, I assure you. . . . Wait until Oliver begins and then be as passive as possible. By that I mean do not try to please him. . . . He will resent your expertise. Do not ever touch Oliver's penis without his permission, and don't try to be alluring or subtle or spectacular. He will hate you if you invent variations or unusual techniques. On the other hand, you must never reject Oliver's advances even if they seem sudden or brusque. . . . Be appreciative but not active. Don't howl. . . . You must leave it up to Oliver. That is the main thing. (223)

This forced intimacy of Oliver and the reader, which requires "*you*" to feel Oliver's touch upon your body, is complicated by the further erosion of the narrator's psyche into that of Oliver in "the community of we." (For example, there is a chilling scene at the end of the book in which, after Oliver has disappeared, the narrator one day changes places with the "Edith" that Oliver has constructed and left on the bed. "I" thereby becomes the construction of femininity, the life-sized doll, which, as she has pointed out earlier in the book, looks a lot like many of the women in "your world."

When the narrator assumes the doll's place and identity, she finds her own personality fading, her curiosity, intelligence, and stubborn rebelliousness all dissolving: "Once it began, there was no stopping it. Eventually I behaved as the dials ordered, assimilated Oliver's chemicals, became inert and lost all autonomy. No heartbeat, hunger, desire—I became the creature that Oliver desired who could in no way disturb him" (207). In this macabre moment and many others throughout the text—and I can't stress enough how many there are—female identity becomes thoroughly problematized as feminist reader (you, not "*you*") and patriarchal victimizer (the him you are to find) become inextricably entangled. Pronouns become hopelessly amalgamated: The "I" of this text, we learn at the end, is probably the real Edith, who was in a mental hospital; "I" also is the construction of "Edith" on the bed and, even in her most mutinous mode still, like "Edith," a product of Oliver and part of him.

Most disturbing of all is the insistence that "I" is "*you*" and vice versa. In a passage near the end of the book, the narrator describes herself as a voyeur and eavesdropper, the one "listening to intimate conversations in restaurants . . . [,] staring into your window with a pair of binoculars, and listening at the door." She, like you, is a reader of texts: "There I am reading entire books in the bookstore, never buying any. You can see me reading them with a look of glee on my face; that is how I must have looked while reading Oliver's letter from Van Gogh or Edith's letters to Oliver. Habits are not easy to break. . . . Just invite me over and you will see. If you disappear for ten minutes, I will find your secret letters; I have an instinct about such things. . . . Be very careful because I read upside down almost as well as I read the regular way" (200–201).

Find Him! thus travels the space of "*you,*" not only reading your mind, not only reading your own reading practice as a questionable enterprise with questionable motives, not only putting you physically and emotionally where you don't want to be, but requiring that you *accommodate* yourself to those spaces in which "I" has situated you, if indeed you still have a sense of who "you" is, having slipped into that gap of "*you*" created by the imperative of this text.

It is indeed difficult to disengage from this text—to find yourself and get the hell out—because you have been so thoroughly enmeshed in it and dismantled by it and because *Find Him!*'s real message is that, for "*you,*" out is in. Certain accommodations are made in "your world" that are identical to or more bizarre than those the narrator has made in Oliver's world. "*You* feel it for me," our narrator demands (215), and you do. Oliver's construction of "Edith" wasn't so crazy, the narrator insists; women are made every day: "I have seen similar things out here. I have seen women or girls who look like something Oliver or someone else constructed. Not only in the street but in the movies and on television. Only Oliver did it from the beginning" (192).

These are obvious examples, but the tension that *Find Him!* builds around the reader's identity—that awful slippage between reading feminist subject and disempowered female object—leads one—you will notice how my pronoun shrinks from this prospect—to ponder the extent of one's "madeness" in the former position as well as recoil from the terrors of the latter. The two are made to cohere in a surprisingly sticky way. To layer female identity as a montage of subject-object relations raises the question of one's relation to the other: does the feminist subject (you) help make the female object ("*you*")? Does one have a metonymic relation to the other? And, if so, what kind of "community of we" do we have here? Which is the part and which is the whole?

At the close of the novel, the narrator confides that, long after she had left Edith's house, having been abandoned there with some food but not too much ("It was the slow hunger, the slow realization of what had happened that saved my life, that forced me to find the DOOR and go" [220]), she returned to the house after a passage of time to find Oliver snoring loudly on the bed. She killed him by inserting carefully folded pieces of cloth into his nose and mouth. She is now in jail for his murder. "Can you picture it?" she asks. "Me—finding Oliver sleeping there, after all that searching, after all that worrying, after all the time I waited for him with Edith? *You* feel it for me" (215). It was not so much murder ("I" never uses the word *murder*) as a deepening of Oliver's noisy, open-mouthed, adenoid-laden sleep: "Wooden cylinders cloth-covered white inserted silently into his dry hairy nostrils made little difference to him as breath came in and out of his wet mouth" (235). Then a precisely folded piece of cloth inserted "in between the poor triangular glottis slit, a flower hole to suck breath for filling up his lungs. . . . 'Glottis is the DOOR to the Trachea,' said the wise giraffe, knowing how I hate the word DOOR" (236). The narrator, she confides, *is* the mad giraffe.

But in the end, reader, Oliver still walks, tap-tapping with his cane down the streets and alleys of this book. As in the Ron Kolm poem, "Dad" is still "a memory / we're trying to keep / alive." The father still potent in his own dissipation; he is never seen but always leaving a trail.

"Are you going to kill Oliver?" the narrator asks and then begs you not to: "You know what such a thing would do to me, Oliver being all I have, and my hope of finding him and of living with him once again beneath dead tapestries. I will give up everything for him. You are too kind to do that. He was just asleep, I know, I am certain of that—never mind what was stuck in his mouth and nose, taking away the sweet breath of Oliver. No one must know because if it is proven to be a fact, I would vanish" (233). For the narrator to vanish as a result of Oliver's death would mean that her story would vanish and "*you*," reader, with it. That, perhaps, is what you (by "you," I mean me, one lone feminist reader) are left with, reading *Find Him!* on the cusp of the millennium: that the well-traveled story of the father's death is dangerous to believe, not just because there are Olivers still making their Ediths or walking the streets or teaching the children, but because "*you*" are so implicated in that story that you cannot live with it or without it.

A Traveling Text: Keri Hulme's Bone People

> We are transit points and blubbery highways and temporarily fluid screens; indeed we are a finity of things to every light wave and every light particle and sonic particle and sonic wave, but mainly somewhere to pass through in a hurry without so much as a by-yr-lve or a pardon.
>
> —Keri Hulme, *Te Kaihau: The Windeater*

The Bone People is a space traveler—a big novel that took New Zealand author Keri Hulme a dozen years to write on her first typewriter, a gift from her mother. Hulme, who describes her ancestry as Orkney Scots and Lancashire English as well as Kai Tahu, the South Island Maori tribe, pounded it out at night after working days in the Moteuka tobacco fields. Her first book, *The Bone People* was rejected repeatedly over a period of six years by New Zealand's major publishers for being "too large, too unwieldy, too *different* when compared with the normal shape of a novel" (Hulme, preface to 1984 ed.). (The book, including its glossary of Maori words and phrases, is 450 pages in rather small—and varied—type, although originally it was much longer.) One feminist publisher thought it insufficiently feminist for her list (Covi 219). Its rescue from oblivion came in the form of the feminist Spiral Collective, developed by three Wellington women specifically to publish this book (iv). Their efforts were not in vain. In 1984, the year of its publication, *The Bone People* won the New Zealand Book Award and, crucial to its subsequent travels to the United States and other countries, the Pegasus Prize for Literature, which is designed to introduce American readers to distinguished works from countries whose literature rarely receives international recognition.

So it was that in 1985, when such long-distance travels of postcolonial fiction were not as common as they are today, Hulme's book embarked over land and sea to begin its publication history in the United States. In 1985 it was brought out by Louisiana State University Press—a publisher of excellent fiction and poetry—and then picked up by Penguin in 1986, in the meantime garnering its author a grant from the NEA, Britain's prestigious Booker Prize, and a cover blurb from Alice Walker that says, "This book is just amazingly, wondrously great." Widely reviewed and circulated internationally within both academic and trade circles, it remains in print today, still trailing in *Books in Print,* though not on its current paperback cover, the cocky but apt subtitle *A Masterful Story of Myth and Emotional Healing.*[7] In her preface to *The Bone People,* Hulme, whose wide range of reading in Eastern, Western, and indigenous literature and history is apparent, beguiles us with the pleasures of readerly travel. She writes: "To those used to one standard, this book may offer a taste passing strange, like the original mouth of kina roe.[8] Persist. Kina can become a favorite food."

Sounds enticing. But kina isn't all that's on this plate. *The Bone People* is a brilliantly troubled postcolonial novel that, everywhere, forces us to journey beyond its borders. It is a "splendid failure" in the Faulknerian sense (and to my mind, there's no higher praise) in that it ultimately wants to take its readers on a specific journey away from violence, isolation, displacement, and despair and toward mythical resolution as per the promise of its subtitle. But *everything* in the book—memory, language, character, narrative—works against such a resolution. I think of this book in terms of conflicting urges.[9] It propels me in two directions simultaneously. Hulme has said that she wanted the book to be "a bridge" between the two sides of her family, Maori and Pakeha (European), and that she wanted "to make explicit, explicable, the spiritual world" (Hulme and Turcotte 153). I want to believe in her happy ending mythically configured in Maori tradition (there is literal dancing in the street), but the book is haunted by the ravages of Judeo-Christianity: the abusive father, the constantly crucified son. I want to believe in the good father (or at least the rehabilitated father), figured as a laughing trickster; I want to believe in the Maori sense of reciprocity and accommodation to the other, figured in the resurrected son; I want to believe in home, wherever it may be found. I want to believe that the woman artist of the novel who is so Woolfian in her piercing sense of reality can lead father and son to this destination. Everything in this book works toward this ending. Everything works against it. In this sense, *The Bone People* bears a marked similarity to *Find Him!* in that it brings intensely conflicting urges to bear on the reading process. It insists that I go in several directions at once. The question, then, for the traveler/reader of *The Bone People* is not so much one of destination but what to make of the gap between conflicted journeys.[10]

There are no edges to *The Bone People.* It is a beautiful yet slippery novel, blending languages that sing and sob, kill and heal, solidify identity and disassemble it. All is depth and flux, wave and particle. All lines blur. To block out any part of this process and frame it critically is to commit an act of violence. Gender must travel in this book because everything else does.

The book's multiple spatial dimensions compel the reader to travel in several directions at once: between mythic systems (primarily Maori and Christian); toward a conflicting geography of place and displacement, settling and wandering (New Zealand, North and South Islands, town and countryside); into an ecology of extremes (the great earth mother Papa, the omnipresent pull of the sea, a simultaneous violence and tenderness toward others). Layered throughout are the tormented corporeal and emotional realities of all three main characters, whose separate yet intertwined senses of being in the world and living in their own skins become the space that this narrative wanders through and worries over.

One feels a readerly urge to roam these spaces—cultural, material, psychological—without settling, despite the book's movement toward resolution. *The Bone People* is always displacing its own narrative; displacement tropes its way through the book, materially as well as psychologically. Despite a deep pull toward physical and cultural geography, the novel's statements of location are vague, tied to land and ocean, country and town, rather than specific places. Place names are used very sparingly, although New Zealand emerges as both actual and mythical setting connected to the archetypal and cultural work of healing. But a strange linguistic edginess and the piercingly acute memory of what it is to wound and be wounded often take me, when I least expect it, someplace else.

Although never expressed directly, the Maori origination myth of perilous journeying seems to undergird *The Bone People*'s precarious mobility. Nearly all the Maori peoples tell stories of original voyages to Aotearoa, a name denoting first the North Island ("the land of the long white cloud") and now generally referring to all New Zealand, paddling *wakas,* or canoes, from the mythical homeland of Hawaiki, in the East, where human life was believed to have been first created (Orbell 28, 50). These were astonishing sea travels involving great danger and initiated out of necessity after quarrels or warfare in the mythical homeland. Sometimes an individual would ride a whale or a piece of pumice. The ancestors brought the *kumara,* or sweet potato, and other plants, birds, volcanic fire, moth caterpillars, and sacred objects such as the *mauri,* which is a complex symbol taking physical shape, usually as a stone, and believed to hold the life force of an individual or group (Orbell 50, 117). (It is indicative of the novel's insistence on paradox that Joe Gillayley, onetime vicious beater and perhaps molester of his adopted son, is the keeper of the *mauri,* which in the end sinks into the ground, becoming, he thinks, "a sort of pricket and tremble in our gut" [445].)

The pricket and tremble in my European readerly gut derives more from the book's Christian symbology, which *seems*—and I stress that I am not sure about this—constructed in opposition to Maori principles of reciprocity and interconnection. Here are the characters: adoptive father and Maori Joe Gillayley (read Joseph of Galilee), the violent abuser; his adopted European son, Simon (fisher of men?), who appears again and again as a wounded Christ figure and who actually seems to undergo rebirth; the female artist-creator and part-Maori Kerewin Holmes (mother, home, holy spirit?). The book's original title was taken from a short story entitled "Simon Peter's Shell" (preface). Gender itself travels metaphorically dangerous seas—but from where, toward what? Can this novel be read as a devastating critique of God the Father and an abusive system governed by patriarchal power? Is the counter to such a system the classic Maori principle of reciprocity, *utu*, which still plays a significant part in contemporary Maori interpersonal and intergroup relations? (Metge 67)

However we approach these questions, we can surely say that *The Bone People* is a profoundly multicultural story about appropriation and accommodation, overlap and exchange. Powerful mythic elements from a variety of sources offer a way of living within historical and cultural overlays; there are spiritual messages and artifacts from Asian as well as Christian and Maori belief systems. Even within the characters' own families, meaningful interactions between cultures and belief systems occur in a contemporary postcolonial setting. I am especially interested in how the book's articulation of questions of accommodation and reciprocity, so intensely experienced by the characters, are configured spatially and how those spaces are conflicted and paradoxical. This is a book set on an island, but a book that interrogates the presence of borders; characters (and readers) must traverse certain landscapes and cross certain emotional and spiritual demarcations to restructure their relations with others.

Yet these transactions remain vexed. *The Bone People* comes to U.S. feminism from a long distance and is *about* the problem of distance itself, its journeyings, like Maori belief systems and unlike Judeo-Christianity, conceived in spatial terms that relate the human and spiritual worlds "as different but interlocking dimensions" (Metge 57). Life and death thus "define and complete each other," and the individual is always part of the group, with his or her life and death as part of a continual process of an ongoing spirit that extends beyond the individual (Metge 56–57). Such a philosophy of experience translates to all things. *Papa* (the earth) and *Rangi* (the sky) mourn their enforced separation (Orbell 133). All things are connected in time and space in the great spiral of existence and in that necessary motion of the imagination which links one to another.

In its own dynamic spatiality, *The Bone People* functions both within and outside of these reciprocal dimensions. The bone people are felt everywhere in this book; they emerge at crucial moments as healers and teachers; they are the dead who make life full. Their tribal presence raises questions of home and homeland, interior and exterior. As Hulme points out, the Maori word *iwi* means both "tribe" and "bones." *Wairua,* quasi-human beings who help people, are called "the bones" (Hulme and Turcotte 142). For all three characters, who are resurrected from a death of spirit, there is the journey toward an attentiveness to and an accommodation of what one is not. They bear their illnesses, malaise, wounds, and guilt down the road, to the pub, to the sea, to the ledge of the cliff, to the brink of slow, painful death.

In the end they are miraculously put together again and become a trinity (again Christian symbology) of joy and reciprocity. They come together, still in motion, continuing their travels: the child abuser Joe; the child Simon, now lame and nearly deaf from his last beating, who still loves the man who nearly killed him; the troubled artist Kerewin, who, having torn down her tower of isolation and narcissism, leads father and son to reunion and reconciliation. The first three short sections of the book, entitled "The End at the Beginning," depict each—the man, the child, and the woman—in motion: walking down the street, smiling and at peace, first separately and then together, in a kind of allegory of their longer journey, which has brought them back to "change and curve and hope" (3). With these three poetic segments, which cluster together on its first page, *The Bone People* poises itself to undertake its own narrative journey, a journey that seems to go in many directions at once. It twists and turns and circles back onto itself, beginning at the end and ending at the beginning. There are spirals (a ubiquitous shape throughout) and designs (tattoos, scars, writings, carvings, sculptures). The book overflows in many whirls and eddies of consciousness, history, and geography. It travels back in time to the bone people (the revered ancestors) and forward to a new conception of family and tribe, which is itself continually pulled or dragged back by memory. Mysterious figures who occupy dimensions that are neither here nor there but both at once appear throughout; they are the healers and truth-tellers, the multidimensional and quasi-gendered bone people, who live in the overlapping expanse between the spiritual and physical worlds.

But the memory of violence has its own mysterious and terrible wanderings in this narrative. I can move beyond it only temporarily and inadequately.

There are other difficult journeys for the feminist reader to make as well. The novel's three central characters, especially Joe, are so enigmatic, abrasive, and violent that they create (for me, at least) intensely conflicting feelings of attraction and repulsion. As in *Find Him!* but to a greater though more subtle degree, the feminist reader is confronted with a highly problematic male character, and in Hulme's novel one travels his mind throughout. One finds oneself traveling gender, but not in a particularly pleasant way. Moreover, gender itself becomes dismantled in a complicated book about complicated problems. Questions of reciprocity—the Maori sense of being in relation to others—and a hopeful movement toward accommodation to what one is not are particularly fraught. (Interestingly the term *utu*—originally meaning reciprocity—has partly lapsed in usage among contemporary Maoris, possibly because Pakehas commonly translate it as "revenge," giving it a purely negative cast [Metge 67]).

One question *The Bone People* poses, as do *Find Him!* and *Bird-eyes,* is how far accommodation can or should go. Can or should a child maimed and almost killed, perhaps sexually abused, still love the man who did it? What is the community's relationship to such deeds? Can there be healing for such terrible wounds, forgiveness for the perpetrator and a cessation of suffering for the wounded? These are the deeply human questions that entail a spatial dimension. Are there not real consequences of the violent invasion of bodied space that cannot be undone, whether such an invasion takes the form of familial violence or historical intervention? Can the spaces of identity and social relations be read as cultural spaces in the sense that Hulme suggests in her statement about bringing together Maori and white traditions? These questions have rather obvious feminist and postcolonial implications, and they buzz like troublesome insects around the edges of this narrative.

Further complicating this text, these sites of trouble in *The Bone People* cluster in a murky and liminal queer space, creating a troublingly conspicuous opposition of queerness and health, spiritual and psychic, that gnaws at the balance of things finally achieved and the accommodative, reciprocal impulses undergirding that balance. An aura surrounds queerness in this text that makes me question how far *The Bone People*'s journey toward true reciprocity goes. Like the conflicting mythical stories that float in and out of this novel, *The Bone People*'s queer spaces—as I discuss at the end of this section—further disturb this already unsettled narrative.

But let me embark, engaging the spiral at its entrance:

At the beginning of the novel, Kerewin Holmes's distance from the world is vast. She is a (definitely) reclusive, (maybe) asexual artist in her thirties who, despite or perhaps because of her wealth, has lost her ability to paint and who for a decade has isolated herself from the rest of the community by living in a six-story medieval-style tower, "gaunt and strange and embattled," which she herself designed and built "on an almost island in the shallows of an inlet, tall in Taiaroa" (7).[11]

> It was the hermitage, her glimmering retreat. No people invited, for what could they know of the secrets that crept and chilled and chuckled in the marrow of her bones? No need of people, because she was self-fulfilling, delighted with the pre-eminence of her art, and the future of her knowing hands.
>
> But the pinnacle became an abyss, and the driving joy ended. At last here was a prison.
>
> I am encompassed by a wall, high and hard and stone, with only my brainy nails to tear it down.
>
> And I cannot do it. (7)

Kerewin drinks to excess and is bitterly estranged from her family. She hates being touched or bothered, owns a phone on which she can call out but no one can call in, and has a well-stocked wine cellar, a collection of exquisite jewelry, and a library that contains "just about everything." When she's not drinking, fishing, or both, she spends most of her time trying to draw or sculpt, but "nothing grows under her anxious hands. She feels empty and sour" (45). Although her ancestry is only one-eighth Maori, she says, "By heart, spirit, and inclination, I feel all Maori . . . or used to. Now it feels like the best part of me has got lost in the way I live" (62). Kerewin is an intellectual who has partaken of many cultures in her search for pattern and design: "Futureprobes, Tarot and I Ching and the wide wispfingers from the stars. . . . A broad general knowledge, encompassing bits of history, psychology, ethology, religious theory and practices of many kinds. Her charts of self-knowledge. Her library. . . . None of them helped make sense of living" (90). In her determined narcissism she has created her own claustrophobic interiority, engaging continually in talking to herself about herself—"mirrortalk," as she calls it (one of Hulme's chapters carries this name [261]). The one good painting she produces during the period of life encompassed by the early part of the book is a self-portrait.

When Simon Gillayley, "a right stubborn illnatured mess of a child" (45), enters her tower through a window, her life is permanently transformed by the boy, who is probably around five and does not or cannot speak, and his adoptive father, Joe, a widower who rescued him from a mysterious shipwreck and calls him "jetsam." She finds the boy framed in her window, a Christlike figure looking down on her, intent on entering her zealously guarded space: "In the window, standing stiff and straight like some weird saint in a stained gold window, is a child. A thin shock-headed person, haloed in hair, shrouded in the dying sunlight" (16). Simon is Pakeha, but his original identity isn't known. He has a reputation in town as a destructive, antagonistic thief with a penchant for throwing stones and setting fires. As Kerewin comes to discover, Simon is actually an intelligent, delightful child who is hiding the fact that he is undergoing intense battering at home. He believes he deserves it, and he doesn't want anyone to know how "bad" he is. Despite an extended family that is quite involved in his life, Joe feels, like Kerewin, that "the Maoritanga [Maori spirit] has got lost in the way I live" (62). Another heavy drinker, Joe deeply grieves the death of his wife and their young son. He is considered a likable sort with a difficult child to raise alone, although, as Kerewin later finds out, Joe's family, especially his brother, Piri, has become increasingly worried over Simon's welfare. (Hulme does everything she can to make me like Joe, and more often than not I do, even after I find out what he's doing to his son.)

Simon has special powers. He can see auras, "lights on people." Although connected by name and situation to Christian belief systems, he also seems linked to the Polynesian trickster, Maui, who, like Simon, came out of the sea—legend having it that he was a miscarried fetus that developed in the ocean. Maui, again like Simon, had a lack of respect for authority and liked to play tricks and steal. Simon's hobby at the beginning of the book is to skip school, break into people's houses, and steal whatever catches his eye. Maui's legendary accomplishment was to catch the land—the North Island of New Zealand—and fish it up out of the sea after considerable effort with a hook made from the jawbone of one of his grandparents (an act that breaks *tapu*). It is said that the land is still in the shape of the fish (Orbell 114–16).

In an important scene around the middle of the book, Kerewin and Joe take Simon to the ocean for a three-week vacation. They take him out in a boat for the first time since he was almost drowned in the shipwreck. Like Maui and Simon Peter of Galilee, the boy becomes a fisher par excellence, catching an enormous grouper as big as he is. This whole episode carries Christian and Maori resonances, and the reader is urged to travel back and forth between competing systems of belief. Although Simon finally manages to pull in the big fish, a moment later, in another struggle with the fish inside the boat, he sticks the hook deep into his thumb. The hook is large and deeply embedded, but Simon is scared of doctors, so Joe removes it from the soft bone himself. The wound and the intense pain it gives are indicative of Simon's many woundings, which are unnaturally gotten and threaten death: continual crucifixions.

Here, then, are the images of wounding—the bloody hands—of Christian tradition versus the trickster's antics, which are constantly aimed at overturning the natural order of things. The reader is urged in both mythic directions—tragic and comic—at once. For example, even Maui's death has a comedic element: he tried to crawl inside the body of the "great woman the night" Hine-nui-te-po but was trapped when she shut her legs and died, then, in the space of birth (Orbell 117).

Stories of the trickster Maui are important to Hulme. In an afterword to her 1986 short story collection, a rather rollicking poem called "Headnote to a Maui Tale," she tells one version of the myth that begins with Maui's development from the sea and ends with the question of whether Maui was actually killed in this incident with the "beady-eyed" Hine-nui-te-po. Hulme's poem ends by suggesting that there are many versions of the myth. Maui's fate is dependent on what story is being told. What Hulme requires in *The Bone People* is that we hear several stories at once, layered one on top of another. Nor can we choose among them. *The Bone People* insists on the multiple layer, the journey back and forth.

In a deadly serious way, Simon's story, like Maui's, becomes one of diminishing space. His inability to speak makes the tightening enclosure of violence even more debilitating and helps to create the acute tension between the experiences of this progressing violence as Hulme moves back and forth between the consciousnesses of the brutally abusive father and the beaten, broken son. These scenes of violence are repeated again and again; they sometimes happen in narrative sequence and sometimes come in the form of memory, but the memory of them stays alive throughout the book. And, despite Hulme's characters' turn toward reconciliation and love, my journey through this beautiful and terrible book is so directed by the vividness—the terror and pain—of Simon's beatings that, although I am tempted by such resolutions, I cannot always travel their path. I am urged in two directions: one, to follow the novel's movement toward resolution; another, to turn back, examine these deeds in all their ugliness, and wonder how such wounds can ever be healed. I must believe in miracles, in resurrection, but *The Bone People* leads me to doubt, too.

These memories of violence rattle around the final pages of the novel, haunting its joyous dance of life and renewal. One enormous difficulty with reading the novel is the way it, like most of the other texts I have discussed, summons an embodied reading of violence. At times scenes of excruciating brutality are rendered poetically, almost like hymns. Here is the child being beaten, entrapped within a spiral of agony—crucifixion within crucifixion, consciousness disassociating from itself:

> The world is full of dazzlement, jewel beams,
> fires of crystal splendour.
> I am on fire.
> He is aching, he is breaking apart with pain.
> The agony is everywhere, hands, body, legs,
> head.
> He is shaking so badly he cannot stand.
> The hard wood keeps grinding past him.
> . . .
> The lights and fires are going out.
> He weeps for them.
> The blood pours from everywhere.
> He can feel it spilling from his mouth, his
> ears, his eyes, and his nose.
> The drone of flies gets louder.
> The world goes away.
> The night has come. (308–9)

Simon is indeed "like some weird saint"; the mythical resurrection of his still terribly wounded child's body at the end of the book is a partial miracle offering spiritual as well as corporeal renewal. But one must cast aside memory to believe in miracles.

Let me return to the characters' travels. After knowing one another for only a short time, the three travel together to the South Island for three weeks—a time that is fraught with tension and violence after Kerewin discovers Simon's wounds from prior beatings. Several months later, after Joe almost kills Simon, the three travel in separate directions. Following a long and only partial recovery in the hospital, Simon is displaced further from his Maori adoptive extended family, including grandparents, his uncle Piri, and cousins, all of whom care deeply for him. Because they are Maori and he is not, he is not allowed to return to them but is instead put in an orphanage and later a foster home. Wherever he is "placed" as a ward of the court, he runs away, determinedly seeking his father and Kerewin.

During the extended period while Simon is still in the hospital, the two adults, driven by guilt and remorse, tear down Kerewin's tower. Before setting out on her journey, Kerewin creates a sculpture of the heads of all three individuals, the two adults intertwined in Simon's long hair; when she finishes the work, she places it in the middle of the tower's wooden ruins and sets it afire. After months in jail Joe travels to the seashore on an isolated point of the North Island and attempts unsuccessfully to kill himself. On the South Island Kerewin, meanwhile, has become very ill with a strange, seemingly malignant growth in her belly. By the book's end both Kerewin and Joe—traveling in opposite directions—have recovered from their physical and emotional wounds. The mysterious hard lump in Kerwin's abdomen has vanished after her near-death experience and intervention from a strange, ungendered figure with a burned scar over half its face. She finds herself able to draw and paint, and one of her first undertakings is to rebuild a Maori meeting house nearby. Joe's broken arm, which he injured trying to kill himself by jumping off a bluff, is also healed by a liminal figure—a very old man, "the *kaumatua*," or elder, with an archaic tattoo of two blue lines across his face, who tells Joe he has been waiting all his life for Joe to appear and who dies before Joe is gone. The *kaumatua* is the keeper of the *mauri*, the life principle associated with the remains of an original *waka* and "a little god." Before he dies, he turns this responsibility over to Joe. Their journeying brings both Kerewin and Joe to the brink of death but also back to life and to a growing sense of reciprocity and responsibility toward others.

Such renewal comes for Kerewin at the hand of an androgynous figure, "a thin wiry person of indeterminate age. Of indeterminate sex. Of indeterminate race" (424). For Joe, the *kaumatua* serves the same purpose of providing what is necessary for healing: providing "the little god"—one of many and thus a replacement for a monolithic patriarchal figure. Each of these liminal figures is marked: the small, androgynous, unraced person, with a massive burn scar over half its face; the elder, with the archaic blue tattoo. Again here are conflicting (and conflicted) myths that raise questions concerning what it means to be marked by a wound and what purpose wounding serves. The keloid burn scar, the double-lined blue tattoo: these are at once forms of wounding and forms of beauty, signs of scarring and signs of redemption.

All these travels eventually come full circle with the reunion of Kerewin, Joe, and Simon and their families and friends. In the end the shell house that Kerewin builds around the ruins of her tower "holds them all in its spiralling embrace" (442)—a newly shaped home space that contains the memory of evil but also testifies to transformation. At the reunion Joe sees his own guilt mirrored in everyone's eyes, with "memory in all the eyes round him, furtive glances that rake him, all saying, The quick light is dimmed, the dancer's grace is gone. Damn you." In his wounded son's eyes, however, he finds "no sign of reproach": "The unlevel gaze is bright, brimming, but every time I look, the loveshine's there" (443). And so these perilous, near fatal journeys end in reconciliation and accommodation, or seem to. The memory of the quick light, the dancer's grace, remains, as does the reader's memory of wounds, of what making wounds and being wounded feels like.

So the ending of this book is both believable and unbelievable. The kind of traveling I am required to undertake as a reader of this text, whether Hulme intended it or not, prepares me for this unsettling ambiguity, this insistence on a thick complexity that is both cultural and psychological. I am overtaken by, submerged in, the consciousness of each character: the mere twitch of an impulse, a tooth-grinding fury, the buzz of a fly in the ear. I learn things that no one else knows: that Simon's secret name for himself, probably from his past life, is "Clare"; that Joe, who has had at least one sexual relationship with a man, may have sexually abused Simon; that Kerewin spends the day as a mute to try to understand the child's reality. *The Bone People* requires that you read it to the bone for what is below the surface, for what keeps rattling. And that is why, even though I've seen evidence to the contrary, I sometimes believe that such things can happen: towers can be rebuilt into spirals. The wounded can walk (although he is still crippled). North and South can become connected by travel. People can journey from what they are to what they are not.

Yet this book's optimism is disturbing as well. Its turn toward one belief system is haunted by the wounds of another. Its journey is perilous because its destination is so alluring. The novel works brilliantly against its own desires. There is a spatial contingency, a permeability here—an opening to something else. I am compelled to read beyond this ending.

The persuasiveness of such a journey lies in my willingness as a reader to travel both inside and outside the experiences of these characters, to gauge the architectonics of distance as well as contiguity. It is necessary to withhold judgment. Nor am I allowed to linger anywhere long enough to get comfortable, to rest. Constant mobility is required; I am always conscious of fluctuation and instability, both within these characters' minds and in what passes between them, and between them and myself as reader. Hulme expresses this process of mutability in the foreword to her second book, a collection of stories entitled *Te Kaihau: The Windeater:* "We are transit points and blubbery highways and temporarily fluid screens; indeed we are a finity of things to every light wave and every light particle and sonic particle and sonic wave, but mainly somewhere to pass through in a hurry without so much as a by-yr-lve or a pardon" (10). This kind of fluidity is true also of the cultural space of this book. *The Bone People*'s insistence on bilingualism—the Maori words, which I must look up in the glossary, are often the most important utterances on a page—gives a sense of a book without borders; what is "native" and what is "foreign," what is Western and what is indigenous, become so complexly intermingled that distinguishing one from the other is impossible.[12]

This book passes through us as much as we pass through it. So what I have said thus far about *The Bone People*—these matters of fact, myth, interpretation—are only part of the journey I would like to compel you to take with this book. Let me begin again, following its spiraling directions, this time mapping the interior journey, the space down through consciousness rather than the path across cultures. One moment. One afternoon. A woman and a boy survey each other.

First the woman, Kerewin.

When she first discovers the child, Simon, in her window, she sees him as within a frame: "Nasty, Gnomish." A "cold cutting anger" sweeps through her (16). How dare "it" invade her inner sanctum, the borders of her invincible tower? The next day Simon appears again, however, standing on her doorstep with a peace offering of four mutton birds and a valuable rosary that he insists on giving her. She allows him to stay, and they manage to communicate: she speaks and he writes on his pad. She has noticed that one side of his mouth is toothless.

Then the child, Simon.

He is lying this afternoon on Kerewin's floor thinking about the day before. He had been on the window sill, framed, the ground far below. If he had jumped in or out, he would have badly injured his already wounded body. So he remained, "stiff and horribly scared" (72). Simon is remembering this fearful experience as he lies quietly on Kerewin's floor, having charmed his way into her good graces. Kerewin and Joe have met, and Simon is hopeful that they will be friends. He will have somewhere to go. He is thinking about beginnings. A visionary, he sees Kerewin as "big and strong . . . stronger than Joe . . . covered with flames like knives . . . a fierce hidden flame inside it, that sometimes dimmed taking all the overlights with it" (73). Wordless as always, he has just kissed her hand. Kerewin, who hates to be touched, is appalled.

This particular afternoon Kerewin gives Simon a pencil so that he can draw, but he instead lies quietly on the floor, flat on his face, thinking his hopeful thoughts. Kerewin is drawing with charcoal. "Near an oily-looking smudge," she suddenly knows that for the first time in a long while she has captured something. When she supplies a border of red-brown chalk, the drawing becomes charged with viciousness and spatial entrapment—"an encroaching fungus that spreads gradually but with terrible sureness to the thing that whines and wriggles and can't get out from between the prisoning chasms that bite down to it like knives" (73).

Her vision violently resists affinity. Like Maui trapped within the woman's body, it is sealed, airtight.

As Kerewin struggles with her drawing, Simon keeps still and quiet because he wants to stay. He is overwhelmed with joy that Kerewin and Joe have become friends, but "the horror was still at home in him. It was almost always there. The only defence he could raise against the dark and the horror and the laughing terrible voice were his golden singers, the sounds and patterns of words from the past that he had fitted to his own web of music. . . . So he lay prone on the floor, and listened to them, and made Kerewin part of them, part of his heart" (73). His sound waves open Simon to Kerewin. Through sound, he frames (inaccurately) her openness to him. His golden singers erase borders; her painting enforces them. We are simultaneously drawn in two directions, toward openness and toward closure. We are not sure which will prevail.

As "the hours sing by" for Simon, Kerewin meanwhile has sprayed varnish over the "creeping fungus with its screaming centre," solidifying it. She tries to work on a pattern of scrolls and curves, to no avail. She is pleased with her fungus drawing and its harsh, thick border, however, thinking: "Another real thing! I am not dead yet! I can still call forth a piece of soul and set it down in color, fixed forever" (74). Hours later she suddenly remembers that Simon is in the room and asks him to come look at the drawing. His response is instantaneous: "He doesn't like it, his face whitening, and his eyes going darker still. He cups one finger in his other hand, tightens the hand as the finger tries to get away" (74). Yet Kerewin is pleased by his dramatization of spatial entrapment; obviously she wants him to get the message that she is closed to his entreaties, and so she

> grins with triumph and delight. "That is it!" hands on hips. "That is exactly what I wanted to show. And even you see it!" "What have you done?" and picks up the pad before he can take it. "Nothing?"
>
> Nothing. (74)

Simon's dreams—of a beginning, an opening—do seem at this point to come to nothing, as he himself realizes when he sees Kerewin's drawing. (Note the fluctuating consciousnesses here: "'Nothing?' Nothing.") While he has been doing such dreaming, Kerewin has been grinding in her screaming border, until it becomes the violent signature of her own enclosure. Simon sees this in a flash. Weeks later when she looks at her canvas, she also will see it for what it is:

> She stares at the screaming painting.
> The candlelight wavers.

> The painting screams silently on.
> She hates it.
> It is intensely bitter.
>
> O unjoy, is that all I can do? Show
> forth my misery? (91)

This interchange between Simon's dreaming and Kerewin's art is a material excavation of the spatial project of *The Bone People:* the novel's redesign of the architecture of the border. Created from grief and guilt after Simon is in the hospital, Kerewin's sculpture connecting the three of them invents another dimension in which borders are not so much erased as attenuated. Kerewin's emotional spatiality has changed, and so has her art. The sculpture, however, must cover over memory to show Simon's unbroken smiling face; Kerewin's last views of Simon, after his beating, were quite different. As she tries to find the boy's unbroken face under her hands, she remembers the last two times she saw him: "The bloody swollen mask on the floor, broken nose and broken jaw. And the horrible indentation in the side of his skull where he had been smashed against the door frame. Or neatened, whitened, bandaged with care, but looking lifeless. O, his eyes had opened several times, but the seacolour had gone and he didn't see her. He didn't see anyone or anything. His eyes look dead" (314).

So the sculpture is both an optimistic and a troubling icon. It is heavy with the memory of violence that it has covered over; it makes whole the face of the broken one. When Kerewin makes the sculpture, it is believed that Simon has incurred irreversible brain damage. He is also blind and deaf from his injuries (he recovers somewhat by the end). She is pressed by guilt over her culpability in Joe's act. Deeply angered at Simon because he had stolen her prize knife and broken her treasured guitar, she agreed with Joe, who had promised not to beat Simon again without her permission, that he should physically punish Simon even though she knew full well that Joe would brutalize the boy. (That day, unknown to either Joe or Kerewin, Simon had found a local pedophile dead in a pool of his own blood and, in a fury of unexpressed fear, broke shop windows all over town.) Kerewin is culpable in Simon's injuries, and she knows it. The sculpture thus speaks both Kerewin's guilt and her overwhelming wish that this story had ended differently. "For the first time in a year, she knows exactly what she wants to make and how to make it. Beads of clay flattened, beads of clay raised. Day by day, the three faces grow. The blunt blind features become definite, refined, awake. Back of head to back of head to back of head: a tricephalos" (314).

At different points both Joe and Simon find the sculpture. Joe sees it before his trial, when the clay faces are still dark and damp. As he circles the triple head, he sees how Simon's long hair curves to link Kerewin to Joe. Joe covers the tricephalos with trembling hands, thinking, "Aue! She saw us as a whole, as a set. And soon we'll be parted forever. (Not forever, not forever, not forever.)" (315). When Simon runs away from his foster home after being released from the hospital, he finds his way back to what has become the ruins of Kerewin's tower and comes across the sculpture in the midst of the ashes and cinders before he is recaptured.

> Gone beyond thinking, drawn forward by his hands, he kneels in front of the thing. There are shadows and voices coming towards him, from all sides over the lawn. It is Kerewin, it is Joe, turning around the third face, aiee it is me, and even though he is moaning aloud, somewhere in the cloudy anguish a thready voice says, Together, all together, a message left for you, and he clasps it to his chest as hard as he can, and will never let it go. Not even when the hands come down on his shoulders, and take him again. (410)

Kerewin's three-faced, multigendered sculpture becomes the spatial incarnation of the resolution *The Bone People* spirals toward; this is a story of great emotional urgency, a story not of romance or sexual relation but of a profound spiritual union of three people—a union *that moves outside the space of social relations built on gender.*

The question for readers becomes: how do we move around this icon? Do we gather it up, in comfort? Do we, like Joe and Simon, embrace its beauty, its narrative of reconciliation and accommodation? Can we also see it as a brilliantly vexed woman artist's (Kerewin's? Hulme's?) depiction of a trinity whose intactness relies on the crucifixion of the son, who can indeed be resurrected whole? Hulme seems to want us to see Kerewin's sculpture as the spatial embodiment of book's new ending, a new beginning. "*We're nearing the end now, soul of the book. We're coming to the new beginning,*" Kerewin tells us (435). What has happened is "past, but we live with it forever," Joe thinks in the last scene of reunion, when he sees the memory of his deeds in the eyes of relatives and friends. The end is the beginning; the spiral brings the return and the expansion, the reaching out and the drawing in. The consolation and the consolidation. So Joe thinks as he watches his wounded son and sees only joy and forgiveness: "Hupe nose and eyes dripping as though this is a tangi, not a return. So gather him up, gather him in, arms tight full, and spin round and round and round in a giddy dance of ecstasy, aching with love to give, smothered by love in return" (443). Kerewin's dream during her recovery, in which "the land is clothed in beauty and the people sing" (428), has come true. There is a redemptive quality to this ending/beginning: "It is dawn, indeed it is dawn, and bright broad daylight braiding our home" (445).

This newly born triad does not mark the home of a heterosexual nuclear family. Kerewin has adopted Simon, but he is very much the child of an extended Maori family. She loves Joe, but not romantically. Their end is perhaps the beginning of another kind of family, a redefinition of what family can become within the spiral that attenuates rather than fixes borders. This is, as I've said, a book that works at being hopeful.

What has been excluded in this final moment in which the space of the sculpture becomes the space of life? The end of the book suggests an answer to this question. There is an odd passage near the end, the culmination of a series of passages that have to do with homosexuality. Joe has a homosexual cousin, Luce, who is depicted throughout the book as a sleazy, repulsive man. He makes his last appearance about a page from the end of the book when, "elegantly dressed in katipo colours," he glides up at the reunion to Joe, Simon, and Joe's brother, Piri. Here is the conversation and Joe's thoughts during it:

> "Happy, Hohepa?"
> "Yes, Luce." Get lost.
> "With everything, cos? Every tiny thing?"
> "No, Luce." Bugger off.
> [Luce] stirs [Simon's] silvergold hair with one cool finger. Not deep enough to touch the skull, enough to make his cool point.
> The gentleness goes from his tired son's eyes, and something iron and quick takes its place. The fingers veer up into Luce's face, effoff. Right on, tama.
> "Manners need mending too," lidded mean gaze turned back to Joe.
> "Piss off, Luce," says Piri, handing the child back. Right on, Piri. (But all the while, the old man while, instinct fought against my clavicle and told me sin, hop in, the livin' water's warm. No way. Not that way ever again.) (444–45)

I have quoted this passage in full because I find Joe's parenthetical thoughts puzzling. Let me situate them in relation to several other similarly troubling scenes earlier in the text. Both Luce and the pedophile Binny Daniels occupy a space of trouble in the text. Each of Luce's two prior appearances in the text precipitates a beating for Simon. In an earlier scene, Luce tells Joe, whom he calls his "kissing coz," that by going to Binny Daniels' house Simon is following in Joe's footsteps, adding, "Well maybe *not* footsteps but you'll gather my meaning hmmm?" Joe is furious and threatens Binny, calling him a "stinking old faggot" (133–

34). He then goes home and beats Simon "until he grovels on the floor, gone beyond begging for it to stop" (136).

Luce's reference to the son's following in the father's footsteps is further elaborated in a later scene that occurs during the three weeks that Kerewin, Joe, and Simon spend at the beach at Moerangi, on the South Island. Joe is lying in bed with Simon sleeping in his arms. As he lies there holding his son, he realizes that he is aroused and begins to masturbate and think back to a conversation with Luce which had ended in a fight with his cousin, after which he went home and again beat Simon until the boy fainted. In the conversation Luce had reminded Joe of his affair with a man named Taki and teased him about kissing his son:

> "The look in your eyes, Hohepa, when you talk and kiss, my god, it's hot enough to turn me on at twenty paces distant, let alone the pretty child himself. . . . And the way he kisses back . . . did you teach him? From Taki? Not from Hana, I guarantee. . . ."
>
> "Shut your mouth about Hana and shut your mouth about Taki. That's dead past and not to be spoke. . . ."
>
> "O, I told him, dear. And do you know? He giggled. Fondly. Dear old Daddy, he loved the idea. Positively delighted in—" (174)

Another ambiguous passage. Did Luce tell Taki that Joe was kissing Simon? Did he tell Simon that his father had been in a relationship with Taki? Whatever they mean, Luce's comments provoke Joe to punch his gay cousin in the nose, get very drunk, and go home to jerk Simon from bed and viciously beat the boy. What is even more disturbing is the sense that, in beating his son, Joe is trying to purge his own homosexual desire.

Here is the father beating the son.

> Muttering "Fallen boy, fallen boy," and remembering the sadsweet months with Taki. I knew it was wrong. I know it was unnatural, but he was gentle, he was kind, I loved him and it was good. . . . The child had crawled part way back to his bedroom. The tired sick way he moves, the mess of him, his cringing, the highpitched panting he makes instead of any normal cry—e this thing is no child of mine, levering the body to his feet and pinning him against the wall, and punching him in the face and body until he whitens horribly and faints a second time. And he had picked up the unconscious child with no feeling except hate in his heart, and thrown him on the bed. He had fallen loose and broken, and lay unmoving, sprawled still as if dead for hours. (175)

Back to the present. Joe is still masturbating in the bunk with Simon in his arms (itself a disturbing image) and Luce's comments on his mind:

"His rage mounted. Laugh at me, will he? Laugh, eh?" Joe's thoughts turn to Simon: "I kiss him too much. I hold him too much. Don't think on it, play each day as it comes. . . . don't drink so much, don't do such things again. Forget it" (175). He then begins to cry and whisper: "Ka nui taku mate, ka nui taku mate" (175; the glossary translates this as "I'm really sick" [448]). Again there is ambiguity. When Joe tells himself, "don't do such things again," I'm not sure whether he means violence and sex or just violence. Regardless, Joe seems to have conflicted sexual feelings about the boy, which result in extreme brutality. The final parenthetical eschewal of "sin" leaves me wondering what specific sin, what "livin' water."

This queer space in the text also emerges less obtrusively in connection with Kerewin, who is far from being traditionally feminine. She beats Joe in her anger over his violence with his son. She builds her own tower and tears it down. She "grew up in a boat" (207) and teaches Joe and Simon about fishing. In the end it is she who takes responsibility for Simon and gives him her name. She claims not to have sexual feelings—clearly she seems to have none for Joe—but is called a lesbian in bars and receives (but evades) sexual overtures from lesbians. After the healer of indeterminate sex leaves her, she ponders indeterminacy while giving herself her first bath after recovering: "The neuter personal pronoun; ve/ver/vis, I am not his, vis/ve/ver, nor am I for her, ver/vis/ve, a pronoun for me, (slopping another tin of water out ready)" (426). Her connection with Joe at the end of the book is neither romantic nor sexual; instead, it has to do with a sense of responsibility and family: "Art and family by blood; home and family by love . . . regaining any one was worth this fiery journey to the heart of the sun" (428).

The Bone People leaves me pondering the indeterminate relation of its contradictory queer spaces. Its already uneasy feminist and postcolonial resolutions are further complicated by these gender travels. Like Hulme's manipulations of conflicting mythic and cultural systems of belief, these contradictions—intensified by memory, desire, and guilt—keep the narrative unsettled and troubled. Joe seems to hate his own sexual impulses and equate homosexuality with pedophilia, perhaps because Luce's taunts about his behavior with his son are true. Yet Kerewin triumphantly carries her gender trouble with her as she leads Joe and Simon away with a song at the end of the book, "throwing away sparks of words" (445).

To its final words, "TE MUTANGA-RANEI TE TAKE" (445), "the end—or the beginning," *The Bone People* works against its own drive toward resolution and salvation and continues to insist on the multiple dimensionality of life, on the complexity of sex, violence, love, and power. The novel rattles with indeterminacy. Violence and remorse can occur in the same moment. The child beater or molester can also love his child, and the child can love him back. Sexuality, like everything else, must be marked by responsibility to and for another. Nothing alive can be accommodated within the bounded verticality of the tower; everything is imaginable within the perpetual motion of the spiral. "Even paired, any pairing, they would have been nothing more than people by themselves. But all together, they have become the heart and muscles and mind of something perilous and new, something strange and growing and great" (4).

But what is that something? It is surely strange; it is surely perilous. It is what Barbara Johnson calls "those impossible contradictions that cannot yet be spoken" (*Feminist Difference* 13) but are crucial for feminist engagements with the complexity that is cultural work. That something—that something *else*—seems to reside in the gap between the journey toward what we want to find, the lost and lovely nest of home, and the memories and wounds that take us on another journey, a hidden quirk in the spiral: destination unknown.

EPILOGUE: CLIMBING *THE WALL*, KEEPING THE HOUSE

Each time I read Marlen Haushofer's *Die Wand* in its 1990 English translation,[1] I have to tell myself it's only a book. With this most recent reading, the space of *The Wall* perforated the tender thread of summer. It made this insidiously sunny time, this bright early onset of global warming, seem clutched by some giant hand and twisted into darkness. Now at night I dream that I am an unnamed middle-aged woman who, on a weekend in the Austrian countryside, finds herself cut off from the world by a transparent wall, behind which living people, including her two daughters, have been turned to stone. This woman writes her "report" of two and a half years, bereft of all human companionship, until her paper runs out; then the book is over.

This sounds like a simple, accessible book, but it is not. Hugo Caviola has rightly noted that *Die Wand* is an aesthetically and philosophically complex postmodern text which makes complicated demands on its readers (102). Reading *The Wall* I have felt keenly apart. This is a vast loneliness, not easily shaken or explained.

The Wall is about entrapment, anxiety, isolation, writing but receiving no reply. But in its own time and space this book grows into something else, its cumulative effect being akin to something hidden in the yard that seems to emerge overnight and out of nowhere, large, full blown, and shockingly beautiful. A hibiscus perhaps. "Loneliness led me, in moments free of memory and consciousness, to see the great brilliance of life again," writes the narrator. This is what the book does; it impels one into a space where the narrator's loneliness and almost tangible perception of the incommensurable dilute and elide the demarcation lines of identity. Reading *The Wall* one journeys across a great divide, beyond the self. "Sometimes," the narrator writes, "my thoughts grow confused, and it is as if the forest has put down roots in me, and is thinking its old, eternal thoughts with my brain. . . . It was almost impossible, in the buzzing stillness of the meadow, beneath the big sky, to remain a single and separate Self, a little, Blind, independent life that didn't want to fit in with a greater Being" (161).

It is loneliness for those who are not ourselves that sends us out to travel such spaces. It is also loneliness that keeps us inside and moves us to shore up the house. *The Wall* reminds me of Marilynne Robinson's *Housekeeping,* where loss becomes so large that the lonely ones cannot settle, and there must be an end to housekeeping. For the girl Ruthie and her aunt Sylvie, adrift in train boxcars, loss and need blossom so lushly that need becomes the lost thing itself. Desire sets in motion the imagined compensation: "to wish for a hand on one's hair is all but to feel it" (Robinson 153). Loss requires that desire stay in motion, so the production of *Housekeeping* is a vortex that leads ever outward; "loss pulls us after it" (194). The space of loss is infinite because the imagination is forever producing and reproducing that which has been lost. But there is always the gap between that which has been lost and one's imagining of it, and that gap is what drives the productions of the imagination, keeping Ruthie and Sylvie on the move.

There is this same piercing sense of loss in *The Wall,* but the production that comes from it is of a different sort: here is the production of housekeeping, cultivation, and harvest. Propelled by the death of the mother, *Housekeeping* produces a space of loss so chasmic that no end to it can be discerned. Propelled by what seems to be the death of all humankind, *The Wall* builds its own walls around loss and keeps the house. This is the labor of love, of looking after, of keeping the house for those who require shelter and food. The narrator's keenest losses are felt when housekeeping fails and violence tears the house. But violence ultimately fails in the face of housekeeping. "As long as there's something for me to love in the forest," the weary and heartsick narrator writes in her journal, "then I shall love it; and if some day there is nothing, I shall stop living" (140).

At the end of the story, having lost almost all her animals, including her beloved companion, a Bavarian bloodhound named Lynx, to a murderous stranger with an ax, the narrator ends her report. She has run out of paper. What is on her mind as evening draws nigh? The devastated narrator is thinking about an albino crow, the outcast of a flock that visits daily, isolated by the others, prevented from sharing food. While there is still enough light, she must feed it. The final lines of the book are these: "The crows have risen, and circle screeching over the forest. When they are out of sight I shall go to the clearing and feed the white crow. It will already be waiting for me" (244).

I want to end my book by trying to describe what it is like to read Marlen Haushofer's. Her book is an emergency journey; this reading, an acute form of travel. *The Wall*—originally published in 1963 and pretty much forgotten, republished twenty years later in West Germany, and published in English by Cleis Press in 1990—is about nothing more than the daily, ordinary labor of taking care of one's self and the well-loved animals in one's purview and nothing less than saving the world. The cultural work this book undertakes is immense and profound. *The Wall* is about how to keep the house while the moment of the last piece of paper, the last match, the last breath, draws ever nearer. It is about feeding the white crow, keeping life alive in a world of death. It is about the production, within confinement, of a social space of caretaking that folds into time, into history. In the complicated relationship between the narrator, who writes these messages, and the reader, who replies to them, space pulsates in the moment, containing within it a past and a future. "I can see a little further ahead," the narrator writes toward the end of the book: "I can see that this isn't the end. Everything goes on. Since this morning I've been absolutely sure that Bella will have a calf. And, who knows, perhaps there will be kittens again. Bull, Pearl, Tiger and Lynx will never exist again, but something new is coming and I can't escape that" (243).

Haushofer prematurely left the world she wanted to save. Born in 1920 in Frauenstein, a region in upper Austria, and coming of age during the rise of Hitler's National Socialist party, she died of cancer in 1970 before she turned fifty. She was of my mother's generation of women, the prefeminist generation who knew much more than I do about the precariousness of small places and spaces, the vicissitudes of travel.[2]

> I hear you calling me,
> Lovely Vienna, so gay, so free.
> City of love and sparkling wine,
> You're such a part of this heart of mine.[3]

As I write this, Haushofer would be three months past her seventy-eighth birthday; my mother, who used to sing that song about Haushofer's shattered country though she was never able to heed its call, would be a year younger. The mere first half of Haushofer's half-century of life—her first twenty-five years—spanned the rise of fascism, World War II, and the advent and demonstration of nuclear destruction. The second half she lived in the shadow of the cold war. *The Wall* has been seen as Haushofer's response to the latter—a bleak depiction of nuclear holocaust as well as a "metaphor for the estrangement that women experience in a male-dominated society" (Kecht 11)—but the narrative also seems imbued with an overwhelming and spreading sense of dread that Haushofer's early adult experiences of a rapidly enclosing fascist military enterprise might have elicited in her fiction. A friend who knows nothing of Haushofer's life says: "This book is like living with terminal cancer, except the world is it, rather than it being in you."

The wall, which seals the narrator both in and out, is invisible, like the web of social relations that created it, transparent until touched, "a smooth, cool resistance where there could be nothing but air . . . [,] a terrible, invisible thing" (8). When the narrator first discovers the wall, it is littered on her side with the bloodied corpses of birds that, deluded by its transparency, have smashed into its clear surface. She can see through to death on the other side, a still, timeless world of corpses in halted motion. The moment her hand rests on "something like a window-pane," her body responds viscerally. She writes, "I heard a loud knocking sound and glanced around before realizing that it was my own heartbeat thundering in my ears. My heart had been frightened before I knew anything about it" (8). There is something terrifying about this moment when the illusion of transparency fails, when the spatial misjudgment created by such an illusion is exposed. Why does the narrator's body quake when she touches a thing she can see through? Why is Haushofer's wall transparent instead of stolid and massive, like the Berlin Wall? In some ways the wall is like this text; it seems crystalline but is thickly composed of the invisible social productions that created it to appear so.

One of the first things the narrator does on discovering the wall is to begin marking its boundary with sticks, a labor that takes her miles and miles from her sister and brother-in-law's hunting lodge in the mountains until she understands that the wall is probably infinite. This terror of transparency—the illusion of clarity, the present but unseeable—becomes a cryptic site of fascination and thriving dread in this story. This novel seems to be about something you think you can see through to but can't; something that exceeds and disengages subject-object relations and, in so doing, reconfigures space itself. If one thinks that one can see, then space is absolutely knowable and "wholly representable . . . [,] real, natural and unproblematic" (G. Rose 38): when this illusion is shattered, all other illusions fall away. Space is no longer empty. Danger abounds because space is released into the arenas of time and social relations. This is because the illusion of transparency offers a sense of space as innocent and trustworthy, with nothing hidden or dangerous, with everything available to illumination and contemplation (Lefebvre 28).

It is interesting, then, to consider the extent to which this novel is laden with historical memory. Donald Daviau argues that because Austria had no direct responsibility for Hitler's regime, "there was no necessity in Austria for the writers to remind their readers of their implication in the war," as writers in Germany's "Gruppe 47" were doing in the postwar years (9). Yet Haushofer's novel—and its central metaphor—seems to insist on cultural memory. The wall (and *The Wall*) makes transparency visible, revealing the deceptiveness of a concept of space as static and ahistorical. Space becomes linked to time and the dynamism of social relations, the tangible effects of power. Seeing as a way of knowing—humanism's master narrative—becomes suspect; a perception of space as empty or unchanging, as bereft of social relations, is unthinkable.

When the wall is revealed, the productions that made the wall leap into being, and the spatial becomes the site of the incommensurability in which gender relations, like other social processes, manifest themselves. Haushofer is noted for her depictions of the irreconcilability between male and female spheres (Vansant 141). In her current situation the narrator is afraid of men; she knows they are stronger than she is and can take what they want from her. Despite her loneliness, she hopes to avoid any men who may be alive in the countryside. The narrator's worst fears conspire, and the most terrible things, like the wall itself, happen out in the open spaces where the narrator tries to see but senses she is the seen before the transparency of the potential gaze. (I'm reminded of Daphne Spain's comments on the gendering of structural workplace arrangements, which put women clerical workers either behind glass or on the "open floor," where they can be watched and interrupted [211–12].)

For the narrator of *The Wall,* the hunting lodge in the misty mountain gorge becomes a space of enclosure and protection; the *Alm,* or high open meadow, where she must take her cow and bull in the summer to graze, seems strangely and obversely menacing. So that which is closed, the lodge, seems open; that which is open, the meadow, feels like a trap about to spring. The meadow makes the narrator uneasy, certainly with seeing and by implication with the potential of being seen: "It was strange to be able to survey a wide area, unimpeded by mountains and trees. And it wasn't immediately pleasant and liberating. My eyes had to get used to the distance first" (151). The self cannot hold its own borders in the high mountain meadow and melts within that vast incommensurable space. This experience is epiphanic for the narrator, but she recognizes the incommensurable's threat to housekeeping. She is torn between the meadow, which "lay outside of time," exuding "a mild narcotic called oblivion" (158–59), and the valley, where she can keep house in the hunting lodge: "It was strange; as soon as I was in the valley I thought about the *Alm* almost with fear and revulsion; but from the pasture I couldn't imagine living in the valley. It was as if I consisted of two quite different people, one of whom could exist only in the valley, while the other was beginning to flourish in the *Alm*. It all scared me a little, because I couldn't understand it" (160). The murderous man who kills Lynx and Bull does so in the meadow, in broad daylight, and Lynx is killed because the narrator prevents him from attacking the man. Loyally abiding by his beloved mistress's orders, the dog becomes an easy target for the ax in the middle of the open meadow.

Early on the narrator quickly learns that her physical and mental salvation lies in an opposition to transparency, in daily and seasonal productions of hard labor and social interaction with her animals, in the knowledge that much remains unseen within the dynamic of space-time. She performs this backbreaking work as much for her animals—a crotchety cat with a succession of kittens; Bella, the cow, and her "son-husband," Bull; the beautiful and loyal dog Lynx; and even the white crow—as for herself. As she grows her beans and potatoes, harvests the hay for Bella and Bull, cuts wood for the fire, and nurses her animals' wounds, the narrator and her animals produce a social space that counters the ethic of destruction manifested in the wall. This social space requires dismantling borders between species, and this dismantling seems subtly linked to a radical reconceptualization of relations among living beings.

This space and this book are deeply gendered, but ambiguously so. On *The Wall*'s back cover Doris Lessing writes, "It is not often that you can say only a woman could have written this book, but women in particular will understand the heroine's loving devotion to the details of making and keeping life, every day felt as a victory against everything that would like to undermine and destroy." This is true, perhaps, but the narrator's survival also depends on her *not* being "a woman." Although Haushofer was recognized for her fiction during her lifetime, her complex books with their critical perspectives on Western patriarchy were often misread and dismissed as the trivial records of neurotic women's lives (Horsley 25). When the narrator of *The Wall* looks in the mirror after two-and-a-half years of hard labor and sees herself as "more like a tree than a person, a tough brown branch that needs its whole strength to survive," she remembers her former self as such a woman:

> If I think today of the woman I once was, the woman with the little double chin, who tried very hard to look younger than her age, I feel little sympathy for her. But I shouldn't like to judge her too harshly. After all, she never had the chance of consciously shaping her life. When she was young she unwittingly assumed a heavy burden by starting a family, and from then on she was always hemmed in by an intimidating amount of duties and worries. Only a giantess would have been able to free herself, and in no respect was she a giantess, never anything other than a torment-

> ed, overtaxed woman of medium intelligence, in a world, on top of everything else, that was hostile to women and which women found strange and unsettling. . . . But I should like to grant her one thing: she always had a dim sense of discomfort, and knew that all this was far from enough. (69)

This seems to be a description of a woman who finds herself ill at ease in another kind of transparent space, one that is "strange and unsettling," at odds with self-determination and comfort. This woman was ill at ease in her body, "so ill armed for real life" that she couldn't hammer a nail properly (69). Gillian Rose maintains that transparent space "can be contextualized in terms of the discursive and visual engendering of the feminine body and in terms of the increasing specularity of certain cultures; and its costs for women can be immediate and painful" (159). Rose's statement that "being in space is not easy" provided me with an epigraph to this book. The wall frees the narrator from uneasily being in space in the engendered feminine body; she can now travel and inhabit a completely new world of social relations that exceed not only gender but also species. She has given transparency a shape; gender hangs loosely like an outworn garment: "My body, more skilful than myself, had adapted itself and limited the burdens of my femininity to a minimum. I could simply forget I was a woman. Sometimes I was a child in search of strawberries, or a young man sawing wood, or, when sitting on the bench holding Pearl on my scrawny lap watching the setting sun, I was a very old, sexless creature" (68–69).

I'm not sure, though, that the narrator really forgets she is a woman. And therein lies *The Wall*'s paradox, politics, and pleasure. This is a book that is filled with the dread of violence, and yet the narrator's determination to learn how to live in peace and harmony with the world of living creatures left to her, her insistence on keeping the house, begets a spatial dimension that exceeds the violence of the wall. Her habitation of loneliness is also a refusal of its consequences, a refusal of isolation, replacing it with a continual urge to establish bonds with whatever is left to her: animals, plants, trees. The narrator is compelled by loneliness to travel beyond its borders, even as she is locked inside (or outside) the wall that at once limits and expands her world. This does not mean that the wall disappears, only that it can be climbed. She wants to claim this dimension as female, this lovely, terrible need to take care, keep the "house":

> It was far less likely that I could help the animals to survive in the middle of the forest than that they would die. I've suffered from anxieties like these as far back as I can remember, and I will suffer from them as long as any creature is entrusted to me. Sometimes, long before the wall

> existed, I wished I was dead, so that I could finally cast off my burden. I always kept quiet about this heavy load; a man wouldn't have understood, and the women felt exactly the same way as I did. And so we preferred to chat about clothes, friends and the theatre and laugh, keeping our secret, consuming worry in our eyes. Each of us knew about it, and that's why we never discussed it. That was the price we paid for our ability to love. (59)

From the first the narrator tells us that Lynx and Bull are dead; she makes us know that violence is the cause. The wall itself testifies to a world obsessed with domination and death. "Loving and looking after another creature is a very troublesome business, and much harder than killing and destruction," observes the narrator. "It takes twenty years to raise a child, and ten seconds to kill it. It took the bull a year to grow big and strong, and a few strokes of an axe were enough to dispatch him" (140). Her report, which she has written over the four months of her third winter, is an effort to understand those terrible moments of violence the whole book both flows from and builds toward: not only the creation of the wall itself, with its destruction of humans and animals, but also the stranger who kills her animals and probably would have killed her had she not shot him first. (When I was writing the first draft of this chapter during the second week of August 1998, such questions seemed especially pertinent. Terrorist bombings in Kenya and Tanzania had killed more than 250 people, a large majority of them African, and wounded around 5,000, many critically. Today is 12 September 2001; the estimated death toll from the most recent acts of terrorism is mounting into the thousands in New York and Washington. The United States is planning invasions, strikes, more bloodshed. My neighbors next door have draped a giant American flag across their front porch. I had planned to put my final typescript in the mail today. Instead I stare out the window.) The narrator writes: "I don't understand what happened. Even today I wonder why the strange man killed Bull and Lynx. I'd called Lynx off, and he had to stand there defenceless, waiting for his skull to be caved in. I'd like to know why the strange man killed my animals. I'll never find out, and it may even be better that way" (243). Grimly, numbly, the narrator continues to live out her ethic of care.

> I dug a grave for Lynx in the evening. Under that shrub with the sweet smelling leaves. I dug the hole deep, laid Lynx into it, covered it with earth and stamped the grass down over it. And then I was very tired, more tired than ever before. I washed at the spring, then I went to Bella in the byre. She didn't give a drop of milk, and was still trembling. I gave her a tubful of water, but she wouldn't drink. Then I sat down on the bench

> and waited for the long night. It was a bright, starlit night, and the wind drifted coldly down from the cliffs. But I was colder than the wind and didn't feel the chill.
>
> Bella started roaring again. In the end I fetched my pallet and carried it to the byre. I lay down on it fully dressed. It was only then that Bella fell silent, and I think she fell asleep. (242)

What the narrator does is enclose violence within the complex multidimension of space and time. ("Animals have no sense of time," a pet sitter told me once. The narrator does not believe this, and neither do I. Bella knows that Bull got his skull smashed in that day. He died a terrible death. She remembers.) The narrator buries her beloved dog and comforts a cow that has witnessed her son being hacked to death. This is not transformative. There is no mythic scheme for redemption; this is simply all she can do. In this sense housekeeping becomes not repressive but recuperative; space becomes a nontransparent production of relations: complex and material. Such a feeling for space entails an ability to keep the house and at the same time to travel a tangled web of social relations outside the house. One keeps the house by climbing the wall; one climbs the wall by keeping the house. That which is small is also large; that which is local is also global. And vice versa.

The Wall is a "Global novel" as Maxine Hong Kingston has defined it (41). It is about living, not dying; it is not dependent on tragedy or violence, excitement or crisis, for the narrative pleasure it offers; it gives us "an idea of the humane beings that we may become" (37). A book that is at once profoundly gendered and ungendered, *The Wall* describes a woman who keeps and travels simultaneously and attentively, who is aware of her own smallness and largeness, her dependence and responsibility in the world and in relation to the world's life. This is a story of a metamorphosing identity that moves beyond its own gender, its own species. This woman who looks like a tree is no longer who she once was, the woman with the little double chin. The woman who was afraid to travel.

Throughout the novel the narrator's worst frustration is that she does not believe she can break out a wall in the hunting lodge to convert a bedroom into a byre for Bella, which would connect with the main room of the hunting lodge. She worries about this a great deal, but she does not think she has the strength or skill to attempt such a task. At the end of the book, however, she has come to believe that the project is within her power. "As soon as the weather turns warmer I shall set about converting the bedroom into Bella's new byre, and I'll also manage to break open the door. I still don't know how, but I'll definitely find a way. I shall be very close to Bella and the new calf, and shall watch over them day and night. Memories, mourning and fear will remain, and hard work, as long as I live" (243–44). The day of the last piece of paper has come already for the narrator; the day of the last match will also come. The house that has been kept will pass into dust. But *The Wall* contends that there is never an end to housekeeping—its pain, its pleasure, its politics. Because the transparency of the wall has been made discernible, the wall itself—and the social relations in place and history that both created and concealed it—remains marked, visible.

We are left with a lonely woman who plans to break down another wall. Her loneliness compels her to travel. The opening has not yet been made for the door, but now the opening has one other story. *The Wall* is a story of holding and keeping that travels, and makes travel imaginable and consequential in a world that cannot do without it.

What is a story like this worth?

Maybe everything.

NOTES

Introduction

1. Here Harjo seems to mean specifically the English language, as opposed to the speaker's, presumably Harjo's, Creek Muscogee tribal language. Harjo's question, however, resonates more generally with questions of language's limitations.

2. I discuss specific Deer Dances and Deer Woman stories later in this chapter.

3. Harjo's band, Poetic Justice, has also appealed to a wide audience in the United States and other countries, producing a kind of borderland of music, from jazz to Latin American to Native American, often with a synthesis of rhythms and styles.

4. As Michel de Certeau points out, "In modern Athens, the vehicles of mass transportation are called *metaphorai.* To go to work or come home one takes a "metaphor"—a bus or a train" (115). *The Oxford English Dictionary* traces *metaphor* to the Greek verb meaning "to bear" or "carry."

5. A notable example in recent U.S. feminism is Gloria Anzaldúa's invocation of the sandbar as a spatial metaphor to evoke the fluidity and shifting locations that can provide "more mobility and more freedom" for women of color involved in alliance-coalition work ("Bridge" 224).

6. See Margaret Higonnet's "Mapping the Text" and Kerstin Westerlund-Shands's "Transcending Gynocentric Space" for discussions of this trend, which will be discussed more fully in the first chapter of this book. Examples include Ruth Salvaggio's descriptions of the relations of feminist theory to spatiality and the spatial dynamics of feminist theory ("Theory and Space") and Teresa de Lauretis's notion of "the space-off" residing in "the margins of hegemonic discourses, social spaces carved in the interstices of institutions and in the chinks and cracks of power-knowledge apparati" (*Technologies of Gender* 25).

7. I first felt the guiltiness of the pleasure and sense of possibility I locate in space and space talk at a Rockefeller research conference sponsored by the Southwest Institute for Research on Women and held in Tucson in 1993. Expansively entitled "Making Worlds: Gender, Metaphor, Materiality," the conference drew thirty or so feminist scholars from the fields of geography, history, anthropology, law, architecture and urban planning, communications, literature, philosophy, political science, African American studies, women's

studies, American studies, and cultural studies, in addition to several women writers, artists, and political activists. Amid a landscape of yucca, saguaro, and aloe plants that dwarfed us all, strong claims were made for real spaces: mud huts in Sudanese villages, tribal configurations in Africa, Native American culture in the northwestern United States, Hispano claims to land and water rights in northern New Mexico. Many of those gathered in Tucson were understandably distrustful of the lush undergrowth of spatial language—the linguistic vineiness that has emerged in literary criticism and critical theory—transmogrifying into what a southerner like myself might have felt was a scary variety of kudzu that had overgrown and smothered serious theorizing about real places and real people.

8. Caren Kaplan explains the operation of metaphor thusly: "Metaphor proceeds by drawing upon a familiar and concrete set of meanings to clarify or explain another set of meanings that are far less familiar or distinct" (145). I would argue that certain kinds of writing strangely and beautifully elude such a definition.

9. See the work of Neil Smith and Cindi Katz, whom Kaplan quotes extensively.

10. Over the past decade there have been careful arguments, especially by feminists, that the social sciences have been self-limited by their refusal to acknowledge the constitutive complexities of language. In the field of history, for example, Joan Scott has expressed uneasiness about the way meaning itself—"evidence"—can seem transparent and thus be reproduced without contestation ("Evidence" 368). Scott calls for an analysis of language within the discipline of history, arguing that this is a task for which historians are ill prepared within the borders of a discipline that has constructed itself in opposition to literature. Scott's hope is for more complex, contradictory readings of history, readings for "the literary"—all that is discursively produced as "evidence." Such readings of history "would not assume a direct correspondence between words and things, nor confine itself to single meanings, nor aim for the resolution of contradiction" (383–85), thereby befitting a discipline devoted to the study of change.

More recently, the sociologist Laurel Richardson has noted the tensions and ironies of empirical methods that view language as a tool while simultaneously employing metaphors at a conceptual level to "prefigure judgments about the truth value of a text" (44). Richardson's own method in her book *Fields of Play: Constructing an Academic Life* (1997) is to rupture the control of "science" over all that is "nonscience" by writing science poetically. She tells stories, her own and those of others. She writes poems as ethnographies, ethnographies as poems.

11. I am grateful to Pamela Ryan's article "Black Women Do Not Have Time to Dream: The Politics of Time and Space" for calling my attention to this story.

12. This effect is related to Bakhtin's notion of *chronotope,* the fusion of space and time enacted in literature: "Time, as it were, thickens, takes on flesh, becomes artistically visible; likewise space, becomes charged and responsive to the movements of time, plot, and history" (84).

13. Even as I write this I realize that, of those peoples who inhabit highly or moderately literate cultures, women and other groups in the United States—not to speak of the world—have been excluded disproportionately from literacy. As Deborah Cameron observes, in global and historical terms illiteracy "has been crucial in silencing women and denying them opportunities for creative expression" and for a part in the shaping of culture (6).

More specifically, Alice Walker and Henry Louis Gates (and many others) have discussed in different contexts the profound and complex ways in which the U.S. history of African slavery has affected African American relations to reading and writing. Walker's much quoted "In Search of Our Mothers' Gardens" asks, "How was the creativity of the black woman kept alive, year after year and century after century, when for most of the years black people have been in America, it was a punishable crime for a black person to read or write?" (*In Search* 234). Also Gates's introduction to the 1985 anthology *"Race," Writing, and Difference,* entitled "Writing 'Race' and the Difference It Makes," shows how Europeans delimited writing as the "medium" for expressing reason and then denied Africans access to writing to deny them reason and hence humanity (8–9).

See also Caren Kaplan's book *Questions of Travel: Postmodern Discourses of Displacement,* from which I quoted earlier and which, following the work of James Clifford, Janet Wolff, and bell hooks, interrogates the term *travel* extensively.

14. Smith and Katz critique Clifford's notion of travel as offering a series of locations that do not change, "a multiplication of absolute spaces rather than a radical rethinking of spatial concepts" (79).

15. A Marxist, Lefebvre distrusts language as a facilitator of social transformation. Consider the following: "'Everything must be said! No time limit on speech! Everything must be written! Writing transforms language, therefore writing transforms society! Writing is a signifying practice!' Such agendas succeed only in conflating revolution and transparency" (29).

16. Soja believes that such an ontological situating of the human subject in "a formative geography"—that is, one which considers the mobile personal space of the body *and* "the more fixed communal locales of human settlements"—must necessarily lead to "a radical reconceptualization of epistemology, theoretical construction, and empirical analysis" (8).

17. Certain other themed spaces have been responsible for creating literary histories and thematics that have excluded the writing of women and many other groups.

18. Tracing the use of spatial metaphors in literary criticism, Margaret Higonnet makes a similar claim, citing the need to "multiply the schemes through which we frame our literary analyses [to] escape the confinement of binaries that regulate most of our systems of value" ("Mapping the Text" 210).

19. In the arena of literary criticism, specifically narratology, whose primary concern has been with time (e.g., the movement of plot and the reader's desire for plot), Friedman, drawing on Kristeva and Bakhtin, offers a rather neatly complementary argument—namely, that narrative itself is composed of the

representation of activity within the poles of both time and space ("Spatialization, Narrative Theory" 110). In *Mappings* Friedman examines narrative theorists' privileging of time over space, citing examples from E. M. Forster, Paul Ricoeur, James Phelan, and Peter Brooks (137).

20. Western critical theory has been configured spatially; yet, as Salvaggio has observed, feminist writers and thinkers such as Virginia Woolf, Elaine Showalter, and Julia Kristeva have envisioned their own spatial theories as being outside the metaphysical traditions that feed the production of Western male traditions. Within U.S. feminist theory, spatially oriented theories have emerged on many different cultural fronts. See, for example, Paula Gunn Allen's discussion of space she calls feminine in American Indian traditions (*Sacred Hoop*), Paula Bennett's and Elizabeth Meese's descriptions of lesbian erotic space (respectively, "Critical Clitoridectomy" and *(Sem)Erotics*), bell hooks's return to black women's home talk (*Talking Back*), Rachel Blau DuPlessis's extensions of female narrative spaces that "write beyond" patriarchal configurations (*Writing beyond the Ending*), Anzaldúa's "mestiza consciousness" (*Borderlands*), and Judith Butler's and Eve Sedgwick's queer spaces (respectively, *Gender Trouble* and *Tendencies*).

21. I am grateful to Patricia Clark Smith for information and insights concerning Deer Dances in the Southwest.

22. I am grateful to Beth Bailey for helping me clarify this point in our discussions of this material. Interestingly, in *The Predicament of Culture,* a book that virtually ignores women writers and feminist thinkers, Clifford makes a similar argument about ethnography. His topic, he writes, "is a mode of travel, a way of understanding and getting around in a diverse world" (13).

Chapter 1: Space Travel

This chapter developed as a joint presentation—a series of letters between Angelika Bammer, Cindi Katz, Elizabeth Meese, and myself—for the 1993 Southwest Institute for Research on Women interdisciplinary Rockefeller conference "Making Worlds: Metaphor and Materiality in the Production of Feminist Texts." I am grateful for their responses to my part in this letter-writing experiment, which did much to challenge and change my thinking, as did reactions and suggestions from conference participants and organizers. The chapter was first published in a different version as "Space Travel: The Connective Politics of Feminist Reading" in *Signs* 21.4 (Summer 1996). © 1996 by The University of Chicago. All rights reserved. It was also part of a coauthored essay (with Bammer, Katz, and Meese) entitled "The Place of the Letter: An Epistolary Exchange" in the volume that resulted from the conference: *Making Worlds: Gender, Metaphor, Materiality,* ed. Susan Hardy Aiken, Ann E. Brigham, Sallie A. Marston, and Penny M. Waterstone (Tucson: University of Arizona Press, 1998). © 1998 by the Arizona Board of Regents. Reprinted by permission of the University of Arizona Press. I also very much appreciate the vigilance of *Signs* editors Ruth-Ellen Boetcher Joeres and Barbara Laslett and the exacting questions posed by the anonymous readers of *Signs.*

1. Pondering these complex processes in *Mappings,* Friedman has called for a "locational feminism" to theorize multiple formations of identity and identity politics. In discussions of feminist critical practice and "Third World Women" of the 1980s and early 1990s, Chandra Mohanty has argued that enormous, multiple, and ever-changing networks of power relations connecting race, class, sexuality, and national interests come together in extremely complicated ways to create the way gender is experienced. These "relations of power," Mohanty maintains, "are not reducible to binary oppositions or oppressor/oppressed relations" but are much more intricate and complex (13).

2. The sculpture by Ellen Driscoll was entitled *The Loophole of Retreat* (*New York Times,* 27 Dec. 1991).

3. I hope that such a reading avoids what Carla Kaplan has called, in reference to a wide variety of readings of *Incidents,* an authorization of oneself "as the ideal listener for whom that text has been waiting" and thereby investing oneself with "a juridical position" (57).

4. See also Friedman, *Mappings,* on this point.

5. This is true even of material, built space. As Leslie Weisman has pointed out in relation to architecture and urban planning, space and its allocations in the material world "reflect and reinforce the nature of gender, race, and class relations in society" (1). Here Weisman is elaborating on Shirley Ardener's observations in the early 1980s that behavior and space are mutually dependent (Ardener 12). More specifically, in *Gendered Spaces* Daphne Spain focuses on the way spatial segregation by gender—both geographical and architectural—reduces women's access to knowledge and thus reproduces male power and privilege (3). Spain believes, with Edward Soja, that "space can be made to hide consequences from us, how relations of power and discipline are inscribed into the apparently innocent spatiality of social life" (Soja in Spain 28). Gendered spaces, according to Spain, whether they be the Mongolian *ger* or academic secretarial offices in the United States, contribute to the maintenance of prevailing status differences.

6. Juhasz, too, recounts the experience of going to the public library and returning home with piles of novels, which she would read voraciously in her favorite green chair.

7. The authors of the poem were Zenobia and Ruth Salvaggio.

8. See "The Uses of the Erotic" in Audre Lorde's *Sister Outsider.* More generally, Daniel Boyarin also discusses "the pervasive association of reading in the West with the private social spaces and meaning of the erotic" (19).

9. Barbara Johnson has written that Hurston's novel creates a "threshold" between inside and outside (*World* 172).

10. This is hardly the way we have been taught to read or to theorize about reading. We have learned, as Anzaldúa points out in her introduction to *Making Face, Making Soul/Haciendo Caras,* that theory is a mental viewing, something carried out from a distance with a subject analyzing an object. Feminist critiques of science of the 1980s, such as the work of Evelyn Fox Keller (e.g.,

Reflections on Gender and Science) and Sandra Harding (e.g., *The Science Question in Feminism*), discuss how the scientific method has divorced the perceived from the perceiver and created a binary relationship by making the perceived (all that is not-scientist) the object of the gaze. Nonetheless, Minnie Bruce Pratt writes of the problem of the "constricted eye, an eye that has only let in what I have been taught to see" (17), and Haraway believes that we need to reclaim vision "in order to name where we are and are not, in dimensions of mental and physical space we hardly know how to name" (*Simians* 190).

11. The act of reading texts has been thoroughly and brilliantly (and sometimes tediously) explored by deconstructionists, phenomenologists, reader-response theorists, narratologists, and new historicists, not to speak of feminists in those and other critical arenas. Although both essays are now dated, Jonathan Culler's "Readers and Reading," in *On Deconstruction* (1982), and Patrocinio P. Schweickart's "Reading Ourselves: Toward a Feminist Theory of Reading" (1986) provide summaries of contemporary reader-response and feminist theories of reading. *Gender and Reading,* the volume in which Schweickart's article appears and which was edited by Schweickart and Elizabeth A. Flynn, contains an annotated bibliography of feminist criticism and theory about reading through 1983. Both Culler and Schweickart investigate the political consequences of "reading as a woman," though they come to different conclusions; Culler claims that the text puts into question any authority it may have been given in the production of insight, and Schweickart believes that reading requires both an acknowledgment that reading is always subjective and a "commitment to reading the text as it was meant to be read" (54). Schweickart cites Adrienne Rich's essay "Vesuvius at Home: The Power of Emily Dickinson" as showing how a woman reader may engage in "intimate conversation" with a woman writer without the power struggles between reader and text that concern male theorists such as Georges Poulet in, for example, "Phenomenology of Reading," and Wolfgang Iser in, for example, *The Act of Reading.* Feminist reading by a woman thus becomes "an intersubjective encounter" with another woman, "a mediation between author and reader, between the context of writings and the context of reading" (Schweickart 53–54).

In her comments about the paucity of feminist reading which is self-consciously subjective and personal, Schweickart's article is now more historical than descriptive. Women's narrative texts and feminist theories are now continuing to converge in what Diane Freedman in 1993 called "a paradigm shift" in feminist discourse (44), a shift that becomes obvious in criticism such as Freedman's *An Alchemy of Genres* and *The Intimate Critique,* an anthology she and others edited, as well as in much the work of scholars and writers such as Elizabeth Meese, bell hooks, Paula Bennett, Maria Lugones, Nancy K. Miller, Jane Tompkins, Patricia Yaeger, Alice Walker, Rachel Blau DuPlessis, Gloria Anzaldúa, and Carolyn Woodward, to name but a few who have engaged in reciprocal and highly personal conversations with women's literature.

For a summary of feminist criticism of women's fiction, see Ellen Cronan Rose's "American Feminist Criticism of Contemporary Women's Fiction." Books on feminist theory and women's writing more generally include Laurie A. Finke's *Feminist Theory, Women's Writing* and Susan Sniader Lanser's *Fictions of Authority: Women Writers and Narrative Voice.* As I've discussed, Carla Kaplan's *The Erotics of Talk* is another example of such studies.

12. As Alvina E. Quintana has observed, literature, despite its relations to ideology and social conditions, "is usually dismissed as insignificant when historians or social scientists theorize" (209).

13. This question is becoming ever more worrisome for those who are committed to the profession of teaching and writing about literature in a climate of increasing disdain for literary criticism and the value of literature in a global economy of transnational capitalism.

14. For a discussion of white women's broken promises as reflected in African American women's writing, see Gwin, "A Theory of Black Women's Texts and White Women's Readings, or . . . The Necessity of Being Other."

15. In "Travels in the Postmodern: Making Sense of the Local," Elspeth Probyn confronts the debates over identity and difference and "who gets to speak from where and for whom" (502) by calling for the development of a "wild" sense of self as an opening to a relational perspective: "Instead of standing on our differences and wearing our identities as slogans we need to put the images of our selves to work epistemologically and ontologically" (511).

16. Two pivotal essays on the subject of identity politics have been Rich's "Notes toward a Politics of Location" and Pratt's "Identity: Skin Blood Heart." Work on the shifting arenas of identity are many and varied, ranging from Anzaldúa's *Borderlands/La Frontera,* to Williams's *The Alchemy of Race and Rights,* Judith Roof's *A Lure of Knowledge: Lesbian Sexuality and Theory* and Haraway's *Simians, Cyborgs, and Women: The Reinvention of Nature,* to mention but a few. Caren Kaplan's *Questions of Travel: Postmodern Discourses of Displacement* and Friedman's *Mappings: Feminism and the Cultural Geographies of Encounter* move questions of identity and identity politics to the arena of transnational critical practices that are specifically located.

17. Fluctuations in the "identity" half of the phrase "identity politics," are, as Henry Louis Gates has warned, "just as volatile and dynamic as the 'politics' half is." The fluctuation of "identity" puts the two terms in dialogue; otherwise, "we should be prepared for the phrase to be revealed as an oxymoron" ("Beyond the Culture Wars" 9).

18. hooks argues, in fact, that travel may indeed be "a way to hold on to imperialism." "Travel," she writes, "is not a word that can be easily evoked to talk about the Middle Passage, the Trail of Tears, the landing of Chinese immigrants at Ellis Island, the forced relocation of Japanese-Americans, the plight of the homeless" ("Representing Whiteness" 343). She points out that, from certain positions—including her own as a black woman—"to travel is to encounter the terrorizing force of white supremacy" and cites her personal experiences in traveling abroad as confrontations with terror that bring back memories of the terror of traveling to the white part of town as a child and

the collective journeying of black people, from the Middle Passage to the mass migrations from South to North in the United States (344).

19. Lugones's directions for what she calls "'world'-travelling" are helpful in considering how reading may be a way of being drawn into other spaces, particularly her suggestion that one important way to identify with others is to travel to other "worlds" as a way of seeing their inhabitants as subjects—"*what it is to be them and what it is to be ourselves in their eyes*" ("Playfulness" 401). Lugones primarily directs her remarks to white women, arguing that to enter other worlds white women must relinquish a sense of authority and self-importance, understanding that "we are not fixed in particular constructions of ourselves, which is part of saying that we are *open to self-construction*" (400). In an analogous reference to reading, Christian has pointed to one of its great rewards as "a widening of the self as self" resulting from "the opportunity to enter into other worlds." To read is for Christian "not only to validate the self but also to participate in 'the other's' view of the world, the writer's view" ("Response" 35).

20. Georges Poulet describes reading as an act that temporarily scrambles subjectivity. A "second self," a "usurper," takes over so completely that "I" becomes problematized and displaced. The result, he writes, is that "I am a consciousness astonished by an existence which is not mine, but which I experience as though it were mine" (59–60). This displacement of self through reading, however, is not discussed in terms of gender (although the male gender is assumed for both writer and reader) or in terms of the lasting possibility of shifting positionality. More conservatively, although Paul Ricoeur sees reading as a medium to be crossed through, he also views reading as a search for coherence that, under favorable conditions, "develops the sort of normativity and canonical status that we acknowledge in great works, those that never cease decontextualizing and recontextualizing themselves in the most diverse cultural circumstances" (179). That this coherence and the "great works" said to embody it have been gendered and racialized has been evident through the history of canonization. Michel de Certeau believes the reader "insinuates into another person's text the ruses of pleasure and appropriation: he poaches on it, is transported into it, pluralizes himself in it like the internal rumblings of one's body." De Certeau also describes reading as consumption, as renting—"transform[ing] another person's property into a space borrowed for a moment by a transient" (xxi). All three of these discussions are notable for their invocations of modes of domination in struggles involving the contested terrains of power, normativity, and capitalism.

21. Similarly, as I will discuss more fully later, in Toni Morrison's novel *The Bluest Eye* Cholly Breedlove's sheer rage and despair from his own history of racial and economic persecution drive him to rape his young daughter, Pecola.

22. As I will show, Morrison does the same in *The Bluest Eye.*

23. See the description of Cisneros at the end of the Vintage edition of *The House on Mango Street*: "The daughter of a Mexican father and a Mexican-American mother, she is nobody's mother and nobody's wife."

24. In their essay "Feminist Politics: What's Home Got to Do with It?" Martin and Mohanty discuss *Yours in Struggle: Three Feminist Perspectives on Anti-Semitism and Racism,* by Elly Bulkin, Minnie Bruce Pratt, and Barbara Smith. Martin and Mohanty find that, in its diverse perspectives on racism and anti-Semitism, the volume "unsettles not only any notion of feminism as an all-encompassing home but also the assumption that there are discrete, coherent, and absolutely separate identities—homes within feminism, so to speak—based on absolute divisions between various sexual, racial, or ethnic identities" (192). Pratt in particular shows how identity and positionality shift by telling the story of her own changing relations as a white southern woman to the geographies and communities and families that were and are her homes. As Martin and Mohanty's analysis points out, Pratt's story is constructed on a tension between "being home"—the space of safety and familiarity—and "not being home"—realizing that home may be an illusion based on the repression of difference. All too often, Martin and Mohanty write, "the white middle-class feminist's mode of adding on difference without leaving the comfort of home" has resulted in the continued marginalization of other women (193). (Clearly this is also part of hooks's critique of "travel" mentioned in note 18.)

25. See Houston Baker's discussion of African American cultural space and "the economics of slavery" in *Blues, Ideology, and Afro-American Literature* (1–14).

26. I am paraphrasing Morrison, who told Bill Moyers that there are some things that only artists can do, adding, "And it's our job."

27. This is not to say that such mappings cannot be helpful. In "Spatialization: A Strategy for Reading Narrative," Friedman discusses what she sees as two axes in narrative: the horizontal, which has to do with what happens in the story (e.g., plot, character, action, and closure), and the vertical, which she relates to multiple resonances of a text, whether they be cultural, intertextual, psychodynamic, and so forth. Reading the vertical dimension of a text, which Friedman relates to Julia Kristeva's concept of the semiotic in language—that which produces a text always in process—enables us to read not only what the text offers to us in the form of story but also what the text may be offering in terms of engagement between reader and writer (see Kristeva, *Revolution* 25–30).

Chapter 2: Nonfelicitous Space and Survivor Discourse

Part of this chapter was published as "Nonfelicitous Space and Survivor Discourse: Reading the Incest Story in Southern Women's Fiction," in *Haunted Bodies: Gender and Southern Texts,* ed. Anne Goodwyn Jones and Susan V. Donaldson (Charlottesville: University Press of Virginia, 1997), 416–40. © 1997 by the University Press of Virginia. I am grateful for the editors' help on this part of the chapter. Additional material from this chapter appears as "'Hereisthehouse': Cultural Spaces of Incest in *The Bluest Eye,*" in *Incest and the Literary Imagination,* ed. Elizabeth Barnes (Gainesville: University Press of Florida, 2002). © 2002 by the University Press of Florida.

1. In a 1985 interview with Gloria Naylor, Morrison said that in writing *The Bluest Eye* she was "looking for that dead girl," adding, "I thought I might talk about that dead girl" (Naylor and Morrison 576). I am grateful to Margot Gayle Backus's article "'Looking for That Dead Girl': Incest, Pornography, and the Capitalist Family Romance in *Nightwood, The Years,* and *Tar Baby*" for calling my attention to Morrison's conversation with Naylor.

2. In December 1994 vandals struck Zimmerman Library at the University of New Mexico, defacing books and journals in gay and lesbian studies and feminist studies. About $20,000 worth of volumes such as *Signs* and *The Journal of Homosexuality* were believed stolen. Several days later the missing books and journals were found hidden in the library.

3. I use the term *father* to refer to any male character who functions in the paternal role, such as a stepfather or uncle.

4. Other contemporary fictional texts by U.S. women writers about incestuous abuse of daughters by figurative or biological fathers include, among others, Kathy Acker's *Blood and Guts in High School,* Kathryn Harrison's *Exposure,* Gayl Jones's *Corregidora,* Elaine Kraf's *Find Him!* and Mona Simpson's "Lawns." Also, as Marilyn Wesley has pointed out, eight of Joyce Carol Oates's novels "are concerned with relations incestuous in tone, if not in fact," between young girls and their fathers or figurative fathers, especially *them* and *Angel of Light.* On the international scene, a few such works are Buchi Emecheta, *Gwendolen;* Herbjorg Wassmo, *The House with the Blind Glass Windows;* and Joan Riley, *The Unbelonging.*

5. Kincaid is referring to *The Courage to Heal: A Guide for Women Survivors of Child Sexual Abuse,* by Ellen Bass and Laura Davis (New York: HarperCollins, 1992).

6. Although I use the first-person singular here, I know that I am not alone in this response. Consider, for example, Nicole Brossard's reaction to an autobiographical manuscript sent to her by Canadian Elly Danica, whose account of her childhood sexual abuse by her pornographer father was later published as *Don't: A Woman's Word,* with a foreword by Brossard: "When I first read the manuscript, I experienced a range of feeling—from outrage to utter dejection, from anger to the deepest of sadness. It took me several days to finish reading it, because this is a book that is read with a lump in the throat, a tightness in the heart, tears. Reading this book, we bear the child and the woman in ourselves. Reading this book we share intimately what seems beyond words" (xv).

7. Following Nina Auerbach, Beth Kowaleski-Wallace suggests that the use of the individual father as a metaphor for patriarchy has tended to oversimplify the insidiousness of a complex dynamics of patriarchal power (297).

8. The uneven power dynamic of hysteria works its way through multiple categories of discourse about gender. During the 1980s Jane Gallop, Shoshana Felman, and Luce Irigaray charted its course in the daughterly relation of feminist theory and practice to Freudian and Lacanian psychoanalysis and

argued in varying ways for the necessity of excavating the patriarchal underpinnings of psychoanalytic theories of gender relations.

9. My readings will include the following: Toni Morrison, *The Bluest Eye;* Lee Smith, *Black Mountain Breakdown;* Alice Walker, *The Color Purple;* Kaye Gibbons, *Ellen Foster;* Dorothy Allison, *Bastard Out of Carolina;* and Jane Smiley, *A Thousand Acres.*

10. This is not to say that all six of these narratives are told from the point of view of the victim/survivor. In *Black Mountain Breakdown,* for example, it is often difficult to know what Crystal Spangler is thinking.

11. Two important exceptions are Janice Williamson's essay "'I Peel Myself out of My Own Skin': Reading *Don't: A Woman's Word,*" which provides a provocative discussion of feminist criticism's responsibilities to autobiographical incest narratives; and Deborah Horvitz's *Literary Trauma,* which addresses literary representations of trauma provoked by sexual violence. Horvitz's volume, with its broader topic, was published while this book was in press. Some book-length studies that discuss father-daughter incest in literature include Melba Wilson's *Crossing the Boundary: Black Women Survive Incest,* which reads five women's narratives as part of her larger project of examining incest within the African American community; Mark Taylor's readings of father-daughter incest in Shakespeare's plays, *Shakespeare's Darker Purpose: A Question of Incest;* and Lynda Zwinger's *Daughters, Fathers, and the Novel: The Sentimental Romance of Heterosexuality,* which theorizes the cultural role of the daughter through the reading of texts from *Clarissa* to *Story of O.* In *Forbidden Partners: The Incest Taboo in Modern Culture* James Twitchell is interested in the titillating nature of the incest taboo as it is articulated in nineteenth-century U.S. and British popular culture and (male-authored) literature. Relevant articles include the following: Paula Bennett, "The Mother's Part: Incest and Maternal Deprivation in Woolf and Morrison"; Vanessa D. Dickerson, "The Naked Father in Toni Morrison's *The Bluest Eye*"; Irene Fizer, "The Name of the Daughter: Identity and Incest in *Evelina*" (the latter two in *Refiguring the Father: New Feminist Readings of Patriarchy,* ed. Patricia Yaeger and Beth Kowaleski-Wallace); Christine Froula, "The Daughter's Seduction: Sexual Violence and Literary History"; Hortense J. Spillers, "'The Permanent Obliquity of an In(pha)llibly Straight': In the Time of the Daughters and the Fathers"; and Marilyn Wesley, "Father-Daughter Incest as Social Transgression: A Feminist Reading of Joyce Carol Oates."

12. For example, two particularly fascinating articles on incestuous abuse, with important implications for feminist criticism, are Janet Liebman Jacobs's "Victimized Daughters: Sexual Violence and the Empathic Female Self," expanded in her book *Victimized Daughters: Incest and the Development of the Female Self,* and Linda Alcoff and Laura Gray's "Survivor Discourse: Transgression or Recuperation?" In addition to essays and books cited in note 11, one other volume has been published while this book was in press: Janice Doane and Devon Hodges, *Telling Incest: Narratives of Dangerous Remembering from Stein to Sapphire,* which includes excellent discussions of fiction and autobiography.

13. As I complete this volume, there are such works underway, for example, *Incest and the Literary Imagination,* ed. Elizabeth Barnes, in which my discussion of *The Bluest Eye* appears.

14. Kincaid could have benefited from Alcoff and Gray's analysis, for many of his most cogent points concern the titillating and debilitating effects of sex talk about children.

15. A good example of such reading strategies is Susan Anne Carlson's "Incest and Rage in Charlotte Bronte's Novelettes," in *Creating Safe Space,* ed. Kuribayashi and Tharp, 61–78.

16. Judith Fryer's *Felicitous Space: The Imaginative Structures of Edith Wharton and Willa Cather* takes its title from Bachelard's phrase.

17. Melba Wilson, herself African American and a survivor of father-daughter incest, might resist such a reading. In *Crossing the Boundary: Black Women Survive Incest* she writes that incest and sexual abuse "are excused by some in our communities on the basis they are justifiable outlet valves for the stresses caused by racism. Stresses which are endured by black men, yes, but which occur in double doses for black women" (25). Although Wilson discusses five books about incest written by black women, including Buchi Emecheta, Joan Riley, Opal Palmer Adisa, Maya Angelou, and Alice Walker, *The Bluest Eye* is conspicuously absent from her discussion of black women's fiction and autobiography. Mark Ledbetter finds that the novel creates "a narrative community, where society's victims are most profoundly and uncomfortably presented back to the very society which creates them" (187).

18. See Ruth Frankenberg's *White Women, Race Matters: The Social Construction of Whiteness* for a discussion of the way colonial discourse produces "an unmarked, apparently autonomous white/Western self, in contrast with the marked, Other racial and cultural categories with which the racially and culturally dominant category is coconstructed" (17).

19. In this respect it is interesting to note that, as Russell points out, very little sociological research has been undertaken on race and ethnic differences in the occurrence and characteristics of incestuous abuse (110).

20. As Susan Willis puts it, "Morrison's portrayal of Pecola is the most horrifying example of the mental distortion produced by being 'other' to white culture" (175).

21. I use this term *we* advisedly, but I hope to show that *The Bluest Eye* does actually create a kind of readerly "we."

22. I stress that this is a novel about father-daughter incest because I do not believe the effect of Pecola's rape has received as much attention as have the abuse and disenfranchisement of the black family by white culture depicted in the novel. (For important discussions of the latter, see Dickerson and Willis). In her article "Tiptoeing through Taboo" Trudier Harris disagrees, saying that Morrison's novel treats the subject only as a brief part of the novel "and without much attention to incest *as* incest" (496).

23. This omission may be understandable in the case of *A Thousand Acres,* in which the incest story is unknown both to the reader and the victim/narrator until well into the narrative.

24. Interestingly, *The Encyclopedia of Southern Culture* is silent on the subject of incest. Neither the table of contents nor the subject index contains entries for either *incest* or *sexual violence,* nor does the work discuss sexual violence, except for a brief discussion about the rapes of African American women during slavery.

25. Zwinger generalizes this argument to women writers as well (120).

26. Spillers, as I have noted, might disagree with this analysis.

27. See Herman, with Hirschman, *Father-Daughter Incest,* chapter 8, "The Crisis of Disclosure" (129–43).

28. See two articles by Jacqueline Bobo that summarize controversies around both the book and the film: "*The Color Purple:* Black Women as Cultural Readers" (1988) and "Sifting through the Controversy: Reading *The Color Purple*" (1989).

29. In this sense, the cover photograph of mother and daughter described earlier does tell an important part of the story.

30. I am indebted to Kate Warne for this insight, which makes Anney's decision more understandable.

31. See Janet Jacobs's discussion of victims' negative relationships with their mothers (*Victimized Daughters* 15–18).

32. Both definitions are combined from *The Random House College Dictionary* and *The American Heritage Dictionary.*

33. Jane Baberman connects the obsidian shard with environmental issues.

34. For a more positive reading of the subversiveness of the novel, see Susan Strehle, "The Daughter's Subversion in Jane Smiley's *A Thousand Acres.*"

Chapter 3: Gender Travels

1. The term "compulsory heterosexuality," which has come into wide usage, derives from Adrienne Rich's widely cited essay "Compulsory Heterosexuality and Lesbian Existence."

2. *Bird-eyes* has received scant attention in feminist, gay and lesbian, and mainstream publication markets.

3. In *Tendencies* Sedgwick shows that one definition of *queer* is "the open mesh of possibilities, overlaps, dissonances and resonances, lapses and excesses of meaning when the constituent elements of anyone's gender, of anyone's sexuality aren't made (or *can't be made*) to signify monolithically" (8).

4. Located in New York, the Fiction Collective was formed in 1974 and operated by writers as a "not-for-profit cooperative conduit for quality fiction, the first of its kind in this country." In its early years each writer had to front $3,000 for the first edition of his or her book, but the Fiction Collective was not a vanity press. Both the editorial board and the membership read manuscripts and voted on their publication. In 1989 the collective was reorganized as Fiction Collective Two, which, after several moves, now operates out of Tallahasee, Florida (Foley 36–37).

5. Even Siegle, however, does not include *Find Him!* in his study.

6. I am using Lynne Pearce's term to describe the feminist reader's complex immersion in certain texts. I will discuss this concept more fully later in this chapter.

7. The novel has been the subject of reviews and critical articles in journals in Australia, New Zealand, France, Britain, Canada, India, Germany, and the United States.

8. Kina roe is sea eggs or sea urchin.

9. Gay Wilentz sees the book differently, as "a healing narrative" that enables us as readers to "accept our part in the process of healing and become instruments of change" (143).

10. The fact that Hulme insists on writing between and within both cultures has been the subject of adverse criticism. In a 1985 article in *ARIEL: A Review of International English Literature*, C. K. Stead writes that *The Bone People* is "a novel by a Pakeha which has won an award intended for a Maori" and casts doubt on the "authenticity" of the Maori material in the novel (104). In "Who Can Write as Other?" Margery Fee responds that Stead's "demand for 'authenticity' denies Fourth World writers a living, changing culture" (243).

11. Kerewin strongly resembles Hulme herself as the author is described on the book jacket of her 1986 collection of stories *Te Kaihau: The Windeater*: "She lives in Okarito on the West Coast of New Zealand, in a house she built herself, where she makes her living as a writer, painter, and whitebaiter." On the same jacket Hulme offers a self-description that also strongly evokes the Kerewin who evolves by the end of *The Bone People*: "I am: a rather reticent and timid person who gets fierce about deliberate ignorance, cruelty and intolerance, unnecessary waste, and any threat to any of my family. . . . One day I hope to develop gills."

12. As reviewer Sharon Oard Warner has rightly pointed out, the glossary of Maori terms at the book's end is less than adequate in that it omits some terms found in the narrative and is cryptic in defining others (10L). I suspect that this was a conscious decision on Hulme's part to preserve the novel's sense of distance.

Epilogue

I am grateful to Linda Jane Barnette for sending me a copy of *The Wall* and insisting that I read it, for sending me information on the book, and for reading this epilogue.

1. In recent years *Die Wand* has been translated into French, Italian, Swedish, Dutch, and Czech, as well as English. In the 1980s the novel became a cult book in West Germany and sparked a series of republishings of Haushofer's novels and short stories (Ullom 11). Joey Horsley has noted that the English translation suffers from stylistic problems that belie Haushofer's "unpretentious, seemingly simple style" and from substantive errors (25).

2. Although Haushofer has recently been claimed as a feminist writer and was influenced by the 1951 German translation of Simone de Beauvoir's *The Second Sex,* she died before the women's movement became a force in Europe (Vansant 9).

3. The song is "Wien, du Stadt meiner Träume," or "Vienna, City of My Dreams."

WORKS CITED

Abbandonato, Linda. "A View from 'Elsewhere': Subversive Sexuality and the Rewriting of the Heroine's Story in *The Color Purple*. *PMLA* 106 (Oct. 1991): 1106–15.

Acker, Kathy. *Blood and Guts in High School.* New York: Grove, 1978.

Ainley, Rose, ed. *New Frontiers of Space, Bodies, and Gender.* London: Routledge, 1998.

Alcoff, Linda, and Laura Gray. "Survivor Discourse: Transgression or Recuperation?" *Signs* 18.2 (Winter 1993): 260–90.

Allen, Paula Gunn. "Deer Woman." *Grandmothers of the Light: A Medicine Woman's Sourcebook.* Boston: Beacon, 1991.

———. *The Sacred Hoop: Recovering the Feminine in American Indian Traditions.* Boston: Beacon, 1986.

Allison, Dorothy. *Bastard Out of Carolina.* New York: Dutton, 1992.

———. *Skin: Talking about Sex, Class, and Literature.* Ithaca, N.Y.: Firebrand, 1994.

———. *Trash.* Ithaca, N.Y.: Firebrand, 1988.

Angelou, Maya. *I Know Why the Caged Bird Sings.* New York: Bantam Books, 1970.

Anzaldúa, Gloria. *Borderlands/La Frontera: The New Mestiza.* San Francisco: Spinsters/Aunt Lute, 1987.

———. "Bridge, Drawbridge, Sandbar, or Island: Lesbians-of-Color Hacienda Alianzas." In *Bridges of Power: Women's Multicultural Alliances.* Ed. Lisa Albrecht and Rose M. Brewer. Philadelphia: New Society, 1990. 216–31.

———, ed. *Making Face, Making Soul/Haciendo Caras: Creative and Critical Perspectives by Women of Color.* San Francisco: Aunt Lute, 1990.

Ardener, Shirley. "Ground Rules and Social Maps for Women: An Introduction." In *Women and Space: Ground Rules and Social Maps.* Ed. Shirley Ardener. London: Croom Helm, 1981. 1–30.

Arnold, Madelyn. *Bird-eyes.* Seattle: Seal, 1988.

Awiakta, Marilou. "Daydreaming Primal Space." In *The Poetics of Appalachian Space.* Ed. Parks Lanier Jr. Knoxville: University of Tennessee Press, 1991. 193–211.

Awkward, Michael. "Roadblocks and Relatives: Critical Revision in Toni Morrison's *The Bluest Eye.* In *Critical Essays on Toni Morrison.* Ed. Nellie Y. McKay. Boston: G. K. Hall, 1988. 57–68.

Bachelard, Gaston. *The Poetics of Space.* Trans. Maria Jolas. Boston: Beacon, 1969.

Backus, Margot Gayle. "'Looking for That Dead Girl': Incest, Pornography, and the Capitalist Family Romance in *Nightwood, The Years,* and *Tar Baby.*" *American Imago* 51.4 (1994): 421–45.

Baker, Houston A., Jr. *Blues, Ideology, and Afro-American Literature.* Chicago: University of Chicago Press, 1984.

Bakerman, Jane S. "'The Gleaming Obsidian Shard': Jane Smiley's *A Thousand Acres.*" *Midamerica: The Yearbook of the Society for the Study of Midwestern Literature* 19 (1992): 127–37.

Bakhtin, Mikhail. *The Dialogic Imagination.* Ed. Michael Holquist. Trans. Caryl Emerson and Michael Holquist. Austin: University of Texas Press, 1981.

Bammer, Angelika, ed. *Displacements: Cultural Identities in Question.* Bloomington: Indiana University Press, 1994.

Bammer, Angelika, Minrose Gwin, Cindi Katz, and Elizabeth Meese. "The Place of the Letter: An Epistolary Exchange." In *Making Worlds: Gender, Metaphor, Materiality.* Ed. Susan Hardy Aiken, Ann Brigham, Sallie A. Marston, and Penny Waterstone. Tucson: University of Arizona Press, 1998. 161–202.

Barnes, Elizabeth, ed. *Incest and the Literary Imagination.* Gainesville: University of Florida Press, 2002.

Bass, Ellen, and Laura Davis. *The Courage to Heal: A Guide for Women Survivors of Child Sexual Abuse.* New York: HarperCollins, 1992.

Bell, Vikki. *Interrogating Incest: Feminism, Foucault, and the Law.* London: Routledge, 1993.

Bennett, Paula. "Critical Clitoridectomy: Female Sexual Imagery and Feminist Psychoanalytic Theory." *Signs* 18.2 (1993): 235–59.

———. "The Mother's Part: Incest and Maternal Deprivation in Woolf and Morrison." In *Narrating Mothers: Theorizing Maternal Subjectivities.* Ed. Brenda Daly and Maureen Reddy. Knoxville: University of Tennessee Press, 1991. 125–38.

Benstock, Shari, ed. *Feminist Issues in Literary Scholarship.* Bloomington: Indiana University Press, 1987.

Berlant, Lauren. "Race, Gender, and Nation in *The Color Purple.*" *Critical Inquiry* 14.4 (Summer 1988): 831–59.

Berry, Philippa. "Woman and Space according to Kristeva and Irigaray." In *Shadow of Spirit: Postmodernism and Religion.* Ed. Philippa Berry and Andrew Wernick. London: Routledge, 1992. 250–64.

Betsky, Aaron. *Queer Space: Archeology and Same-Sex Desire.* New York: William Morrow, 1997.

Bhabha, Homi K. *The Location of Culture.* London: Routledge, 1994.

Blunt, Alison, and Gillian Rose. "Introduction: Women's Colonial and Postcolonial Geographies." In *Writing Women and Space: Colonial and Postcolonial Geographies.* Ed. Alison Blunt and Gillian Rose. New York: Guilford, 1994. 1–25.

Bobo, Jacqueline. "*The Color Purple:* Black Women as Cultural Readers." In *Female Spectators: Looking at Film and Television.* Ed. E. Deidre Priram. London: Verso, 1988. 100–109.

———. "Sifting through the Controversy: Reading *The Color Purple.*" *Callaloo: A Journal of African-American and African Arts and Letters* 12.2 (1989): 332–42.

Boyarin, Daniel. "Placing Reading: Ancient Israel and Medieval Europe." In *The Ethnography of Reading.* Ed. Daniel Boyarin. Berkeley: University of California Press, 1993. 10–37.

Boyarin, Jonathan, ed. *Remapping Memory: The Politics of TimeSpace.* Minneapolis: University of Minnesota Press, 1994.

Braidotti, Rosi. *Nomadic Subjects: Embodiment and Sexual Difference in Contemporary Feminist Theory.* New York: Columbia University Press, 1994.

———. *Patterns of Dissonance.* Cambridge: Polity, 1991.

Bronski, Michael. "Dorothy Allison." In *The Gay and Lesbian Literary Companion.* Ed. Sharon Malinowski and Christa Brelin. Detroit: Visible Ink, 1995. 1–6.

Brossard, Nicole. Foreword to *Don't: A Woman's Word,* by Elly Danica. Charlottetown, Canada: Gynergy Books, 1988. 5–6.

Brown, Rosellen. *Tender Mercies.* New York: Viking Penguin, 1978.

Bryson, John. "Keri Hulme in Conversation with John Bryson." *Antipodes: A North American Journal of Australian Literature* 8.2 (Dec. 1994): 131–35.

Bulkin, Ellie, Minnie Bruce Pratt, and Barbara Smith. *Yours in Struggle.* Ithaca, N.Y.: Firebrand, 1984.

Butler, Judith. *Bodies That Matter.* New York: Routledge, 1993.

———. *Gender Trouble.* New York: Routledge, 1990.

———. "A Skeptical Feminist Postscript to the Postmodern." In *Postmodernism across the Ages.* Ed. Bill Readings and Bennet Schaber. Syracuse, N.Y.: Syracuse University Press, 1994. 233–37.

Butler, Sandra. *Conspiracy of Silence.* San Francisco: Volcano, 1985.

Byerman, Keith E. "Untold Stories: Black Daughters in *Absalom, Absalom!* and *The Bluest Eye.*" In *Unflinching Gaze: Morrison and Faulkner Re-Envisioned.* Ed. Carol A. Kolmerten, Stephen M. Ross, and Judith Bryant Wittenberg. Jackson: University Press of Mississippi, 1997. 128–38.

Cameron, Deborah. Introduction: Why Is Language a Feminist Issue?" In *The Feminist Critique of Language.* Ed. Deborah Cameron. London: Routledge, 1990. 1–28.

Carden, Mary Paniccia. "Remembering/Engendering the Heartland: Sexed Language, Embodied Space, and America's Foundational Fictions in Jane Smiley's *A Thousand Acres.*" *Frontiers: A Journal of Women Studies* 18.2 (1997): 181–202.

Caviola, Hugo. "Behind the Transparent Wall: Marlen Haushofer's Novel *Die Wand.*" *Modern Austrian Literature* 24.1 (1991): 101–12.

Champagne, Rosaria. *The Politics of Survivorship: Incest, Women's Literature, and Feminist Theory.* New York: New York University Press, 1996.

Christian, Barbara T. "The Race for Theory." In *Making Face, Making Soul/ Haciendo Caras: Creative and Critical Perspectives by Women of Color.* Ed. Gloria Anzaldúa. San Francisco: Aunt Lute, 1990. 335–45.

———. "Response to 'Black Women's Texts.'" *National Women's Studies Association Journal* 1.1 (1988): 32–36.

Cisneros, Sandra. *The House on Mango Street.* New York: Vintage, 1989.

Clifford, James. *The Predicament of Culture: Twentieth-Century Ethnography, Literature, and Art.* Cambridge, Mass.: Harvard University Press, 1998.

———. "Traveling Cultures." In *Cultural Studies.* Ed. Lawrence Grossberg, Cary Nelson, and Paula Treichler. New York: Routledge, 1992. 96–112.

———. *Writing Culture: The Poetics and Politics of Ethnography.* Berkeley: University of California Press, 1986.

Colomina, Beatriz, ed. *Sexuality and Space.* New York: Princeton Architectural, 1992.

Courtois, Christine A. *Healing the Incest Wound: Adult Survivors in Therapy.* New York: W. W. Norton, 1988.

Covi, Giovanna. "Keri Hulme's *The Bone People:* A Critique of Gender." In *Imagination and the Creative Impulse in the New Literatures in English.* Amsterdam: Rodopi, 1993. 219–31.

Crang, Mike, and Nigel Thrift, eds. *Thinking Space.* London: Routledge, 2000.

Culler, Jonathan. *On Deconstruction: Theory and Criticism after Structuralism.* Ithaca, N.Y.: Cornell University Press, 1982.

Cvetkovich, Ann. "Sexual Trauma/Queer Memory: Incest, Lesbianism, and Therapeutic Culture." *GLQ: A Journal of Lesbian and Gay Studies* 2.4 (1995): 351–77.

Daly, Brenda. *Authoring a Life: A Woman's Survival in and through Literary Studies.* Albany: State University of New York Press, 1998.

Daviau, Donald G. Introduction. In *Major Figures of Contemporary Austrian Literature.* Ed. Donald G. Daviau. New York: Peter Lang, 1987. 1–24.

de Certeau, Michel. *The Practice of Everyday Life.* Trans. Steven Randall. Berkeley: University of California Press, 1984.

de Lauretis, Teresa. *Technologies of Gender: Essays on Theory, Film, and Fiction.* Bloomington: Indiana University Press, 1987.

Dickerson, Vanessa D. "The Naked Father in Toni Morrison's *The Bluest Eye.*" In *Refiguring the Father: New Feminist Readings of Patriarchy.* Ed. Patricia Yaeger and Beth Kowaleski-Wallace. Carbondale: Southern Illinois University Press, 1989. 108–27.

Ditmar, Linda. "Will the Circle Be Unbroken?": The Politics of Form in *The Bluest Eye.*" *Novel* (Winter 1990): 137–53.

Doane, Janice, and Devon Hodges. *Telling Incest: Narratives of Dangerous Remembering from Stein to Sapphire.* Ann Arbor: University of Michigan Press, 2001.

Donovan, Josephine. "Toward a Women's Poetics." In *Feminist Issues in Literary Scholarship.* Ed. Shari Benstock. Bloomington: Indiana University Press, 1987. 98–109.

Douglas, Mary. *Purity and Danger.* London: Routledge, 1966.
Doyle, Laura. *Bordering on the Body: The Racial Matrix of Modern Fiction and Culture.* New York: Oxford University Press, 1994.
DuPlessis, Rachel Blau. *The Pink Guitar: Writing as Feminist Practice.* New York: Routledge, 1990.
———. *Writing beyond the Ending: Narrative Strategies of Twentieth-Century Women Writers.* Bloomington: Indiana University Press, 1985.
Eagleton, Terry. *Criticism and Ideology.* London: Verso, 1975.
Early, Gerald. "*The Color Purple* as Everybody's Protest Art." *Antioch Review* 44.3 (1986): 261–97.
Eisenstein, Hester. Introduction. In *The Future of Difference.* Ed. Hester Eisenstein and Alice Jardine. New Brunswick, N.J.: Rutgers University Press, 1988. xv–xxiv.
Emechata, Buchi. *Gwendolen.* London: Flamingo, 1990.
Enloe, Cynthia. *Bananas, Beaches, and Bases: Making Feminist Sense of International Politics.* Berkeley: University of California Press, 1990.
Evers, Larry. "Notes on the Deer Woman." *Indiana Folklore* 11 (1978): 33–45.
Farley, Tucker Pamella. "Lesbianism and the Social Function of Taboo." In *The Future of Difference.* Ed. Hester Eisenstein and Alice Jardine. New Brunswick, N.J.: Rutgers University Press, 1985.
Fee, Margery. "Who Can Write as Other?" In *The Post-Colonial Studies Reader.* Ed. Bill Ashcroft, Gareth Griffiths, and Helen Tiffin. London: Routledge, 1995. 242–45.
Felski, Rita. *Feminist Aesthetics: Feminist Literature and Social Change.* Cambridge, Mass.: Harvard University Press, 1989.
Fetterley, Judith. *The Resisting Reader: A Feminist Approach to American Fiction.* Bloomington: Indiana University Press, 1977.
Finke, Laurie A. *Feminist Theory, Women's Writing.* Ithaca, N.Y.: Cornell University Press, 1992.
Fizer, Irene. "The Name of the Daughter: Identity and Incest in *Evelina.*" In *Refiguring the Father: New Feminist Readings of Patriarchy.* Ed. Patricia Yaeger and Beth Kowaleski-Wallace. Carbondale: Southern Illinois University Press, 1989. 78–107.
Flynn, Elizabeth A., and Patrocinio P. Schweickart, eds. *Gender and Reading: Essays on Readers, Texts, and Contexts.* Baltimore, Md.: Johns Hopkins University Press, 1986.
Foley, J. R. "Fiction Collective Two." *Poets and Writers* 24.5 (1996): 35–43.
Foote, Donna. "Trouble in Paradise: A Hawaiian Novelist Sparks a P.C. Protest." *Newsweek* 17 Aug. 1998: 62.
Foucault, Michel. *Madness and Civilization.* Trans. Richard Howard. New York: Vintage, 1973.
———. "Questions on Geography." In *Power/Knowledge.* Ed. Colin Gordon. New York: Pantheon, 1980. 63–77.
Frankel, Haskel. "Review of *The Bluest Eye.*" *New York Times Book Review* 1 (Nov. 1970): 46–47. Repr. in *Critical Essays on Toni Morrison.* Ed. Nellie Y. McKay. Boston: G. K. Hall, 1988. 20.

Frankenberg, Ruth. *White Women, Race Matters: The Social Construction of Whiteness.* Minneapolis: University of Minnesota Press, 1993.

Freedman, Diane P. *An Alchemy of Genres: Cross-Genre Writing by American Feminist Poet-Critics.* Charlottesville: University Press of Virginia, 1992.

Freedman, Diane P., Olivia Frey, and Frances Murphy Zauhar, eds. *The Intimate Critique: Autobiographical Literary Criticism.* Durham, N.C.: Duke University Press, 1993.

Friedman, Susan Stanford. *Mappings: Feminism and the Cultural Geographies of Encounter.* Princeton, N.J.: Princeton University Press, 1998.

———. "Spatialization: A Strategy for Reading Narrative." *Narrative* 1.1 (1993): 12–23.

———. "Spatialization, Narrative Theory, and Virginia Woolf's *The Voyage Out.*" In *Ambiguous Discourse: Feminist Narratology and British Women Writers.* Ed. Kathy Mezei. Chapel Hill: University of North Carolina Press, 1996. 109–36.

Frisbie, Charlotte J. *Southwestern Indian Ritual Drama.* Prospect Heights, Ill.: Waveland, 1989 (1980).

Froula, Christine. "The Daughter's Seduction: Sexual Violence and Literary History." *Signs* 11.4 (1986): 621–44.

Fryer, Judith. *Felicitous Space: The Imaginative Structures of Edith Wharton and Willa Cather.* Chapel Hill: University of North Carolina Press, 1986.

———. "Women and Space: The Flowering of Desire." *Prospects: An Annual Journal of American Cultural Studies* 9 (1984): 187–230.

Gage, Nancy. "Crickets." *Frontiers: A Journal of Women's Studies* 13.1 (1992): 170–79.

Gallop, Jane. *The Daughter's Seduction: Feminism and Psychoanalysis.* Ithaca, N.Y.: Cornell University Press, 1982.

Gates, Henry Louis, Jr. "Beyond the Culture Wars: Identities in Dialogue." *Profession 93* (1993): 6–11.

———. "Introduction: Writing 'Race' and the Difference It Makes." In *"Race," Writing, and Difference.* Ed. Henry Louis Gates Jr. Chicago: University of Chicago Press, 1985. 1–20.

Gibbons, Kaye. *Ellen Foster.* Chapel Hill, N.C.: Algonquin Books, 1987.

Graulich, Melody. "Somebody Must Say These Things: An Essay for My Mother." In *The Intimate Critique: Autobiographical Literary Criticism.* Ed. Diane P. Freedman, Olivia Frey, and Frances Murphy Zauhar. Durham, N.C.: Duke University Press, 1993. 175–90.

Gregory, Derek. *Geographical Imaginations.* Cambridge, Mass.: Blackwell, 1994.

Grewal, Inderpal, and Caren Kaplan, eds. *Scattered Hegemonies: Postmodernity and Transnational Feminist Practices.* Minneapolis: University of Minnesota Press, 1994.

Grosz, Elizabeth. *Space, Time, and Perversion.* New York: Routledge, 1995.

Gwin, Minrose C. "Nonfelicitous Space and Survivor Discourse: Reading the

Incest Story in Southern Women's Fiction." In *Haunted Bodies: Gender and Southern Texts.* Ed. Anne Goodwyn Jones and Susan V. Donaldson. Charlottesville: University Press of Virginia, 1997. 416–40.

———. "Space Travel: The Connective Politics of Feminist Reading." *Signs* 21.4 (Summer 1996): 870–905.

———. "A Theory of Black Women's Texts and White Women's Readings, or . . . The Necessity of Being Other." *National Women's Studies Association Journal* 1.1 (1988): 21–31.

Haraway, Donna J. *Simians, Cyborgs, and Women: The Reinvention of Nature.* New York: Routledge, 1991.

———. "Situated Knowledges: The Science Question in Feminism and the Privilege of Partial Perspective." *Feminist Studies* 14 (Fall 1988): 575–99.

Harding, Sandra. *The Science Question in Feminism.* Ithaca, N.Y.: Cornell University Press, 1986.

Harjo, Joy. *In Mad Love and War.* Middletown, Conn.: Wesleyan University Press, 1990.

Harris, Trudier. "From Victimization to Free Enterprise: Alice Walker's *The Color Purple.*" *Studies in American Fiction* 14.1 (1986): 1–18.

———. "On *The Color Purple,* Stereotypes, and Silence." *Black American Literature Forum* 18.4 (1984): 155–60.

———. "Tiptoeing through Taboo: Incest in 'The Child Who Favored Daughter.'" *Modern Fiction Studies* 28.3 (1982): 495–505.

Harrison, Kathryn. *Exposure.* New York: Warner Books, 1993.

———. *The Kiss.* New York: Random House, 1997.

Harvey, David. *The Condition of Postmodernity.* Oxford: Basil Blackwell, 1990.

———. "Grounding Metaphor: Towards a Spatialized Politics." In *Place and the Politics of Identity.* Ed. Michael Keith and Steve Pile. London: Routledge, 1993. 41–66.

Haushofer, Marlen. *The Wall.* Trans. Shaun Whiteside. San Francisco: Cleis, 1990.

Henderson, Mae Gwendolyn. "Speaking in Tongues: Dialogics, Dialectics, and the Black Woman Writer's Literary Tradition." In *Changing Our Own Words: Essays on Criticism, Theory, and Writing by Black Women.* Ed. Cheryl A. Wall. New Brunswick, N.J.: Rutgers University Press, 1989. 16–37.

Herman, Judith, with Lisa Hirschman. *Father-Daughter Incest.* Cambridge, Mass.: Harvard University Press, 1981.

Higonnet, Margaret. "Mapping the Text: Critical Metaphors." In *Reconfigured Spheres: Feminist Explorations of Literary Space.* Ed. Margaret Higonnet and Joan Templeton. Amherst: University of Massachusetts Press, 1994. 194–212.

———. "New Cartographies: An Introduction." In *Reconfigured Spheres: Feminist Explorations of Literary Space.* Ed. Margaret Higonnet and Joan Templeton. Amherst: University of Massachusetts Press, 1994. 1–19.

hooks, bell. "Representing Whiteness in the Black Imagination." In *Cultur-*

al Studies. Ed. Lawrence Grossberg, Cary Nelson, and Paula Treichler. New York: Routledge, 1992. 338–46.

Horsley, Joey. "In a World of Her Own: *The Wall* by Marlen Haushofer." *Women's Review of Books* 9.4 (Jan. 1992): 25.

Horvitz, Deborah. *Literary Trauma: Sadism, Memory, and Sexual Violence in Women's Fiction.* Albany: State University of New York Press, 2000.

Hulme, Keri. *The Bone People.* 1984. New York: Penguin, 1986.

———. *Te Kaihau: The Windeater.* 1986. New York: George Braziller, 1987.

Hulme, Keri, and Gerry Turcotte. "Reconsidering *The Bone People.*" *Australian and New Zealand Studies in Canada* 12 (Dec. 1994): 135–54.

Hurston, Zora Neale. *Their Eyes Were Watching God.* 1937. New York: Harper and Row, 1990.

Ingram, Gordon Brent, Anne-Marie Bouthillette, and Yolanda Retter, eds. *Queers in Space.* Seattle: Bay, 1997.

Irigaray, Luce. *Elemental Passions.* Trans. Joanne Collie and Judith Still. London: Routledge, 1992.

———. *Speculum of the Other Woman.* Trans. Gillian Gill. Ithaca, N.Y.: Cornell University Press, 1985.

———. *This Sex Which Is Not One.* Trans. Catherine Porter with Carolyn Burke. Ithaca, N.Y.: Cornell University Press, 1985.

Iser, Wolfgang. *The Act of Reading: A Theory of Aesthetic Response.* Baltimore, Md.: Johns Hopkins University Press, 1978.

Jacobs, Harriet A. *Incidents in the Life of a Slave Girl* (1861). Ed. Jean Fagan Yellin. Cambridge, Mass.: Harvard University Press, 1987.

Jacobs, Janet Liebman. *Victimized Daughters: Incest and the Development of the Female Self.* New York: Routledge, 1994.

———. "Victimized Daughters: Sexual Violence and the Empathic Female Self." *Signs* 1 (Autumn 1993): 126–45.

Jameson, Fredric. "Cognitive Mapping." In *Marxism and the Interpretation of Culture.* Ed. Cary Nelson and Lawrence Grossberg. Urbana: University of Illinois Press, 1988. 347–59.

Johnson, Barbara. *The Feminist Difference: Literature, Psychoanalysis, Race, and Gender.* Cambridge, Mass.: Harvard University Press, 1998.

———. *A World of Difference.* Baltimore, Md.: Johns Hopkins University Press, 1987.

Jones, Anne Goodwyn. "The World of Lee Smith." In *Women Writers of the Contemporary South.* Ed. Peggy Whitman Prenshaw. Jackson: University Press of Mississippi, 1984. 249–72.

Jones, Gayle. *Corregidora.* Boston: Beacon, 1975.

Juhasz, Suzanne. *Reading from the Heart: Women, Literature, and the Search for Love.* New York: Viking, 1994.

Kalb, John D. "The Second 'Rape' of Crystal Spangler." *Southern Literary Journal* 21.1 (Fall 1988): 23–30.

Kaplan, Caren. "The Politics of Location as Transnational Feminist Practice." In *Scattered Hegemonies: Postmodernity and Transnational Feminist*

Practices. Ed. Inderpal Grewal and Caren Kaplan. Minneapolis: University of Minnesota Press, 1994. 137–53.

———. *Questions of Travel: Postmodern Discourses of Displacement.* Durham, N.C.: Duke University Press, 1996.

Kaplan, Carey, and Ellen Cronan Rose. *The Canon and the Common Reader.* Knoxville: University of Tennessee Press, 1990.

Kaplan, Carla. *The Erotics of Talk: Women's Writing and Feminist Paradigms.* New York: Oxford University Press, 1996.

Kecht, Maria-Regina. "The Language of the Female Self beyond the Boundaries of Discourse: Marlen Haushofer's Re-creation of the Female Archetype." *Osterreich in Amerikanischer Sicht* 7 (1992): 10–18.

Keith, Michael, and Steve Pile, eds. *Place and the Politics of Identity.* London: Routledge, 1993.

Keller, Evelyn Fox. *Reflections on Gender and Science.* New Haven, Conn.: Yale University Press, 1985.

Kennard, Jean E. "Ourself behind Ourself: A Theory for Lesbian Readers." In *Gender and Reading.* Ed. Elizabeth A. Flynn and Patrocinio P. Schweickart. Baltimore, Md.: Johns Hopkins University Press, 1986. 63–80.

Kestner, Joseph. *The Spatiality of the Novel.* Detroit, Mich.: Wayne State University Press, 1978.

Kincaid, James. *Erotic Innocence: The Culture of Child Molesting.* Durham, N.C.: Duke University Press, 1998.

Kingston, Maxine Hong. "The Novel's Next Step." *Mother Jones* Dec. 1989: 37–42.

Kirby, Kathleen M. "Thinking through the Boundary: The Politics of Location, Subjects, and Space." *boundary 2* 20.2 (Summer 1993): 173–89.

Kowaleski-Wallace, Beth. "Reading the Father Metaphorically." In *Refiguring the Father: New Feminist Readings of Patriarchy.* Ed. Patricia Yaeger and Beth Kowaleski-Wallace. Carbondale: Southern Illinois University Press, 1989. 296–311.

Kraf, Elaine. *Find Him!* New York: Fiction Collective, 1977.

Kristeva, Julia. *Revolution in Poetic Language.* Trans. Margaret Waller. New York: Columbia University Press, 1984.

———. "Women's Time." Trans. Alice Jardine and Harry Blake. *Signs* 7 (1981): 13–35.

Kuribayashi, Tomoko, and Julie Tharp, eds. *Creating Safe Space: Violence and Women's Writing.* Albany: State University of New York Press, 1998.

Lamb-Faffelberger, Margarete, ed. *Out from the Shadows: Essays on Contemporary Austrian Women Writers and Filmmakers.* Riverside, Calif.: Ariadne, 1997.

Lang, Sabine. *Men as Women, Women as Men: Changing Gender in Native American Cultures.* Austin: University of Texas Press, 1998.

Lanier, Parks, Jr. "Psychic Space in Lee Smith's *Black Mountain Breakdown.* In *The Poetics of Appalachian Space.* Ed. Parks Lanier Jr. Knoxville: University of Tennessee Press, 1991. 58–66.

Lanser, Susan Snaider. *Fictions of Authority: Women Writers and Narrative Voice.* Ithaca, N.Y.: Cornell University Press, 1992.

Lauter, Paul. *Canons and Contexts.* New York: Oxford University Press, 1991.

Ledbetter, Mark. "Through the Eyes of a Child: Looking for Victims in Toni Morrison's *The Bluest Eye.*" In *Literature and Theology at Century's End.* Ed. Gregory Salyer and Robert Detweiler. Atlanta: Scholars, 1995. 177–88.

Lefebvre, Henri. *The Production of Space.* Trans. Donald Nicholson-Smith. Cambridge: Basil Blackwell, 1991.

Levy, Helen. *Fiction of the Home Place.* Jackson: University Press of Mississippi, 1992.

Lewis, C. S. *An Experiment in Criticism.* Cambridge: Cambridge University Press, 1961.

Light, Alison. "Fear of the Happy Ending: 'The Color Purple,' Reading and Racism." In *English and Cultural Studies: Broadening the Context.* Ed. Michael Green. London: John Murray, 1987. 103–17.

Lloyd, Roseann. "Writing My Self into Existence." In *She Who Was Lost Is Remembered: Healing from Incest through Creativity.* Ed. Louise M. Wisechild. Seattle: Seal, 1991. 71–75.

Longino, Helen E. "Feminist Standpoint Theory and the Problems of Knowledge." *Signs* 19.1 (1993): 201–12.

Lorde, Audre. *Sister Outsider.* Freedom, Calif.: Crossing, 1984.

Lugones, Maria. "Playfulness, 'World'-Travelling, and Loving Perception." In *Making Face, Making Soul/Haciendo Caras: Creative and Critical Perspectives by Women of Color.* Ed. Gloria Anzaldúa. San Francisco: Aunt Lute, 1990. 390–402.

———. "Purity, Impurity, and Separation." *Signs* 19.2 (1994): 458–79.

McDowell, Deborah E. "'The Changing Same': Generational Connections and Black Women Novelists." *New Literary History* 18.2 (1987): 281–302.

———. "Reading Family Matters." In *Changing Our Own Words: Essays on Criticism, Theory, and Writing by Black Women.* Ed. Cheryl A. Wall. New Brunswick, N.J.: Rutgers University Press, 1989. 75–97.

McLennan, Karen Jacobsen. *Nature's Ban: Women's Incest Literature.* Boston: Northeastern, 1996.

McNaron, Toni A. H., and Yarrow Morgan. *Voices in the Night: Women Speaking about Incest.* San Francisco: Cleis, 1982.

Martin, Biddy, and Chandra Talpade Mohanty. "Feminist Politics: What's Home Got to Do with It?" In *Feminist Studies/Critical Studies.* Ed. Teresa de Lauretis. Madison: University of Wisconsin Press, 1986. 191–212.

Massey, Doreen. *Space, Place, and Gender.* Minneapolis: University of Minnesota Press, 1994.

Meese, Elizabeth A. *(Ex)Tensions: Re-figuring Feminist Criticism.* Urbana: University of Illinois Press, 1990.

———. *(Sem)Erotics: Theorizing Lesbian Writing.* New York: New York University Press, 1992.

Meiselman, Karin C. *Resolving the Trauma of Incest: Reintegration Therapy with Survivors.* San Francisco: Jossey-Bass, 1990.
Metge, Joan. *The Maoris of New Zealand Rautahi.* London: Routledge, 1976.
Mhlope, Gcina. "The Toilet." In *Sometimes When It Rains.* Ed. Ann Oosthuizen. New York: Pandora, 1987. 1–7.
Miller, Nancy K. *Getting Personal: Feminist Occasions and Other Autobiographical Acts.* New York: Routledge, 1991.
———. *Subject to Change: Reading Feminist Writing.* New York: Columbia University Press, 1988.
Miner, Madonne. "Lady No Longer Sings the Blues: Rape, Madness, and Silence in *The Bluest Eye.*" In *Conjuring: Black Women, Fiction, and Literary Tradition.* Ed. Marjorie Pryse and Hortense J. Spillers. Bloomington: Indiana University Press, 1985. 176–91.
Mitchell, Juliet. *Women: The Longest Revolution.* London: Virago, 1984.
Mohanty, Chandra Talpade. "Introduction: Cartographies of Struggle—Third World Women and the Politics of Feminism." In *Third World Women and the Politics of Feminism.* Ed. Chandra Talpade Mohanty, Ann Russo, and Lourdes Torres. Bloomington: Indiana University Press, 1991. 1–47.
Molina, Maria Luisa "Paposa." "Fragmentations: Meditations on Separatism." *Signs* 19.2 (1994): 449–58.
Moore, Henrietta L. *A Passion for Difference.* Bloomington: Indiana University Press, 1994.
———. *Space, Text, and Gender: An Anthropological Study of the Marakwet of Kenya.* Cambridge: Cambridge University Press, 1986.
Moraga, Cheríe. *Giving Up the Ghost: Teatro in Two Acts.* Albuquerque, N.Mex.: West End Press, 1986.
Morrison, Toni. Afterword to *The Bluest Eye* (1970). New York: Penguin, 1994. 209–16.
———. *Beloved.* New York: New American Library, 1988.
———. *The Bluest Eye.* New York: Pocket Books, 1970.
———. "Home." In *The House That Race Built: Black Americans, U.S. Terrain.* Ed. Wahneeba Lubiano. New York: Pantheon, 1998. 3–12.
———. *Playing in the Dark: Whiteness and the Literary Imagination.* Cambridge, Mass.: Harvard University Press, 1990.
———. Remarks prefatory to a reading of *Beloved.* Virginia Polytechnic Institute and State University. Blacksburg, Virginia. 6 May 1988.
Naylor, Gloria, and Toni Morrison. "A Conversation." *Southern Review* 21 (July 1985): 567–93.
Oates, Joyce Carol. *Angel of Light.* New York: Dutton, 1981.
———. *them.* Greenwich, Conn.: Fawcett, 1970.
Olivares, Julían. "Critical Commentary." In *Hispanic Literature Criticism,* vol. 1. Ed. Jalena Krstović. Detroit: Gale Research, 1994. 465–68.
Orbell, Margaret. *The Illustrated Encyclopedia of Maori Myth and Legend.* Christchurch, N.Z.: Canterbury University Press, 1995.
Pearce, Lynne. *Feminism and the Politics of Reading.* London: Arnold, 1997.

Peek, Andrew. "An Interview with Keri Hulme." *New Literature Review* 29 (Winter 1990): 1–11.

Pitner, Erin Clayton. *Stones and Roses.* Ed. Minrose Gwin. Albuquerque, N.Mex: Chamisa, 1993.

Poulet, Georges. "Phenomenology of Reading." *New Literary History* 1 (1969): 53–68.

Pratt, Minnie Bruce. "Identity: Skin Blood Heart." In *Yours in Struggle,* by Elly Bulkin, Minnie Bruce Pratt, and Barbara Smith. Ithaca, N.Y.: Firebrand, 1984. 11–63. Repr. in Minnie Bruce Pratt. *Rebellion: Essays, 1980–1991.* Ithaca, N.Y.: Firebrand, 1991. 27–81.

Probyn, Elspeth. "Travels in the Postmodern: Making Sense of the Local." In *Feminism/Postmodernism.* Ed. Linda J. Nicholson. New York: Routledge, 1990. 176–89.

Quindlen, Anna. *How Reading Changed My Life.* New York: Ballantine, 1998.

Quintana, Alvina E. "Women: Prisoners of the Word." In *Chicana Voices: Intersections of Class, Race, and Gender.* Ed. Teresa Córdova, Gilberto Cardenas, and Christine M. Sierra. Colorado Springs: National Association for Chicano Studies, 1990. 208–19.

Rabinow, Paul. "Introduction." In *The Foucault Reader.* Ed. Rabinow. New York: Pantheon, 1984. 3–29.

Randall, Margaret. Preface. In *She Who Was Lost Is Remembered: Healing from Incest through Creativity.* Ed. Louise M. Wisechild. Seattle: Seal, 1991. xi–xiii.

———. *This Is about Incest.* Ithaca, N.Y.: Firebrand, 1987.

Rich, Adrienne. "Compulsory Heterosexuality and Lesbian Existence." In *Blood, Bread, and Poetry: Selected Prose, 1979–1985.* New York: W. W. Norton, 1986. 23–75.

———. "Notes toward a Politics of Location." In *Blood, Bread, and Poetry: Selected Prose, 1979–1985.* New York: W. W. Norton, 1986. 210–31.

———. *Your Native Land, Your Life.* New York: W. W. Norton, 1986.

Richardson, Laurel. *Fields of Play: Constructing an Academic Life.* New Brunswick, N.J.: Rutgers University Press, 1997.

Ricoeur, Paul. *Time and Narrative,* vol. 3. Trans. Kathleen Blamey and David Pellauer. Chicago: University of Chicago Press, 1988.

Riley, Joan. *The Unbelonging.* London: Women's, 1985.

Robinson, Marilynne. *Housekeeping.* New York: Bantam, 1980.

Romines, Ann. *The Home Plot: Women, Writing, and Domestic Ritual.* Amherst: University of Massachusetts Press, 1992.

Roof, Judith. *A Lure of Knowledge: Lesbian Sexuality and Theory.* New York: Columbia University Press, 1991.

Rose, Ellen Cronan. "American Feminist Criticism of Contemporary Women's Fiction." *Signs* 18.2 (1993): 346–75.

Rose, Gillian. *Feminism and Geography: The Limits of Geographical Knowledge.* Minneapolis: University of Minnesota Press, 1993.

Rosenberg, Ruth. "Seeds in Hard Ground: Black Girlhood in *The Bluest Eye.*" *Black American Literature Forum* 21.4 (Winter 1987): 435–45.

Roy, Arundhati. *The God of Small Things.* New York: Harper, 1997.

Royster, Philip M. "In Search of Our Fathers' Arms: Alice Walker's Persona of the Alienated Darling." *Black American Literature Forum* 20 (Winter 1986): 347–70.

Russell, Diane. *The Secret Trauma: Incest in the Lives of Girls and Women.* New York: Basic Books, 1986.

Ryan, Pamela. "Black Women Do Not Have Time to Dream: The Politics of Time and Space." *Tulsa Studies in Women's Literature* 11.1 (Spring 1992): 95–102.

Said, Edward. *The World, the Text, and the Critic.* Cambridge, Mass.: Harvard University Press, 1983.

Salvaggio, Ruth. "Theory and Space, Space and Woman." *Tulsa Studies in Women's Literature* 7.2 (1988): 261–82.

Schwartz, Lynne Sharon. *Ruined by Reading: A Life in Books.* Boston: Beacon, 1996.

Schweickart, Patrocinio P. "Reading Ourselves: Toward a Feminist Theory of Reading." In *Gender and Reading.* Ed. Elizabeth A. Flynn and Patrocinio P. Schweickart. Baltimore, Md.: Johns Hopkins University Press, 1986. 31–62.

Scott, Joan W. "The Evidence of Experience." In *Questions of Evidence: Proof, Practice, and Persuasion across the Disciplines.* Ed. James Chandler, Arnold Davidson, and Harry Harootunian. Chicago: University of Chicago Press, 1994. 363–87.

———. *Gender and the Politics of History.* New York: Columbia University Press, 1988.

Sedgwick, Eve Kosofsky. *Tendencies.* Durham, N.C.: Duke University Press, 1993.

Shea, Renee H. "Lois-Ann Yamanaka: Pidgin Politics and Paradise Revised." *Poets and Writers* 26.5 (Sept.–Oct. 1998): 32–37.

Showalter, Elaine. *The New Feminist Criticism: Essays on Women, Literature, and Theory.* New York: Pantheon Books, 1985.

Sibley, David. *Geographies of Exclusion.* London: Routledge, 1995.

Siegle, Robert. *Suburban Ambush: Downtown Writing and the Fiction of Insurgency.* Baltimore, Md.: Johns Hopkins University Press, 1989.

Simpson, Lewis P. Introduction to part 1. In *The History of Southern Literature.* Ed. Louis D. Rubin et al. Baton Rouge: Louisiana State University Press, 1985. 9–33.

Simpson, Mona. "Lawns." *Iowa Review* 14.3 (Fall 1984): 80–98.

Slicer, Deborah. "Toward an Ecofeminist Standpoint Theory: Bodies as Grounds." In *Ecofeminist Literary Criticism.* Ed. Greta Gaard and Patrick D. Murphy. Urbana: University of Illinois Press, 1998. 49–73.

Smiley, Jane. *A Thousand Acres.* New York: Fawcett Columbine, 1991.

Smith, Lee. *Black Mountain Breakdown.* New York: Ballantine, 1980.

Smith, Neil, and Cindi Katz. "Grounding Metaphor: Towards a Spatialized Politics." In *Place and the Politics of Identity.* Ed. Michael Keith and Steve Pile. London: Routledge, 1993. 67–83.

Smith, Sidonie, and Julia Watson, eds. *De/Colonizing the Subject: The Politics of Gender in Women's Autobiography.* Minneapolis: University of Minnesota Press, 1992.

Soja, Edward W. *Postmodern Geographies: The Reassertion of Space in Critical Social Theory.* London: Verso, 1989.

Soja, Edward W., and Barbara Hooper. "The Spaces That Difference Makes." In *Place and the Politics of Identity.* Ed. Michael Keith and Steve Pile. London: Routledge, 1993. 183–205.

Spain, Daphne. *Gendered Spaces.* Chapel Hill: University of North Carolina Press, 1992.

Spencer, Elizabeth. *The Snare.* Jackson: University Press of Mississippi, 1993.

Spillers, Hortense. "'The Permanent Obliquity of an In(pha)llibly Straight': In the Time of Fathers and Daughters." In *Changing Our Own Words: Essays on Criticism, Theory, and Writing by Black Women.* Ed. Cheryl A. Wall. New Brunswick, N.J.: Rutgers University Press, 1989. 127–49.

Spivak, Gayatri Chakravorty. "Can the Subaltern Speak?" In *Marxism and the Interpretation of Culture.* Ed. Cary Nelson and Lawrence Grossberg. Urbana: University of Illinois Press, 1988. 271–313.

———. *In Other Worlds: Essays in Cultural Politics.* New York: Methuen, 1987.

Stade, George. "Womanist Fiction and Male Characters." *Partisan Review* 52.3 (1985): 264–70.

Stead, C. K. "Keri Hulme's 'The Bone People' and the Pegasus Award for Maori Literature." *ARIEL: A Review of International English Literature* 16.4 (Oct. 1985): 101–8.

Stimpson, Catharine R. *Where the Meanings Are: Feminism and Cultural Spaces.* 1984. New York: Routledge, 1990.

Strehle, Susan. "The Daughter's Subversion in Jane Smiley's *A Thousand Acres.*" *Critique: Studies in Contemporary Fiction* 41.3 (Spring 2000): 211–26.

Taylor, Mark. *Shakespeare's Darker Purpose: A Question of Incest.* New York: AMS, 1982.

Tompkins, Jane. "Me and My Shadow." In *Gender and Theory.* Ed. Linda Kauffman. Oxford: Basil Blackwell, 1989. 121–39.

Trinh T. Minh-ha. *Woman-Native-Other: Writing Postcoloniality and Feminism.* Bloomington: Indiana University Press, 1989.

Tuan, Yi-Fu. *Space and Place.* Minneapolis: University of Minnesota Press, 1977.

Twitchell, James. *Forbidden Partners: The Incest Taboo in Modern Culture.* New York: Columbia University Press, 1987.

Ullom, Carine. "Aspects of Memory in the Novels of Marlen Haushofer." M.A. thesis. University of Wyoming, 1988.

Urgo, Joseph R. "Distraction; or, The Public Value of Literary Study." *Journal X* 2.2 (Spring 1998): 237–59.
Vansant, Jacqueline. *Against the Horizon: Feminism and Postwar Austrian Women Writers.* New York: Greenwood, 1988.
Vickroy, Laurie. "The Politics of Abuse: The Traumatized Child in Toni Morrison and Marguerite Duras." *Mosaic* 29.2 (June 1996): 91–108.
Walker, Alice. "The Child Who Favored Daughter." In *In Love and Trouble.* New York: Harcourt Brace Jovanovich, 1973. 35–46.
———. *The Color Purple.* New York: Pocket Books, 1982.
———. "Finding Celie's Voice." *Ms.* December 1985: 71–72, 96.
———. *In Search of Our Mothers' Gardens.* New York: Harcourt Brace Jovanovich, 1983.
Wall, Cheryl A. "Introduction: Taking Positions and Changing Words." In *Changing Our Own Words: Essays on Criticism, Theory, and Writing by Black Women.* Ed. Cheryl A. Wall. New Brunswick, N.J.: Rutgers University Press, 1989. 1–15.
Warhol, Robyn, and Diana Price Herndl, eds. *Feminisms: An Anthology of Literary Theory and Criticism.* New Brunswick, N.J.: Rutgers University Press, 1991.
Warner, Sharon Oard. "Novel's Terrain Strangely Satisfying." *Kansas City Star* 9 Feb. 1986: 10L.
Wassmo, Herbjorg. *The House with the Blind Glass Windows.* Trans. Roseann Lloyd and Allen Simpson. Seattle: Seal, 1987.
Watson, Sophie, and Katherine Gibson. *Postmodern Cities and Spaces.* Cambridge, Mass.: Blackwell, 1995.
Weedon, Chris, ed. *Postwar Women's Writing in German: Feminist Critical Approaches.* Providence: Berghahn Books, 1997.
Weisman, Leslie Kanes. *Discrimination by Design: A Feminist Critique of the Man-made Environment.* Urbana: University of Illinois Press, 1992.
Wesley, Marilyn C. "Father-Daughter Incest as Social Transgression: A Feminist Reading of Joyce Carol Oates." *Women's Studies* 21.3 (1992): 251–63.
———. *Secret Journeys: The Trope of Women's Travel in American Literature.* Albany: State University of New York Press, 1999.
Westerlund-Shands, Kerstin. "'Transcending Gynocentric Space': Spatial Metaphorics in Feminist Theory and Criticism." *Nora* 1 (1993): 1–7.
Wilentz, Gay. "Instruments of Change: Healing Cultural Dis-ease in Keri Hulme's *The Bone People.*" *Literature and Medicine* 14.1 (Spring 1995): 127–45.
Williams, Patricia J. *An Alchemy of Race and Rights: Diary of a Law Professor.* Cambridge, Mass.: Harvard University Press, 1991.
Williams, Terry Tempest. *Refuge: An Unnatural History of Family and Place.* New York: Vintage, 1991.
Williamson, Janice. "'I Peel Myself out of My Own Skin': Reading *Don't: A Woman's Word.*" In *Essays on Life Writing: From Genre to Critical Practice.* Ed. Marlene Kadar. Toronto: University of Toronto Press, 1992. 133–51.

Willis, Susan. "I Shop Therefore I Am: Is There a Place for Afro-American Culture in Commodity Culture?" In *Changing Our Own Words: Essays on Criticism, Theory, and Writing by Black Women.* Ed. Cheryl A. Wall. New Brunswick, N.J.: Rutgers University Press, 1989. 173–95.

Wilson, Charles Regan, and William Ferris, eds. *The Encyclopedia of Southern Culture.* Chapel Hill: University of North Carolina Press, 1989.

Wilson, Elizabeth. "Not in This House: Incest, Denial, and Doubt in the White Middle Class Family." *Yale Journal of Criticism* 8.1 (Spring 1995): 35–58.

Wilson, Melba. *Crossing the Boundary: Black Women Surviving Incest.* Seattle: Seal, 1994.

Wisechild, Louise M., ed. *She Who Was Lost Is Remembered: Healing from Incest through Creativity.* Seattle: Seal, 1991.

Wolff, Janet. "On the Road Again: Metaphors of Travel in Cultural Criticism." *Cultural Studies* 7.2 (1993): 224–40.

Woodward, Carolyn. "'My Heart So Wrapt': Lesbian Disruptions in Eighteenth-Century British Fiction." *Signs* 18.4 (1993): 838–66.

Woolf, Virginia. *A Room of One's Own.* New York: Harcourt Brace Jovanovich, 1957.

Yaeger, Patricia. "Introduction: Narrating Space." In *The Geography of Identity.* Ed. Patricia Yaeger. Ann Arbor: University of Michigan Press, 1996. 1–38.

Young, Iris Marion. "The Ideal of Community and the Politics of Difference." In *Feminism/Postmodernism.* Ed. Linda J. Nicholson. New York: Routledge, 1990. 300–323.

Zauhar, Frances Murphy. "Creative Voices: Women Reading and Women's Writing." In *The Intimate Critique: Autobiographical Literary Criticism.* Ed. Diane P. Freedman, Olivia Frey, and Frances Murphy Zauhar. Durham, N.C.: Duke University Press, 1993. 103–16.

Zwinger, Lynda. *Daughters, Fathers, and the Novel: The Sentimental Romance of Heterosexuality.* Madison: University of Wisconsin Press, 1991.

INDEX

MINROSE C. GWIN, a professor of English at Binghamton University, State University of New York, is the author of *Black and White Women of the Old South: The Peculiar Sisterhood in American Literature* and *The Feminine and Faulkner: Reading (Beyond) Sexual Difference.* She has written articles on women's literature; gender, space, and reading; feminist theory; and writers of the American South. Most recently she completed a memoir entitled "Wishing for Snow." Her editorial projects include the Norton anthology *Literature of the American South,* with William L. Andrews, Trudier Harris, and Fred Hobson, and *A Woman's Civil War* by Cornelia McDonald.

The University of Illinois Press
is a founding member of the
Association of American University Presses.

Composed in 9.5/12.5 Trump Mediaeval
by Celia Shapland
for the University of Illinois Press
Manufactured by Thomson-Shore, Inc.

University of Illinois Press
1325 South Oak Street
Champaign, IL 61820-6903
www.press.uillinois.edu